ARCHAEOLOGICAL SURVEY OF INDIA, VOLUME XXXVII, IMPERIAL SERIES

BIJAPUR
AND ITS
ARCHITECTURAL REMAINS

ARCHAEOLOGICAL SURVEY OF INDIA, VOLUME XXXVII, IMPERIAL SERIES

BIJAPUR

AND ITS
ARCHITECTURAL REMAINS

WITH AN HISTORICAL OUTLINE OF
THE ADIL SHAHI DYNASTY

BY

HENRY COUSENS, M.R.A.S

LATE SUPERINTENDENT, ARCHAEOLOGICAL SURVEY OF INDIA WESTERN CIRCLE

GYAN

Published by

Gyan Publishing House
5, Ansari Road
Daryaganj, New Delhi-110002
Phone: 011-47034999, 9811692060
E-mail: books@gyanbooks.com

Distribution Network
gyanbooks.com
India, USA, Canada, UK, Australia, France

ISBN : 978-81-212-2674-5 (HB)
First Published, 1916

2nd Impression 2021

Printed at: Gyan Press, Delhi.

Bijapur and its Architectural Remains
Author: Henry Cousens

ARCHÆOLOGICAL SURVEY OF INDIA, VOLUME XXXVII, IMPERIAL SERIES

BĪJĀPŪR

AND ITS

ARCHITECTURAL REMAINS

WITH AN HISTORICAL OUTLINE OF
THE 'ĀDIL SHĀHI DYNASTY

BY

HENRY COUSENS, M.R.A.S.
LATE SUPERINTENDENT, ARCHÆOLOGICAL SURVEY OF INDIA
WESTERN CIRCLE

BOMBAY
PRINTED AT THE GOVERNMENT CENTRAL PRESS
1916

ELEVATION OF THE MIHRAB OF THE JAMI MASJID.

CONTENTS.

LIST OF PLATES.

LIST OF TEXT ILLUSTRATIONS.

PREFACE.

AFTER the sumptuous volumes, brought out some fifty years ago, of *Architectural Illustrations of the Principal Buildings at Bijapur* by Mr. James Fergusson and Captain Hart, R.E., and *The Architecture at Bijapur* by Colonel Meadows Taylor and Mr. Fergusson, it may seem superfluous to bring out another on the same subject. But those volumes, limited, as they were, to a very small edition, are now out of print and are very rare. The first contains no photographs and scant descriptive matter, and, like the second, treats of very few of the buildings of the city. The second is, unfortunately, full of blunders, due, no doubt, to Colonel Meadows Taylor having written up his account at a distance from the place, and some time after his visit, from imperfect notes. For instance, two photographic views of the same mosque, that of Karīm-ud-dīn in the citadel, taken from different points of view, are described as two different buildings. Many of the others are wrongly labelled, and a mosque at Lakshmeśwar, in the Dhārwār district, is described as being at Adoni, to the south of Raichūr. These mistakes have led Mr. Fergusson astray in his remarks upon some of the buildings.

The illustrations, which form the most important feature of this volume, and which will enable the student to form his own ideas and conclusions, have been prepared during the frequent and lengthened visits of the Survey party to the old capital—at first under the direction of Dr. James Burgess, late Director General of Archæology, and, later, under my own personal control. The drawings are the work of Indian draftsmen recruited from the schools of art and further trained to the particular pen and ink work required of them.

Except where otherwise stated, the translations of the numerous inscriptions referred to were made by the late Mr. E. Rehatsek who was, for many years, Professor and Examiner in Persian and Arabic in the University of Bombay.

The printing of the volume has been entrusted by the Government of Bombay to their Central Press, at Bombay, for the letterpress, and to the Government Photozincographic Department, at Poona, for the illustrations. To the Superintendents of both establishments I tender my best thanks for the very great pains they have taken to turn out the best possible results.

HENRY COUSENS.

TEDDINGTON, *July*, 1913.

HISTORICAL OUTLINE

OF THE

'ĀDIL SHĀHI DYNASTY OF BĪJĀPŪR.

As a history of the 'Ādil Shāhi dynasty this account will appear very meagre; but this volume does not profess to deal with the history of the state, but rather with a description of its architectural remains. A short outline is, however, needful, to make the description of the buildings and references to individuals more intelligible.

The short-lived dynasty of Bījāpūr, the 'Ādil Shāhi, passed through a period of incessant wars without its walls, and of constant faction brawls within. Not only was the fair face of the country, around, ploughed up by cavalry and artillery, ever on the move, but the very courts, within the citadel, were frequently dyed with blood during civil strife. At no time could any man's life be said to be safe; and hardly a ruin now remains which has not been the site of some treasonable plot or dastardly assassination. The very air reeked with blood. Yet during all those troublous times there were intervals of comparative calm, when time was found for the erection of those grand piles of architectural splendour to the memory and glory of its kings and nobles.

The better to understand the early history of the dynasty, it is necessary to go to far away Turkey, at the time when Henry VI. sat upon the English throne. The Ottoman *masnad* was then occupied by Sultān Murād II. (A. D. 1421—1451). Tradition tells us that, following the custom of the time, orders were issued, at his death, for the execution of all his male children, save the heir, but that the mother of one of them succeeded, by stratagem, in saving the life of her child. Smuggled out of the country, this boy, after many adventures, and led, it is said, by some prescience, derived from dreams, of his future fortunes, found himself landed in Hindustān, at the port of Dābul. Journeying thence to the capital of the Bīdar kings, he was taken on as one of the king's retainers. Yūsuf, for such was his name, once started in life, was not long in rising into favour and higher positions under his new sovereign.

Another account tells us that Yūsuf was the son of Maḥmūd Beg, governor of the province of Sāvah; and that, when the latter was killed in battle, and his family and adherents were dispersed, Yūsuf Beg was brought up as a child at Iṣpahān, whence he was taken to Shīrāz, and afterwards to India. But, from the fact that the crescent, the Turkish national symbol, surmounts the old state buildings of Bījāpūr, it would appear that his descendants believed in their princely descent. Nevertheless he is known in some of the old writings as Yūsuf Sāvah, but this may be due to his having been educated at that place.[1]

After passing some time in various military appointments under the Bīdar government, he was selected by the king to fill the post of governor of the Bījāpūr province, with the honorary title of 'Ādil Khān.[2]

The last years of Sulṭān Maḥmūd saw the decline of the Bahmanī kingdom of the Dakhan, and the loosening of the grasp of central control upon the provincial governments. Upon his death dissensions spread rapidly throughout the Bīdar territories. Yūsuf 'Ādil Khān, collecting around him a strong force of Turks and Mughals, began, by degrees, to sever his connection with the central government; and, finally, in A. D. 1489, like the governors of other provinces, he openly declared his independence by ordering the *khuṭbah*[3] to be read in the public mosques in his own name.

YŪSUF 'ĀDIL SHĀH (A. D. 1489—1510) did not long enjoy his new honours before the avenging hand of his rejected sovereign reached him. Qāsim Barīd, minister at Bīdar, aided by the Hindu ruler Timrāj of Vijayanagar, marched against him, but was unsuccessful in his efforts to recover the lost province. Soon after this he was attacked by Timrāj, and, henceforth, Vijayanagar became a thorn in the side of Bījāpūr, its territories marching for some two hundred miles or more with those of the Muḥammadan kingdom. Repelling him successfully, and having captured the forts of Mudgal and Raichūr, he returned to Bījāpūr with much booty, which helped him very materially in his efforts to put his house in order. Relieved for a time from anxieties without, he began to introduce innovations within, amongst these being the introduction of the Shī'ah doctrines in which he had been brought up in Persia. The Dakhani Muḥammadans being Sunnīs, and very jealous of their belief, this attempt to subvert their faith brought trouble upon him, and he was forced, for a time, to fly from the vengeance of the Bahmanī king, aided by the forces of the newly constituted Niẓām Shāhi king of Aḥmadnagar, and those of the Quṭb Shāhi king of Golkondah. About this time the Portuguese appeared upon the shores of India and took possession of Govah or Goa, a Bījāpūr port on the western coast. In the twenty-second year of his reign Yūsuf died, having had his son Ismā'īl crowned in his presence in the death-chamber. Ismā'īl,

[1] Firishtah, in giving an account of a quarrel between Ismā'īl 'Ādil Shāh and Burhān Niẓām Shāh, quotes a letter sent by the former to the latter, in which he reminds him that, unlike him, whose title of "Shāh" was conferred upon him by the kings of Gujarāt, he derived his royal lineage from a race of sovereigns, and was so styled by the kings of Persia descendants of the Prophet.—Briggs' *Ferishtah,* Vol. III, p. 227.

[2] 'Ādil, the "Just".

[3] This is the sermon delivered in the mosques on Friday, at the time of midday prayer in which the name of the acknowledged ruler is brought in for a blessing, after those of the Prophet and Companions.

being a minor, his minister, Kamāl Khān Dakhanī, was entrusted with the administration of the state. At his own request Yūsuf was buried near the tomb of Shāh Chanda Ḥusainī in Gogī, a village he had received in *in'ām* from the Bīdar king Maḥmūd Bahmanī. Firishtah's date for Yūsuf's death is generally accepted as correct, *viz.* A. D. 1510.

Fig. 1. Yūsuf 'Ādil Shāh, from an old drawing.

Bījāpūr does not seem to have been a place of much importance before the time of Yūsuf. The earliest authentic records of it are contained in the old Kanarese inscription on the tablet and columns at the entrance to the citadel. These columns and other fragments are remains of one or more Hindu temples which once existed on or near this spot. The Muḥammadans probably found these shrines more or less in ruins, and set about using the materials to construct their gateways, guardrooms, and mosques. They did the same in Gujarāt and other parts of the country, frequently desecrating and despoiling temples, still in use, for the purpose. The principal inscription is a well-inscribed stone slab which had been built in, low down, on the left or south side of the inner gate of the citadel.[1] It is of the time of the Western Chālukyan king Bhuvanaikamalla or Someśvara II., and is dated in *Śaka* 996 (A. D. 1074-75). From this inscription it appears that Bījāpūr was then included in the district known as the Taddevāḍi[2] Thousand, and was at that time the capital of the provincial *daṇḍanāyaka* or governor, Nakimayya. It records the building of the temple of the god Śrī-Svayambhū-Siddheśvara at Vijayapura, and a grant of land within the borders of Bijjanhalli.[3] The last few lines of this inscription are of a later date, and were added at the time of Vikramāditya VI. Bījāpūr, under the original name of Vijayapura, was thus a Western Chālukyan possession in the 11th century; and, from inscriptions of subsequent date, on some of the pillars in the gateway, we find that it must have passed into the hands of the Yādavas of Devagiri,[4] in whose possession it was in the latter half of the 12th and beginning of the 13th centuries. During the invasion of the Dakhan by Malik Kāfūr, 'Alā-ud-dīn's general, about A. D. 1300, the Muḥammadans occupied Bījāpūr, and an inscription on a pilaster in the converted temple, near the entrance to the citadel, tells us that Malik Karīm-ud-dīn erected the upper part of the mosque in

[1] It is now in the Bījāpūr Museum, and has been published in the *Indian Antiquary*, Vol. X, p. 126.

[2] On the south bank of the Bhīmā, 36 miles north of Bījāpūr.

[3] On an old manuscript Persian map of the city of Bījāpūr is a village Bajkanhalli, one of seven which were absorbed in the new city.

[4] Daulatābād, near Aurangābād.

Śaka 1242 (A. D. 1320).[1] Karīm-ud-dīn was the son of Malik Kāfūr, and appears to have resided at Bījāpūr as governor.

From the Chālukyan inscription it is plain that the name of the place was originally Vijayapura, or "city of victory", probably so-called on account of some victory having at one time been obtained here; and this name has been retained, with brief intermissions, to the present day under the Muḥammadan form of Bījāpūr. In the vernacular it is generally written Vījāpūr. The intermissions were, if the old name was really ever dropped for the time being, when Ibrāhīm II., in A. D. 1603, gave it the name of Badyapūr, and when Sulṭān Muḥammad called it Muḥammadpūr.[2]

ISMĀ'ĪL 'ĀDIL SHĀH (A. D. 1510—1534) is said to have been about twelve or thirteen years of age when he succeeded his father. Under the regent Kamāl Khān Dakhanī, the Sunnī faith was re-established. Ismā'īl's reign opens with a tragedy within the palace walls. Kamāl Khān, intoxicated with the power entrusted to him, soon began to carry things with a high hand, and even attempted to dethrone the youthful king. But in this attempt he failed, and was assassinated within his own room by an emissary of Ismā'īl's mother. An unsuccessful siege of the palace by Kamāl Khān's party ensued. During this struggle one of Ismā'īl's most faithful adherents was Khusrau Āqā, a Turk, to whom he gave the title of Asad Khān, with the fort of Belgaum in *jāgīr*. Of this noble we shall hear more, for he played a very important part, for many long years, in the history of Bījāpūr.

Ismā'īl soon set to work to consolidate his little kingdom and to attend to home matters; but he was not long engaged in this occupation before he began to think of extending his possessions by further conquests. Accordingly, he first raided the districts of Qāsim Barīd, having previously disbanded all Dakhanīs and Ḥabshīs (Abyssinians), employing Mughals in their place, who were excellent archers and spearmen. It is said that he re-introduced the Shī'ah faith. This expedition was followed by a retributory attack upon him by the combined forces of the other Dakhan states, which he succeeded in repelling. Asad Khān now comes to the front as Ismā'īl's commander-in-chief, and does good work as general peacemaker in the broils that followed between Bījāpūr and the neighbouring kingdoms. Friendships were, to some extent, cemented by matrimonial alliances, and Ismā'īl's three sisters were given in marriage to Aḥmad Shāh Bahmanī of Bīdar, Sulṭān 'Alā-ud-dīn 'Imād Shāh of Khāndesh, and Sulṭān Burhān Niẓām Shāh of Aḥmadnagar respectively. His crushing defeat of Amīr Barīd, who had now dispossessed the Bahmanī family at Bīdar, having taken possession of Bīdar itself and seated himself upon the Bahmanī throne, was, perhaps, the most important military expedition of his reign. During the siege of Golkondah Ismā'īl fell sick, and, his case becoming hopeless, he rapidly sank, and died at Sāgar in A. H. 941 (A. D. 1534).[3] His body was sent to Gogī and laid beside that of his father.

Firishtah thus sums up his character on the authority of Sayyid Aḥmad Hiravī: "Ismā'īl 'Ādil Shāh was just, prudent, patient, and liberal; and, from the abundance of his magnanimity he gave rewards without too minutely inspecting the condition of his treasury.

---

[1] Another account says A. H. 716 (A. D. 1316).

[2] In a Devanāgari inscription, on a wall near the Ibrāhim Rauza, written in the time of Sultān Muḥammad, Bījāpūr is called Vidyāpura, "city of wisdom" or "city of learning". But this is probably no more than a conceit of the *Pandit* who composed the inscription. On an old manuscript Persian map it is called Dārul Zafar, "abode of victory", just a translation of Vijayapura.

[3] Another writer says he died in A. H. 931.

He was extremely generous also, frequently pardoning state criminals, and averse from listening to slander. He never used passionate language. He possessed great wit to which he added a sound and acute judgment. He was an adept in the arts of painting, varnishing, making arrows, and embroidering saddle cloths. In music and poetry he excelled most of his age. He was fond of the company of learned men and poets, numbers of whom were munificently supported at his court. He was delighted with repartee in conversation, and had a great fund of humour, which he often displayed in his intercourse with his courtiers: no other king of the Deccan equalled him in this respect. He was fonder of the Turkish and Persian manners, music, and language, than the Deccany: he seldom made use of the latter tongue." [1]

Ismā'īl is said to have founded the village of Chandapūr [2] in A. H. 926 (A. D. 1520), and to have built the Champa Maḥall in A. H. 927 (A. D. 1521), of which no vestige now remains, unless under a changed name.

MALLŪ 'ĀDIL SHĀH (A. D. 1534), Ismā'īl's eldest son, succeeded to the throne, in accordance with his father's wishes. But the people were so dissatisfied with him, and disgusted with his evil ways and dissolute habits, that it became no difficult task, for those who were particularly desirous of it, to dispose him. So, after a short reign of seven months, the libertine, Mallū, was set aside and blinded,[3] and his younger brother Ibrāhīm, the favourite, was hailed king in his stead.

IBRĀHĪM 'ĀDIL SHĀH I. (A. D. 1534—1557) soon won the confidence of his subjects, being a brave man and a good soldier. He was more or less engaged in strife with his Dakhanī neighbours throughout his reign. It is said he was ever on the alert, and hardly slept at night, being always in a state of unrest, and in perpetual fear of sudden surprisals by his enemies. It is told of Ṭahmāsp, king of Persia, that he used to say that two kings, Afrāsiyāb Turk and Ibrāhīm 'Ādil Shāh, had no other rivals in deeds of bravery and heroism. Ibrāhīm inaugurated his reign by introducing drastic measures of reform in the civil administration of the state. He once more restored the Sunnī form of faith, and dismissed from office most of those whom his predecessors had brought in to swell the number of the Shī'ahs. He re-employed Dakhanis and Abyssinians in place of the discharged Persians and others; and the Hindu element in the public offices was considerably strengthened. Persian was made the official language of the court.

Bhoj Tarmal, the rightful sovereign of Vijayanagar, who had been ousted from his throne by his minister Rāmrāj, called upon Ibrāhīm to assist him against the latter. When, however, Ibrāhīm moved his troops towards the southern capital, Rāmrāj made a show of submission. Deceived by his assumed humility, Bhoj Tarmal sent forty or more lakhs of *hūns* to Ibrāhīm to compensate him for the expenses of his expedition, and besought him to return. Ibrāhīm, perhaps as well pleased with ready cash as with an uncertain campaign, returned to Bījāpūr; but he was no sooner gone, than Rāmrāj returned to Vijayanagar, murdered the too confiding Bhoj Tarmal, and assumed full powers of royalty.

---

[1] Briggs' *Ferishtah*, Vol. III, p. 72.

[2] A village a few miles south of Bījāpūr.

[3] The blinding of kings and princes was a common practice in India; for, where the stronger party dared not commit the crime of murder, the lesser outrage most effectually prevented the victim from taking further active interest in politics. Moreover, it was generally considered that any physical defect disqualified a man for sitting upon the throne.

Ibrāhīm, on his return home, is said to have laid out part of the money thus obtained in strengthening and completing the citadel fortifications, which is confirmed by the inscriptions on the walls.

Ibrāhīm, hearing of the death of Bhoj Tarmal, and probably thinking that he had as much right to some of the Vijayanagar possessions as Rāmrāj, despatched Asad Khān, with considerable forces, to capture the much coveted fort of Ādoni. This little enterprise being brought to a very successful issue, Ibrāhīm honoured Asad Khān by marrying his daughter, and declaring that should he have male issue by her, that son should be his heir. About this time 'Ain-ul-Mulk Kan'āni,[1] one of Ibrāhīm's nobles, driven by the king's injustice to him, rebelled and took possession of several districts adjoining his own *jāgīr,* which was somewhere near the seashore; but the king promptly confronted him, and compelled him to flee to the court of Niẓām Shāh, where he expected to find favour and asylum. Niẓām Shāh, being at this time unwilling to have any cause of quarrel with Ibrāhīm, had 'Ain-ul-Mulk put to death. His tomb stands a conspicuous object upon the plain, some little distance to the east of Bījāpūr.

Asad Khān's prosperity soon made him many enemies, who were ever ready to impugn his loyalty to his master, and for a time they were successful in their evil machinations and alienated the king's favour from him. But, through the friendly intervention of 'Imād-ul-Mulk, he was reinstated in his old relations with his master. It was not long before Ibrāhīm was again in sore need of his favourite's advice and assistance—this time against a confederacy of Aḥmadnagar, Golkondah and Vijayanagar, the ostensible reason for the attack upon him being the recovery of the fort of Sholāpūr by Niẓām Shāh. The readiness of the other states to join in these combined attacks was more due to their delight in raiding and looting a neighbour's territory than to their wish to assist the one with whom they combined. This was specially so with the Hindu rulers of Vijayanagar, who were well pleased with any prospect of paying back old scores, and attacking the hated Muḥammadans. Asad Khān brought off this little business with great *éclat* and much credit to himself, and returned to Bījāpūr in triumph. The restless spirit of Niẓām Shāh once again induced him to try conclusions with Ibrāhīm, only to be ignominiously defeated upon the banks of the Bhīmā, where immense loot was taken.

Ibrāhīm's fiery temper, and very harsh and vindictive nature, meting out the most severe punishment for the most trivial offence, was the cause of a plot being laid to dethrone him in favour of his brother 'Abdullāh. Again he lost faith in his old servant and suspected Asad Khān of being implicated in it; but, being subsequently assured of his loyalty, he set out on a journey of penitence to visit him in his fort at Belgaum. Before he reached that place, his old general had gone to his last account. Ibrāhīm mourned his loss much, and distributed goods and jewels amongst Asad Khān's sons. Asad Khān Lāri is said to have been over a hundred years old, and to have served the state of Bījāpūr forty or fifty years. He died in A. H. 956 (A. D. 1549) and was buried in the tomb he had built for himself near the fort of Belgaum. Asad Khān was one of the greatest men in Bījāpūr story; and, since

[1] This is the name as given in a copy of the *Basātīn-i-Salāṭīn.* Firishtah calls him, according to Col. Briggs' translation, "Seif Ein-ool-Moolk Geelany" and says he was Burhān Niẓām Shāh's commander-in-chief, who was won over by Asad Khān to Ibrāhīm's service. He also says he was celebrated throughout the Dakhan for his courage, and for the efficiency of his party of horsemen, with whom he lived on the terms of a brother.—Briggs' *Ferishtah,* Vol. III, p. 238.

his death, for some reason or another, he is still remembered and treated as a *walī* or saint, religious discourses being occasionally delivered at his tomb.

Fig. 2. The Maqbara at Gogī, containing the tombs of Yūsuf, Ismā'il and Ibrāhīm I.

Further trouble ensued between Burhān Nizām Shāh and Ibrāhīm: several forts were taken and re-taken. The former king dying, peace reigned for a time between Ibrāhīm and Husain Nizām Shāh, his successor. In A. H. 965 (A. D. 1557) Ibrāhīm died a miserable death, being deserted by those of his physicians who had not already been put to death for not curing him. His body was carried to Gogī and interred in the family vault at that place.

Fig. 3. The graves in the Maqbara at Gogī— (1) Tomb of the queen of Ibrāhīm I.; (2) Tomb of Ibrāhīm I.; (3) Tomb of Ismā'il; (4) Tomb of the queen of Yūsuf; (5) Tomb of Yūsuf.

Although Ibrāhīm possessed such a vindictive nature yet he treated his soldiers well, and was courteous and urbane to learned men. He had four sons and two daughters, but their order of birth is not very clear, Ismā'il, apparently, being older than 'Ali. The former was dull and stupid, while the latter was bright and active; and the king, not caring for the heir to be seen to such disadvantage by contrast with his younger brother, had the latter confined in the fort of Miraj for nine years. The other sons were Aḥmad and Ṭahmāsp. His daughters were married to Niẓām Shāh and 'Ali Barīd.

He colonised Ibrāhīmpūr, a suburb to the south of Bījāpūr, in A. H. 933 (A. D. 1527), and built the mosque in that village in the same year. He also built the Solah Thami Maḥall in A. H. 935 (A. D. 1528), which is not at present existing; added to the fortifications of the citadel, and erected a mosque called the Ghālib Masjid, which was adorned with 1,303 niches for lamps. Another building of his was his Jāmi' Masjid, near the tomb of Hazrat Ja'far Saqqāf, built in A. H. 958 (A. D. 1551), which still exists.

'ALI 'ĀDIL SHĀH'S release from the fort of Miraj, and his accession to the throne, was hailed with satisfaction by most of his subjects.[1] It is said that endeavours were made by his father to set him aside in favour of Ṭahmāsp, grandson of Asad Khān Lāri, but that these were thwarted by the nobles, whose preference was for 'Ali. Ṭahmāsp was blinded, and thus put out of the running. A strong reason for Ibrāhīm's aversion to 'Ali was that the latter, despite his father's many threats and commands, was a firm adherent to the Shī'ah faith, and this was fostered by the companionship of Khwājah 'Ināyat Ullāh Shīrāzī, his preceptor, and his successor Mullā Fatḥ Shīrāzī. 'Ali answered his father's arguments by retorting that if the king thought proper to depart from his father's faith it was quite as admissible for him to do the same; so, on ascending the throne, he again introduced the Shī'ah faith, and invited men of that persuasion, from Persia and elsewhere, to Bījāpūr in order to strengthen his party. The Sunnīs were on the point of proclaiming a *jihād*, or holy war, and civil strife was imminent; but he at length won over the populace by his justice, liberality and kindly manner. He did not spare his treasury, but lavished his wealth freely.

The heritage of war and ancient feuds was passed on from father to son, and it was not long ere 'Ali was embroiled in quarrels with his neighbours. He began by cultivating the friendship of Rāmrāj, and even paid a visit of condolence to him at Vijayanagar on hearing of the death of his son. By this means he won over the assistance of the Hindu king in an attack upon Burhān Niẓām Shāh, who had offended him by not sending the usual letter of congratulation upon his accession; and, moreover, he was bent upon winning back the forts of Kalyāṇi and Sholāpūr. But Rāmrāj's men could not resist the temptation to pillage, and he laid the country waste wherever he went, in the Bījāpūr territory as well as that of Aḥmadnagar. His excesses were so great, not only in this campaign, but also in a subsequent one in which 'Ali had again invoked his aid against Niẓām Shāh, that the former could bear with it no longer. He had become thoroughly disgusted with the arrogance and overbearing of this *kāfir* king, and induced both Niẓām Shāh and Quṭb Shāh, who also had good cause to desire Rāmrāj's extermination, to join with him in a great expedition and holy war against this infidel. Matrimonial alliances cemented the friendship of these kings, whose forces were augmented bv those of 'Ali Barīd of Bīdar. In A. D. 1564, the whole combined force marched in the direction of Vijayanagar, but were checked in their progress at the Krishna river where they found Rāmrāj with immense forces, encamped

[1] His full name, as given in old inscriptions at Raichūr fort, is Abū-l-Muẓaffar 'Ali 'Ādil Shāh.

upon the opposite side and holding the fords. After several futile attempts at crossing, the Muḥammadan troops at length succeeded by a ruse, which drew the enemy away from the ford. Battle was joined near Talikot, which resulted, mainly through the use of artillery, in an overwhelming victory for the four kings. The Muḥammadans followed up the enemy for miles, and the country between the field of battle and Anagundi was strewn with the dead and dying. It is estimated that, without exaggeration, there must have been at least 150,000 troops engaged in this battle. The confederate kings followed up the victory by marching upon Vijayanagar, where they remained some time in possession. The greater part of the capital was destroyed, and it was henceforth blotted out of the roll of living cities.[1] Rāmrāj had been beheaded on the field, and Niẕām Shāh is said to have sent his head to 'Imād-ul-Mulk, as a significant warning, as he had been plundering his districts in his absence.[2]

Fig. 4. Head of Rāmrāj.

'Ali obtained possession, by this victory, of the forts of Raichūr and Mudgal; and, after enforcing his authority in these places, and leaving them in capable hands, he returned to Bījāpūr, where, with the great wealth he had obtained in the general plunder of Vijayanagar, he began and carried out that most desirable work—the walling in, and fortifications of, the whole city of Bījāpūr. Hitherto, the only completely defended portion of the capital was the citadel, but a considerable town had grown up around it, which was entirely at the mercy of an invader. This undertaking was completed in A. H. 973 (A. D. 1565).

The avarice of 'Ali 'Ādil Shāh led him to think of following up the defeat of Rāmrāj by an attack on Palganda, to which his family had retreated and established themselves; and, for this purpose, he despatched an army under Kishwar Khān to invade the south. Quṭb Shāh, becoming jealous of 'Ali's continued acquisitions of territory, induced Niẕām Shāh to join him in seizing upon the opportunity to attack Bījāpūr when its main forces were scattered and so far afield; but Kishwar Khān, returning suddenly, utterly discomfited them; but only for a while, Niẕām Shāh returning shortly after and taking his revenge, when Kishwar Khān met his death. Other expeditions were undertaken by 'Ali 'Ādil Shāh with varying success.

During the reigns of Yūsuf, Isma'il, and 'Ībrāhīm I., the Bījāpūr troops had been brought into contact with a new power on the coast. Goa, and the coast districts, had

---

[1] For a full account of Vijayanagar, see *A Forgotten Empire,* by R. Sewell.

[2] The head seems, afterwards, to have been kept at Aḥmadnagar for some time. A stone representation of Rāmrāj's head existed at Bījāpūr. Mr. Jas. Bird says that it was set up in the citadel wall, on the right of the gate at entering (Capt. Sydenham says, in the curtain wall outside the east gate, inclining downwards), but having been removed thence by the Rājá of Sātāra, it was thrown into the ditch (*Journ. Bom. Br. R. A. S.,* Vol. I., p. 376). I was told some years ago that it had been thrown into the Tāj Bāuri, and, confirming this, is the fact that, subsequently, when the *bāurī* was being cleaned out for the first time in its history, perhaps, a large stone head, shewn in Fig. 4, was discovered in the mud at the bottom. It is now in the local museum. There appears to have been a tradition that there was also an equestrian statue of Rāmrāj at Bījāpūr, for Capt. Sydenham says "I neither saw nor heard of the equestrian statue of Rāmrāj at Bījāpūr, which has been mentioned in a former work, though my guide of his own accord pointed out to me the head" (*Asiatic Researches,* Quarto Ed., Vol. XIII, p. 447.)

fallen to the lot of Yūsuf 'Ādil Shāh on his revolt, it having been, up to that time, an outlying province of the Bahmanī kingdom. A fleet had been collected, which cruised along these shores, and these ships Vasco de Gama came into contact with when he came in sight of the Indian coast in A. D. 1498. In 1510 Affonso de Albuquerque arrived before Goa with a great fleet, and, after some resistance on the part of the Bījāpūr troops, took possession of it. Three months after this an expedition was despatched from Bījāpūr, which soon drove the Portuguese back to their ships; but, before the year was out, the latter, strengthened by a fresh squadron from Europe, appeared once more before the fort and taking it by assault, drove the king's troops from the city with great slaughter. Albuquerque put the city into a thorough state of defence, and overhauled its forts, turrets, and bastions. 'Ali 'Ādil Shāh, turning his attention to this port, with 100,000 men and 2,140 elephants, besieged the city for ten months, but was, in the end, obliged to retire.

He next sent Ankus Khān against the celebrated fort of Adoni, hitherto considered impregnable, but which, after a long blockade, surrendered to the Bījāpūr troops. After this, having entered into a compact with Murtazā Nizām Shāh, by which he was to overrun the Vijayanagar territories in return for non-interference with Nizām Shāh in his designs upon Berār, 'Ali marched against the forts of Torgal, Dhārwār, and Bankapūr, wresting them from the feudal chiefs. Leaving Mustafā Khān in charge of Bankapūr, and reinstating the other chiefs as his own vassals, he returned to Bījāpūr after an absence of three years. Several minor expeditions followed this.

In a dispute with a slave from Gulbargah, regarding the return of certain jewels, which had belonged to his daughter, 'Ali 'Ādil Shāh was struck in the bowels with a dagger, from the effects of which he died.[1] This happened in A. H. 988 (A. D. 1580), and he was the first king of his line to be buried in Bījāpūr, being laid to rest within a very plain-looking tomb in the south-west corner of the city. Many works of utility are ascribed to him, amongst which are, as has already been mentioned, the walls around the city; the Gagan Mahall; the Chānd Bāurī; the great Jāmi' Masjid, which was left well in hand; the Ānand Mahall; and his own tomb. On one of the bastions of the fort of Raichūr is an inscription of his reign recording the building of the same by Tāhir Khān in A. H. 978 (A. D. 1570).[2] He built the fort of Shāhdrug in A. H. 966 (A. D. 1558). The suburb of Shāhpūr was laid out under the direction of Kishwar Khān, whose private grounds were somewhere near this. He built the Harya Mahall in 968 (A. D. 1560); the fort of Dhārwār in 975 (A. D. 1567); the forts of Shāhanūr and Bankapūr in 981 (A. D. 1573); and he laid out the Bārā Imām and Fadak gardens in A. H. 974 and 976 (A. D. 1566 and 1568) respectively. Aqueducts, conveying water through the streets, are also ascribed to him. A chronogram gives the date of his death in the equivalent of the words "He saw oppression", A. H. 988.

Kishwar Khān is said to have been put in charge of the walling in of the city, for which work he gathered masons, stone-cutters, and skilled artizans from other parts of India. He is credited with having been in charge of the construction of the Jāmi' Masjid, the stone and lime having been obtained at a place two *farsakhs* distant from the city. It was two years and a half in progress. We are told that the circuit of the Hisār, or

---

[1] A rather different version of his death is given by Capt. J. S. King, Bo. S. C., in the *Indian Antiquary*, Vol. XVII, p. 221.

[2] *Indian Antiquary*, Vol. XI, p. 130.

fortified walls of the city, was 6 *farsakhs*, its breadth 18 yards (probably cubits), and height 20 yards. There were 120 bastions with 6,000 *kanguras* (merlons of the battlementing), 6 main gates and 70 sally-ports—the gate towards the *qiblah* being named the Makka gate, while the others were called after towns near by, or to which the road through them led. A deep broad *khandaq* or ditch was dug around the walls to contain water. The citadel was supplied with water, and, beside the gardens already named, other two, the Bāgh 'Alavī and Bāgh 'Ali, were also laid out. Near the fort was constructed a large tank called Kāranjah, which was always filled with water and much used by the townspeople.

Rafī'-ud-dīn Shīrāzī, who was employed as steward, treasurer, and *ḥavildār*, for some twenty-one years, in the household of the king, and who was an eye-witness of his death, sums up his character thus: "The king was gentle, good-natured, and of a religious turn of mind. He was matchless in his generosity and liberality, and delighted in the company of learned men, whom he invited to Bījāpūr, from Persia, and elsewhere, and sent away well rewarded. He was kind to his servants; was not particular about his dress, it only costing him about two *hūns*, and used to dress as a *faqīr*, calling himself 'Ali Sher Qalandar ('Ali lion-*faqīr*)."

Immediately upon the news of 'Ali's death becoming known, there was great alarm and confusion in the city. The nobles gathered in groups, and whispered their misgivings, and eagerly questioned one another as to what was about to happen. The king had left no issue, and it was doubtful who should succeed him. By common consent they appealed to Afzal Khān, who convened a meeting of some of the leading men with the result that they decided that the young Ibrāhīm, the king's nephew, and son of his brother Ṭahmāsp, was next-of-kin and should be installed as king. Accordingly, and without further loss of time, Ibrāhīm was brought forth, was seated upon the *masnad*, and the royal umbrella was raised above him. Here he received the salutations of the people, and was hailed as king IBRĀHĪM II. He was generally called Ibrāhīm Jagat Gīr (the holder of the world), but sometimes Ibrāhīm Jagat Guru, *guru* being a Hindu devotee and teacher, Ibrāhīm having been accused of leanings towards Hinduism.

Kāmil Khān, an officer of high standing, took upon himself the care of the state, while the widowed queen Chānd Bībī acted as Regent, the king being but a lad of nine years of age. But Kāmil Khān's star was not long in the ascendant. By his haughty and insolent behaviour he gave offence to the queen, who urged Kishwar Khān[1] to rid her of him. This, Kishwar Khān promptly did, murdering him as he fled towards Gulbargah. The appointment of a successor to Kāmil Khān became a cause of strife among the nobles, who fell out and fought within the palace precincts.

These internal quarrels gave an opportunity to Nizām Shāh and Quṭb Shāh to renew their attacks upon Bījāpūr. At this conjuncture, Afzal Khān was chosen to lead an army of defence, and, marching against each opponent in turn, before they could coalesce, he defeated both. News reached the nobles in the field of the wrong doings of Kishwar Khān at home, and they, in communication with the queen, appointed Mustafā Khān Ardistānī, governor of Bankapūr, to supersede him. But Kishwar Khān, getting news of this, sent

[1] It must be remembered that Kishwar Khān is but a title, and, like many more similar ones, passed on from one noble on his death or disgrace, to another.

off a small force against Mustafā Khān, which, after storming Bankapūr, seized and murdered him. More impudent and daring now than ever, he had the temerity to transport the queen herself to Sātāra, where he imprisoned her.

It may be as well to say a word about the queen, Chānd Bībī, who was one of the noblest figures in Bījāpūr history. She was the daughter of Ḥusain, king of Aḥmadnagar, and was given in marriage to 'Ali 'Ādil Shāh at the time that the confederacy of the four kings was formed against Rāmrāj of Vijayanagar. She soon began to take an active interest in all her husband's doings, and was, indeed, his constant companion in the field as well as at home. She was used to war's alarms, having been at his side in several skirmishes. She was not secluded, as was the usual custom at the time among respectable Musalman women, but, in deference to public opinion, she wore a light flimsy veil. She was more or less versed in Persian, Arabic, Marathi and Kanarese, and was no mean artist with her brush. Meadows Taylor, who was familiar with the scenes of Bījāpūr story, and who lived a hundred years nearer to the events he describes in his works, writes thus of this "Noble Queen":

> "Few in England know that the contemporary of our Queen Elizabeth in the Deccan kingdoms was a woman of equal ability, of equal political talent, of equal, though in a different sense, education and accomplishments, who ruled over a realm as large, a population as large, and as intelligent, and as rich as England; a woman, who, surrounded by jealous enemies, preserved by her own personal valour and endurance her kingdom from destruction and partition; who through all temptations and exercise of absolute power, was at once simple, generous, frank, and merciful as she was chaste, virtuous, religious and charitable—one who, among all the women of India, stands out as a jewel without flaw and beyond price."

Nemesis quickly overtook Kishwar Khān. When the news of this treachery reached the army in the field, Ikhlās Khān, with a large force, immediately returned to Bījāpūr, only to find Kishwar Khān gone. He had gathered up his belongings, and had made for Aḥmadnagar, where, however, they would have nothing to do with him, and drove him from the place. On entering Quṭb Shāh's territory, he was recognised and murdered by a man of Mustafā Khān's household. Chānd Bībī's release and return to the capital followed Ikhlāṣ Khān's arrival at Bījāpūr.

Yet again was Bījāpūr territory invaded by Nizām Shāh and Quṭb Shāh, the opportunity being irresistible, since the army was scattered—part under Afzal Khān Shīrāzī in the north, part away on the expedition that was sent against Mustafā Khān, and the rest retained by Kishwar Khān at the capital for his own purposes. At this time a general scramble was going on at Bījāpūr, accompanied by bloodshed and imprisonments, for possession of the higher offices of state, and especially for that of *vakīl* or prime minister. So much engaged were they with these troubles in the city, that no resistance was offered to the enemy in the field, and Bihzād-ul-Mulk brought up a force and invested Bījāpūr, Afzal Khān having retreated within the walls. Afzal Khān was arrested, imprisoned, and eventually put to death. The confederate forces outside could, nevertheless, make little impression upon the city, and, the rainy season coming on, they raised the siege and returned to their respective homes.

In this manner things went on—invasions from without and civil strife within—and it is unnecessary here to go further into the details of all the surprises and skirmishes between Bījāpūr and its neighbouring states, or the jealousies, depositions, and assassinations among its nobles. Another noble, Dilāwar Khān, had risen to power, who probably held greater domination over the state, the king, and the queen than any before him. He even meditated dethroning Ibrāhīm and putting the king's brother Ismā'īl in his place; but this rebellion was nipped in the bud, and Dilāwar Khān was for a time in dire disgrace. About this time a rebellion broke out at Aḥmadnagar, through an attempt to seat another Ismā'īl, son of Burhān Shāh, on the throne. Ibrāhīm 'Ādil Shāh espoused the cause of Burhān Shāh against Ismā'īl and his supporter Jamāl Khān, and Dilāwar Khān having been taken into favour again by Ibrāhīm, was despatched with an army against the rebel force, which was defeated, Burhān Shāh being placed upon the throne. But Dilāwar Khān became very arrogant and overbearing, and his conduct towards his sovereign caused the latter to deprive him of his office, and, the nobles deserting him, he was obliged to flee from Bījāpūr.

The plot to dethrone Ibrāhīm 'Ādil Shāh, and place his brother Ismā'īl on the *masnad,* came to a head under the leadership of 'Ain-ul-Mulk and Ankus Khān, who succeeded in seizing the fort of Belgaum, where Ismā'īl was in confinement, and proclaiming him king. But this rising was quelled by Ḥamīd Khān, whom the king despatched against them, when 'Ain-ul-Mulk was killed, and Ismā'īl blinded and imprisoned again. Soon after this the throne of Aḥmadnagar passed, by death, from Burhān to Ibrāhīm his eldest son, who, treating certain Bījāpūr ambassadors with insult, forced Ibrāhīm 'Ādil Shāh to take the field against him. In an action that was fought, the former was killed. This happened about A. D. 1595. Ibrāhīm 'Ādil Shāh being, for the time, relieved of outside worries, applied himself to the business of civil government, and was very assiduous in its execution, attending many hours daily in public *darbār,* where he heard and disposed of petitions, and dispensed justice to the poor. Bījāpūr had a long spell of freedom from turmoils, and king Ibrāhīm was able to devote more time to that splendid memorial of his—the mausoleum to the glory of his queen, Tāj Sulṭāna. Trade had increased and prosperity reigned within the state.

Chāṇd Bībī had made the journey to her old home at Aḥmadnagar with her niece, Khadijah Sulṭāna, on the occasion of the marriage of the latter to Murtazā Niẓām Shāh, and she never again returned. The story of her management of affairs during the civil broils and unsettled conditions at that capital, which followed Ibrāhīm's death, and her noble defence of the fort against the Mughals, with her shameful death by assassination, are part of the history of the Niẓām Shāhi dynasty. The tragic passing of the queen forms one of the most heart-stirring episodes in its history.

In the year A. D. 1599 Ibrāhīm 'Ādil Shāh conceived the idea of transferring the seat of government from Bījāpūr to a pleasanter and more salubrious spot some four miles to the west of the city walls, where he began to build a new city. An account of this enterprise, which was eventually abandoned, will be found further on under the description of Naurasрūr.

A cloud was now forming in the north which, though small at this time, was destined soon to grow to greater proportions, and to bring down with it a storm which was to carry everything before it. The imperial Mughals were on the southward war path, and were beginning to interfere with the Dakhanī kingdoms. Flimsy pretexts were sufficient. When Akbar penetrated into the Dakhan and besieged Aḥmadnagar, he sent such a message to

Ibrāhīm as is said to have astounded the Bījāpūr court, regarding the non-payment of an annual tribute which the Mughals had wrung from the state.[1] But matters were temporarily patched up by the betrothal of Sulṭāna Begam, Ibrāhīm's daughter, to Prince Dānyāl.

Malik 'Ambar, minister and commander-in-chief at Aḥmadnagar, though frequently assisted in his military expeditions by Ibrāhīm, grew so intoxicated with his successes, and his behaviour became so very overbearing and offensive, that the king determined to bring him to his senses. But the army he sent against him was defeated, and the next year, A. D. 1624, Malik 'Ambar followed up his advantage by invading Bījāpūr territory and carrying destruction and desolation up to the very walls of the capital. Nauraspūr, the new city, not then completely walled in, fell an easy prey to his arms, and was plundered and ruined. About this time Ibrāhīm contracted a very serious disease which his own physicians could not cure. He then summoned a European physician who was at Bījāpūr, but he, too, failed to relieve him, and the king died in A. D. 1627.

It is said that Ibrāhīm was handsome, liberal, and careful for his subjects' welfare. He patronized learning and the fine arts, and was passionately fond of music and singing; and it is said by some, that it was due to the company of Hindu musicians and singers, whose patron goddess is Sarasvatī, that he acquired his liking for and leanings towards this deity. Like Akbar, he was charged with the neglect of his own religion. During his reign, a saint, named Hazrat Shāh Ṣibghatullāh, arrived from Medina, who was so shocked at the debauchery and dissipation he witnessed in the public streets, that he severely reprimanded the king for allowing it. He also took him to task for his predilection for music and Sarasvatī.

During his reign were built the Sāt Khan-kā-Maḥall (Sāt Manzil) in A. D. 1583, and, in the same year, the Dilkushā Maḥall and the Ḥaidarī or Uprī Burj. The Malikah Jahān Masjid was erected in 1587; the Ānaṇd Maḥall, for dancing and singing, in 1589; and the Sangat or Nauras Maḥall, and other buildings in Nauraspūr, between 1599 and 1624. He is said to have possessed 52,000 horse, 100,400 infantry and 955 elephants. Bījāpūr attained its high water-mark of prosperity during the reigns of Ibrāhīm II. and Sulṭān Muḥammad. The city is said to have then contained 984,400 persons, and to have possessed 1,600 mosques. The state revenue was upward of 10,000,000 sterling.[2]

Although Darvesh Pādshāh was Ibrāhīm's eldest son, he was set aside, and MUḤAMMAD, a younger son, was raised to the throne in his stead, in A. D. 1627, at the immature age of fifteen. The two ministers chiefly instrumental in this move were Mirzā Muḥammad Amīn Lāri, who was given the title of Muṣṭafā Khān, and Daulat Khān, who was called Khawāṣṣ Khān. No sooner was Muḥammad seated upon the throne than he took the field against Aḥmadnagar. Ibrāhīm did not live to wreak vengeance upon that state for the destruction of Nauraspūr. Muṣṭafā Khān, whose father-in-law had been executed by Malik 'Ambar, was also burning for revenge; and, against the better judgment

---

[1] Pietro Della Valle, an Italian, who travelled in India in 1623-24, during the reign of Ibrāhim, writes: "But indeed *Adil-Sciah* fears the Moghol, yea he fears and observes him so much that he pays him an annual tribute; and when the Moghol sends any letter to him, which is always brought by some very ordinary Souldier or Slave, he goeth forth with his whole army to meet the letter and him that brings it, who being conducted to the Palace sits down there, whilst *Adil Sciah* stands all the time, and the letter being lay'd upon a carpet on the pavement, before he offers to put forth his hand to take it up, he bows himself three times to the earth, doing reverence to it after their manner."—*Travels of Pietro Della Valle in India*, Ed. by Edward Grey for the Hakluyt Society. Vol. I, p. 148.

[2] *Architecture at Beejapoor*, by Fergusson and Taylor, p. 57.

of Khawāṣṣ Khān and other nobles, invited the Mughals to assist him in breaking up and sharing the Aḥmadnagar kingdom. This suicidal policy very soon brought the Mughal army down upon Bījāpūr, and for a time they invested the city itself. But they were, in the end, repulsed and driven off, being followed up as far as Parandah.[1]

The Mughals were now very active in the Dakhan, the Aḥmadnagar state receiving the first brunt of their attacks. The almost impregnable frontier fortress of Daulatābād surrendered to them; and its fall, and the capture of king Ḥusain Shāh practically wiped out that kingdom. Had these states actively united against this their common foe, the establishment of the power of Delhi, south of the Narmadā, must have been indefinitely postponed. But their jealousies and petty selfish motives, on all occasions, kept them apart, or rendered abortive whatever half-hearted aid they offered each other. The better trained Mughal troops were never slow to take full advantage of this disunion, and every year found them in further possession. There was now a great scramble for the Aḥmadnagar territory. These events, as they were bound to do, brought about ill-feeling and misunderstandings between the two ministers Khawāṣṣ Khān and Muṣṭafā Khān, who forthwith quarrelled, when the former, getting the upper hand, imprisoned the latter in the fort of Belgaum.

Shāh Jahān again took personal control of his troops in the Dakhan, dividing his army into two divisions, one of which he sent against the Marātha insurgent Shāhjī, while the other was directed against Bījāpūr. Muḥammad Shāh, unable to meet the imperial troops in the field, shut himself up within the city, after having destroyed all forage and provisions within twenty miles around the capital, which he was unable to store himself, and emptied the tanks, leaving the country so barren and desolate that it was impossible for an enemy to remain long in it. Though thus thwarted in their attempt upon the city, the Mughals were able to wring from Muḥammad an annual tribute of twenty *lakhs*, and the promise not to assist Shāhjī. The latter, however, was soon taken into favour and was given a command in the Bījāpūr service.

During the period which succeeded, from A. D. 1636 to the death of Muḥammad in 1656, Bījāpūr enjoyed comparative immunity from troubles within or without; and the king used this time in completing his own colossal mausoleum, the Gol Gumbaz, and erecting many other buildings throughout the city. Under the superintendence of Afzal Khān the water-supply of the city was considerably increased by a conduit from a fresh source, the Begam Talāo, to the south of the town. Muḥammad built the Āthār Maḥall as a Court of Justice, but it was subsequently used as a repository for the sacred relics—two hairs of Muḥammad, the Prophet—which are said to be still safe within its walls.

Shāhjī was now employed as one of the Bījāpūr chiefs in the Karnatic. He possessed his hereditary estate near Poona, where he had left his wife, Jījī Bāī, a most ambitious woman, and his son, Śivājī. As the latter grew up, a restless and crafty character, fired with an ambition to found a Marātha kingdom, he gradually gathered around him associates willing to share his fortunes and privations. He eventually became strong enough to take possession of several of the old mountain forts of the Western Ghāts, affecting to do so in the name of the king. But, having intercepted some treasure, and committed other

[1] It was while Murāri, the Bījāpūr officer in command of the troops, was at Parandah that orders were issued for the great Malik-i-Maidān gun to be brought to Bījāpūr from that fort.

high-handed offences, he was denounced as a rebel, and his father, Shāhjī, was recalled and imprisoned on the suspicion of being concerned in his son's misdoings.

Prince Aurangzeb, his father's deputy in the Dakhan, returned in 1650, to his government of those districts, and very soon got mixed up with the affairs of Golkondah, and marched against it with his troops. While there, in the year 1656, the news arrived of the death of Muḥammad 'Ādil Shāh.

The treaty by which Bījāpūr remitted an annual tax to Delhi constituted, in the eyes of Shāh Jahān, a reason for interfering in its affairs, and controlling it, to a certain extent, as a tributary state. Great offence was thus given to the emperor by the succession of 'Ali, without any previous reference to him, and he accordingly seized upon the opportunity for active interference. He denounced 'Ali as spurious, and contended that Muḥammad had no male offspring, and hence the state had lapsed to the empire for want of a legitimate heir. Aurangzeb marched from Golkondah against Bījāpūr, laying waste and ravishing the country as he proceeded, and laid siege to the capital. He pressed the siege with vigour, but just as the outlook was beginning to appear very gloomy to the besieged, he got news of his father's serious illness and hurried back to Delhi to secure to himself the succession in the event of Shāh Jahān's death, after hastily concluding a peace with Bījāpūr.

'ALI 'ĀDIL SHĀH II. was not long at peace with his neighbours. Śivājī, who had thrown off all allegiance to Bījāpūr, had been backed in his ever-increasing aggressions by the Mughals. He was now making things very unpleasant for Bījāpūr ; he was plundering and raiding its territory, and carrying on a predatory warfare against Dakhanis and Mughals alike, only intent upon setting up a kingdom for himself and exterminating the unclean Moslem. It was, therefore, decided to send out an expedition against him. Afzal Khān was selected as commander-in-chief in succession to Khān Muḥammad, who, owing to his treachery during the late Mughal investment of the city, was executed ; and, when all was in readiness, the troops marched for Śivājī's retreat. It was a fatal enterprise which ended in disaster, and the death of Afzal Khān. The mountain chief lured the Muḥammadan army into the hills of the Western Ghāts, where Śivājī, with his own hands, treacherously murdered Afzal Khān, after inducing him to meet him under the flag of truce. The Marātha hordes, hidden in the jungle and surrounding the Bījāpūr troops, at a given signal, swept down upon them and practically annihilated the whole force. A remnant only escaped.[1]

This was followed up by the despatch of a fresh expedition, which, however, made little impression upon the Marāthas, who, whenever pressed, were always able to retreat to their mountain fastnesses, every inch of the ground being perfectly familiar to them. It was, therefore, deemed advisable to come to terms with Śivājī, and a treaty was signed confirming him in his possession of the whole of the Konkan and a good slice of the Dakhan. But he could not rest. He was tempted to cross swords with the Mughals, but soon joined them in their campaign against Bījāpūr, which, however, had to be abandoned. 'Ādil Shāh now began to think it time to propitiate the emperor, since these repeated invasions were becoming very serious. Hitherto the yearly tribute had fallen into arrears,

---

[1] *The Basātīn-i-Salāṭīn* gives another account of Afzal Khān's death. It states that Śivājī affected submission, and Afzal Khān, being deceived thereby, concluded peace with him, and accepted his invitation to visit him on Partābgarh fort with twelve attendants, when Śivājī offered him poisoned sherbet to drink which brought about his death.

and this was a constant excuse for Aurangzeb's reprisals. A treaty was entered into by which Bījāpūr lost much of its possessions in the north, including the fort of Sholāpūr. An understanding was also come to with Śivājī, who was preparing to levy *chauth*, and it was agreed to pay him three *lakhs* of rupees in consideration of his refraining from the collection of this blackmail.

In A. D. 1672 the king died of paralysis, brought on, it is said, by lustful indulgences, in the thirty-fifth year of his age, and after a reign of sixteen years. He had received from his father a kingdom intact and flourishing, but to his son SIKANDAR, now only five years of age, he left a shattered heritage, shorn of some of its best possessions, by Śivājī on the one hand and the Mughals on the other. He commenced a mausoleum for himself, which, had it been completed, would have been one of the most elegant buildings in the city; but either because he began it too late in life, or was too often interrupted in its construction, it was never finished, and it now remains conspicuous upon its lofty basement, the finest ruin in the city. He was buried in the vault of the unfinished building, which also contains the graves of his wife and many others, probably members of his household.

Not much remains now to be told of Bījāpūr story, the falcon was hard upon its prey, and was about to make a final swoop. No worse luck could have befallen the state at this time than to pass into the hands of a minor. Its very existence was seriously threatened by the Mughals, and its peace continued to be disturbed by the ever restless and treaty-breaking Śivājī. Khawāṣṣ Khān, the son of the traitor Khān Muḥammad, was left as regent to manage the affairs of the state. But his treachery in attempting to sell the kingdom to the Mughals met with its due punishment. He was executed and buried beside his father, and Karīm Khān was appointed in his place. Śivājī took advantage of the party strife that naturally accompanied the regency, and stripped Bījāpūr of many more of her districts. He had now become sufficiently powerful to be crowned Mahārājā in A. D. 1674, and to make treaties with the English Factors of Bombay, who thus acknowledged his position. He even extended his field of operations as far south as the forts of Gingi and Vellur, and eastward to Golkondah, traversing Bījāpūr territory with impunity. At Golkondah, he made a treaty with Quṭb Shāh for the division of 'Ādil Shāh's southern provinces. An attack upon Golkondah failed, and the Bījāpūr troops had to beat a retreat. Long arrears of pay had spread discontent and disorder throughout the Bījāpūr army, so that great numbers deserted to the Mughals and Marāthas, where they were paid more regularly. Once again was the city besieged by the Mughal troops, and again, owing to Śivājī's assistance, they were compelled to abandon the siege. In A. D. 1680 Śivājī died.

Faction quarrels again broke out in the city as soon as the enemy withdrew. In 1683 Aurangzeb marched out of Delhi with an immense army, intent upon accomplishing himself what his generals had failed to do—the overthrow of Bījāpūr and the complete conquest of the Dakhan—but it was not until 1686 that his operations were crowned with success, by the unconditional surrender of the city. Sikandar, the last of the 'Ādil Shāhis, who was taken prisoner at the same time, lived some few years longer, when, with his death, the dynasty ceased to exist, and the kingdom was merged in the greater empire of Delhi.[1] He was buried in a simple grave, which still exists, not far from the Dakhanī 'Īdgāh.

[1] It is said that he was poisoned in A. H. 1111 (A. D. 1699).

Aurangzeb remained for some years in the city after its fall. When Nizām-ul-Mulk proclaimed his independence in 1724, it became part of his possessions. In 1760 it was ceded to the Peshwā. During the period it was under the Marāthas, the city suffered severely. They found in its public buildings a mine of material which they immediately proceeded to appropriate. The palaces were stripped of all their woodwork; beams, doors, windows were ruthlessly torn out and carted away; and so, when we look upon the remnants of these old structures today, the marks of the ravaging hand of man upon them is but too painfully apparent, beside which the disintegrating process of time is as nothing. Famines visited the now forlorn city at frequent intervals and still further decimated its population. Many old families left it and took up their abode in distant towns where their descendants still live. A few of the leading families remained behind, and their representatives are now very poorly off. In 1818 Bījāpūr passed into the hands of the Rājā of Sātāra; and, later on, together with the rest of the Marātha kingdom, it reverted to the British. It was then for some time part of the Sātāra collectorate, after which it was handed over to Sholāpūr, and finally became a *taluqa* or sub-division of the Kalādgī district. Subsequently Kalādgī was given up as the headquarters station, and Bījāpūr was selected as such. It is now the chief town of the Bījāpūr collectorate of the Bombay Presidency; and, at it, reside the Collector, Judge, and other local Officials. *Sic transit gloria mundi!*

DESCRIPTION OF THE CITY.

GENERAL ASPECT.

BĪJĀPŪR, its history, and its monumental remains, are little known beyond the limits of the Bombay Presidency. Yet there are few spots in India of more absorbing interest than this 'city of the plain', which was, a hundred years ago, not inappropriately called the 'Palmyra of the Deccan'.[1] This expression was applicable up to within a few decades ago, before its restoration to prosperity, and before its salubrious position and tempting material marked it out for conversion into a district headquarters in place of the unhealthy and less centrally placed town of Kalādgī.

The town is situated in north latitude 16° 50′, and east longitude 75° 52′, at an elevation of 2,000 feet above sea-level; or, as the crow flies, it lies about two hundred and forty miles south-east of Bombay. It is immediately surrounded by almost barren, treeless plains, intersected, here and there, by scarcely less unfertile valleys, whose stream beds are moist for but a very short period during the rainy season. A few miles, however, to the south is the Dhon river, whose valley, in good seasons, has been so productive that it constituted the granary of Bījāpūr.

In the early days of British occupation, situated, as it was, far from the rail and the busy haunts of men, it was an almost forgotten spot. Its extensive ruins, thickly overgrown with rank vegetation, were the abode of the owl and the jackal, and the undisturbed and happy hunting ground of the village vandal. Within its crumbling walls, with a girth of over six miles, the remains of the city presented a scene of utter desolation—lines of ruined houses and fallen palaces, overturned gravestones, disclosing gaping holes where bodies once reposed, all choked with the exuberant growth of cactus and noxious weeds. Out of this chaos, festooned and bound into inextricable masses by persistent creepers—a wilderness of tangled jungle—rose the truncated forms and shattered remains of the greater tombs, mosques, and palaces of the 'Ādil Shāhis. The visitor then needed a guide

[1] *Asiatic Researches*, Quarto Ed., Vol. XIII, p. 433.

to trace the intricate windings of the uncertain footpaths leading to the various buildings, even within the Ārk-qil'ah or fort. Save for the soft lowing of village cattle, the cooing of doves in the bush, and the occasional shrill note of the distant kite, silent solitude brooded over all. Under such conditions did the writer first set foot within the deserted city forty years ago.

Meadows Taylor, who visited the place in the early years of the last century, thus describes it as it was then :

"Mournful as it is, the picturesque beauty of the combinations of the buildings, the fine old tamarind and peepul trees, the hoary ruins, and distant views of the more perfect edifices, combine to produce an ever-changing and impressive series of landscapes. Nowhere in the Deccan, not even at Beedar, at Goolburgah, or in the old fort of Golcondah, is there any evidence of general public taste and expenditure, like that proved by the remains in Beejapoor—and for days together the traveller, or sketcher, will wander among these remains with his wonder still excited and unsatisfied. It is not by the grandeur of the edifices now perfect, noble as they are, that the imagination is so much filled, as by the countless other objects of interest in ruin, which far exceed them in number. Palaces, arches, tombs, cisterns, gateways, minarets, all carved from the rich brown basalt rock of the locality, garlanded by creepers, broken and disjointed by peepul, or banian trees, each, in its turn, is a gem of art, and the whole a treasury to the sketcher or artist. . . . . The interior of the citadel is almost indescribable, being nearly covered with masses of enormous ruins, now almost shapeless, interspersed with buildings still perfect. All those which had vaulted roofs are sound, but all in which wood existed are roofless and irreparably ruined. . . . . In the citadel the visitor, if he be acquainted with its past history, will have many a scene of historical interest shown him. The court which the devoted Dilshad Agha, and her royal mistress Booboojee Khanum, Queen of Yusuf Adil Shah, clad in armour, and fighting among the soldiers, defended against the attempts of the treacherous Kumal Khan to murder the young king Ismail ; the place where the son of Kumal Khan stood, when the young king pushed over a stone from the parapet above, which crushed him to death ; the window where the dead body of Kumal Khan was set out, as if alive, to encourage the soldiery in their brutal assault ; the place on the ramparts where Dilshad Agha threw over the ropes, and the faithful bands of Persians and Moghuls ascended by them and saved the Queen and her son. All these will be pointed out with every accompanying evidence of probability and truth ; as well as the apartment whence the traitor Kishwar Khan dragged the noble-hearted Queen Chand Beebee to her prison at Sattara. Then in a lighter vein, the visitor will be told of the merry monarch Mahmood ; he will be shown the still entire and exquisitely proportioned and ornamented room where happy hours were passed with the beautiful Rhumba ; and though it was much defaced when the Rajah of Sattara began with his own dagger to scrape the gilding from the walls there are still traces of the picture of the jovial king and his lovely mistress. Such, and hundreds of other tales of wild romance and reality which linger amidst these royal precincts, will, if the visitor choose to listen to them, be told him by descendants of those who took part in them, with as fond and vivid a remembrance as the Moorish legends of the Alhambra are told there.

"For such legends of that beautiful memorial of past greatness, an interest for all time has been created ; but no one has succeeded in awakening for Beejapoor any corresponding feeling, and far grander as its memorials are, accounts of them are listened to with a cold scepticism or indifference which hitherto nothing has aroused. And yet, inspired by the effect of these beautiful ruins with the glory of an Indian sun lighting up palace and mosque, prison and zenana, embattled tower and rampart, with a splendour which can only be felt by personal experience, it may be hoped that some eloquent and poetic pen may be found to gather up the fleeting memorials of traditions which are fast passing away, and invest them with a classic interest which will be imperishable. Above all, however, these noble monuments may serve to lead our countrymen to appreciate the intellect, the taste, and the high power of art and execution which they evince, to consider their authors not as barbarians, but in the position to which their works justly entitle them ; and to follow, in the history of those who conceived them, that

Divine scheme of civilization and improvement, which, so strangely and so impressively, has been confided to the English nation."

This is now all changed. The hum of busy life pervades the atmosphere ; the jungle is well-nigh all cleared away ; well-made roads take the place of tortuous paths through bush and brake ; modern residences and *bāzārs* cover the once ruinous sites ; factory chimneys rise in unlovely contrast with graceful minarets ; and the railway discharges its living freight at the very gate of the town.

It may not be out of place to give, here, a little vision of the past as conjured up by a modern writer[1] :

"The Bijapore which we see today is not the Bijapore which Ferishta saw in 1589, exactly three hundred years ago. We now see its ghost. But from the Palace of the Seven Stories we can see the ground he often travelled over and the place he made his home. That great street nearly three miles in length, which bisects the city now crowded on either side with the ruins of tomb, mosque or mahal, was then alive with thousands of people. We are not left in doubt on this point, for we have an exact description (Assad Beg, 1604) by one whom Ferishta knew, for he travelled with him that year to Berhampore. The bazaar which lined this great street was filled with shops, brimful of every commodity that the East and the then West could furnish. Cairo or Damascus today may exhibit its counterpart, but not its extent. All the luxuries and necessities which the ingenuity of man could devise—crystal goblets, porcelain vases, gold and silver ornaments, rare essences and perfumes, double distilled spirits from Dabul or Goa, tobacco also and the finest wines from Portugal, with groups of pleasure-seekers, fair-faced choristers and dancing girls ; everything to fill with wonder the stranger from distant provinces. As he passed the great suburbs of Shahapur and Torvi, now a white heap of ruins, he saw indications of what awaited him in the palaces of the nobles and the garden houses of the rich, embowered in greenery, flowers of every hue and creepers trailing up to lattice and jalousie, with bubbling springs of water, fountains and streams which transported his mind to the Koran Paradise and the garden of God.

"The Ibrahim Roza which we see today, battered with age, the elements and Aurungzebe's cannon, had then the appearance of a forest of bamboos, covered here and there by tattered screens to hide the workmen from the heat and his mason craft from the public gaze. Amid piles of timber and masses of stone, hewn and unhewn, the design of the architect was dimly creeping out, and through the network the skeletons of a half finished minaret or bulbous dome that was to be projected, their outlines. But the din was overpowering from hammer, anvil and bellows, and the work was never to cease day or night for the next twenty years : 5,000 men were engaged on it when Ferishta entered the city of Bijapore. He saw the Juma Mosque, and was doubtless at the earliest opportunity among its 5,000 worshippers who bent the knee to the one God ; and he was in Bijapore when the two hairs of the Prophet (he does not say of his beard) arrived from Mecca. He saw the lovely Mehtar Mehal spick and span, not one cornice or frieze abraded, not one line blurred or effaced, a perfect gem of exquisite purity and grace. The moat in the picture in Ogilby's Atlas (1680) is full of open-mouthed crocodiles : but he does not mention them. One building he did not and could not see, and that was the Dome of Mahmud. Mahmud succeeded Ibrahim. He could walk round Nagar in half-an-hour. He found half-a-day was too little for the circumference of Bijapore."

The grand old citadel has all but disappeared : its hoary old ruins, that were so picturesquely clothed, have been stripped of the mantle nature so generously wove for them, and have been laid bare in all their naked uncomeliness. Some have been cleared away entirely, while the exigencies of the public service have caused others to be adapted and converted to modern requirements. It was in 1877 that the first extensive clearance in the citadel was made, when it was carried out as a famine relief work. Subsequently

[1] James Douglas in the *Pioneer*, 1889.

great lengths of the walls were demolished to let in more air to the buildings within the fort, which were being converted to public use. Government have, however, for many years past, taken a special interest in the proper conservation of these old relics and have not stinted expenditure upon them. Consequently, the loss of the picturesque combinations of crumbling walls and luxurious jungle are now more than compensated for by the neat and pleasant surroundings, and more stable condition of the buildings. There are still extensive areas within the city walls that have not yet been encroached upon by cultivation or modern masonry, and over these may still be traced many an old road and street between the heaps of ruins of fallen walls. Prickly-pear, that once held full possession of the place, and which took hundreds of convicts, many a long month, to make any impression upon, still asserts itself, and, where undisturbed, jealously encompasses and guards the crumbling ruins. Captain Sykes, who was encamped at Bījāpūr in 1818, was told that there were then, within the walls, " 700 wells with steps (bowries), 300 without steps (kooahs), 700 mosques and tombs of stone, and 700 of bricks and chunam ".[1] The present population which is fast increasing, has spread itself across the west end of the city, round about the Jāmi' Masjid, and through a few small scattered hamlets, the remains of the *bāzārs* of the former wards of the city. Without the walls are several suburbs, the largest being that of Shāhpūr on the north-west.

From the high ground to the north and north-east of the walls, a grand uninterrupted view of the city is obtained. The various buildings of note stand out sharply against their sombre backgrounds, the great dome of the tomb of Muḥammad, the Gol Gumbaz, close at hand, overshadowing and dominating those in its vicinity. It is difficult to conceive why such a position was ever selected for a city that had to defend itself against many enemies. There is nothing whatever in the natural features of the ground to give it any claim to preference; rather the reverse. It doubtless grew from small beginnings; and Yūsuf Khān, with whom its story opens, found it an important military post, and a fairly large town, when he was sent there as its commandant and governor by the Bahmanī king of Bīdar. It was, indeed, at a later time, intended to move the seat of government to Nauraspūr, a few miles to the west of Bījāpūr, and Ibrāhīm II. began to build palaces and fortifications on the new site; but the ever officious astrologers stepped in with their warnings and the project was given up. It would appear, indeed, that Bījāpūr, such as it was, was within an ace of falling into obscurity at its very outset, for it is related that after Yūsuf 'Ādil Shāh retook Goa, soon after its capture, for the first time, by the Portuguese, he " had such a predilection for this place [Goa] that he not only resided there frequently, but also, owing to the great advantage of its position and the beauty of its port, at one time resolved to make it the seat of his government ".[2]

The whole of the eastern and northern quarters are completely overlooked and commanded by the higher ground on these sides, which surrounds, and is close up to the walls. A few batteries entrenched along these ridges would, in a short time, have laid the city in ruins. We can only suppose that guns were little used at the time the site was selected as the headquarters of a province by the Bīdar government; and that, for some time after they did come into use, they were such primitive weapons, and were so poorly

---

[1] *Transactions of the Literary Society of Bombay*, Vol. III, p. 57.

[2] Fonsera's *History of Goa*, p. 131, and *Commentaries of Albuquerque*, Vol. II, p. 96.

served, that the town was comparatively safe. When, however, Aurangzeb came down upon it, with his superior artillery, the city soon succumbed to his attacks.

The area of the whole city covers about two and a half square miles, the walls having a circuit of about six and a quarter miles. It is stated that seven village sites were absorbed, namely, those of Gajkanhallī, Bajkanhallī, Chandankirī, Kyādgī, Khatarkirī, Kūrbūrhattī, and Kūzankūtī.[1]

THE CITADEL.

The most interesting spot of all is the citadel, or Ārk-qil'ah [2] as it is generally called, for within this small, and almost circular enclosure, were the palaces and private apartments of the king and his family, various public buildings such as the civil and criminal courts, the military and revenue offices, and treasury, interspersed with courts and gardens, fountains, cisterns and running water. Within it have been enacted some of the most stirring events and darkest tragedies in Bījāpūr history, and many a treasonable plot and villainous intrigue have there been planned. The buildings, when Bījāpūr came into our hands, were in such a state of ruin that, with the exception of a few of the principal ones, it was impossible to trace or identify the dilapidated remains of many that are mentioned in local historical accounts, or to follow, with any pretence at accuracy, the changes of residence of successive kings from one palace to another. Nor are we able to say, except in the case of three or four, and this on tradition mainly, for what purpose each building was intended. Possibly these palaces were put to different uses by different kings just as the whim seized them at the time. The better known structures are the Sāt Manzil, the Gagan Maḥall, and the Ānand Maḥall, which, with the Makka Masjid and the old mosques, converted from Hindu materials, are described in the following pages. We get a little further light upon the minor ruins, many of which were converted into residences or offices, from early European visitors to the city. Mr. James Bird, writing about 1844, says that the 'Adālat Maḥall, or 'Adālat K͟hāna, now the Collector's residence, was the place where the kings usually received the congratulations of the multitude and the petitions of the poor. It consisted of two stories, with wide verandahs, elevated on large wooden pillars, and was standing when he first visited Bījāpūr; but in consequence of the building falling quickly to decay, the Rājā of Sātāra had the whole taken down, and the only remaining part then to be seen were the ruined fountain in the garden and the terrace where people were usually allowed to present themselves. The building, he says, was erected by 'Ali I. Close to it, on the north side is a small mosque, perched upon a high platform, which is said to have been erected by Aurangzeb. To the right of it was the Sonā Maḥall, or Gilded Palace (probably the block No. 271 shewn on the plan), which was burnt down. Beside the 'Adālat Maḥall on the west, and now represented by the Collector's servants' quarters, was the Sūraj Maḥall, where there are some extensive underground apartments. To the west of the Ānand Maḥall, Mr. Bird tells us, was the "Dhobi Mahal," and to the south the "Sejadah Mahal" or "Sat Khandi" (The Sāt Manjli), called the "Sejadah Mahal," he says, from being a

---

[1] These names are as entered upon an old manuscript map found at Bījāpūr. A list given at the end of a copy of the *Basātīn-i-Salātīn* is as follows: Gachānalli, Bachaknallī, Chandankirī, Kyādgī, Khīrkiri, Kūrbūrhattī, and Kurankūtī. The differences between the names in the two authorities are due to the omission or unnecessary addition in one or the other of the dots above or below the letters.

[2] It is also written *Arg-Qil'ah,* the Arg Fort, and *Qil'ah-ārk*. The term *Ark* or *Arg* is not peculiar to Bījāpūr; it is used in other parts of India for a citadel or fort, but its precise meaning is uncertain.

palace of retirement for the princesses to pay their devotions. The "Dhobi Mahal" must be that block now converted into offices, on the north of the Sāt Manzil, and separated from it by the Jalamaṇdir or little water pavilion. Captain Sydenham, who visited Bījāpūr about the end of the eighteenth or beginning of the nineteenth century, says the 'Adālat Khāna, or court of justice, was situated at the extremity of a court 150 yards long by 80 broad :

"Here the sultans were installed in a balcony projecting from the upper story, where also justice was administered. In front of the building is a large fountain, and at the opposite end of the court is a low range of buildings with a front of 30 arches, in which the Umrahs attended in waiting. There is a black stone a few paces before the centre of this arcade, called the *mujri-gah* from which the officers of the court used to perform their obeisances.[1] On the right of the front of the Adawlat Khana is the Sona Mahl, which, as its name implies, was richly gilded, but now hardly a vestige of this ornament remains. Opposite the Sona Mahl, is the Sicca Mahl in which was kept the privy-seal. Beyond this is the Pani Mahl,[2] built on the brink of the ditch on the northern side of the citadel."

Fig. 5. Entrance to the Citadel.

If we take the 'Adālat Maḥall as having faced south originally, as the space between it and the citadel walls on the north side, hardly suffices for gardens, fountains and waiting halls, then the block of ruins to the right front of it, standing with one's back to the 'Adālat Maḥall, would probably be the "Sona Mahl" (No. 271 on plan). The smaller building in the corner between it and the 'Adālat, used now as outhouses, being the Sūraj Maḥall, while the 'Arsh Maḥall,[3] opposite the "Sona Maḥall," would answer to the "Sicca Mahl". These form a group around an extensive court or garden and probably all looked inwards to it. Then, as he says, the little pavilion on the ramparts, known as the Pāni Maḥall, is beyond it on the north-east.

Upon the south side of the Sāt Manzil, and into which it has been built at the north-west corner, is a great enclosure

[1] Probably one of those now lying at the Āthār Maḥall.

[2] Described further on.

[3] *'Arsh* means a throne or chair of state. The *maḥall* possibly contained a throne room.

surrounded by arcades on the east, west and north, and closed up on the south by a building extending across the whole breadth of the court. This block of ruins has been converted into public offices, but it was known, on account of the great quantities of broken china excavated from around it, as the Chīnī Maḥall. It seems to have been originally the Farākh Maḥall and is said to have been built in A. H. 921 (A. D. 1514) during the reign of Ismā'īl.

The walls of the citadel are amongst the earliest structures raised by the 'Ādil Shāhis at Bījāpūr, after their assumption of independent power. Expecting, as Yūsuf 'Ādil Shāh naturally would, attempts to be made on the part of the Bahmanī king to recover his lost province, he would be anxious to fortify his position as well as he could against attack. And this he, no doubt, proceeded to do by laying the foundations of the walls of the citadel, in solid stone masonry, to form a more lasting protection than its old dilapidated mud walls afforded.[1] His limited resources at that time would have compelled him to restrict the extent of his fortifications to the small area that we find was enclosed—about forty-two acres—but, as buildings were added by successive kings, the fort became very crowded towards the end of the dynasty. It even overflowed when Muḥammad built the Dād Maḥall outside its limits, and bridged the moat in order to get easy access to it. The construction of these walls extended over many years, disturbed as the work must have been, from time to time, by invasions and surprisals by quarrelsome neighbours, and the king's frequent absence on expeditions against them. There are several inscriptions upon them, the earliest dated being in A. H. 920 (A. D. 1514) during the reign of Ismā'īl, and the latest in A. H. 951 (A. D. 1544) during that of Ibrāhīm I. As these record the completion of the several parts, the earliest dated portion must have been finished within four years of Yūsuf's death, so we may safely conclude the work was begun by him. The *Basātīn-i-Salāṭīn* tells us that Ibrāhīm I. rebuilt the citadel of Bījāpūr and made it strong. He made two *ḥiṣārs* (surrounding walls) and two ditches. The *ḥiṣārs* were 20 cubits high, and between them and the ditch he made a little garden, built some houses, and erected a mosque called Ghālib (victorious) with 1,303 niches. This is confirmed by an inscription on the walls.

Our first authoritative statement, however, is contained in an inscription on the outside of the citadel wall on the south-east, between the citadel gateway and the Āthār Maḥall. It is in barbarous and verbose language, and rather disintegrated in parts. Its translation runs as follows :—

> The marking of the date was this which the meanest, humble individual has composed :—In Jumādā the second, month last, year 920 of the Hijrah [A. D. 1514]. Having been ordered to fortify the said citadel by auspicious exalted favour and blessing . . . . . . the fortification . . . . . he considered again and established it by the high command of his majesty . . . . . exalted, that sum and dignity, 'Adil Khān son of 'Adil Khān 'Ali, may Allah perpetuate his monarchy. By order . . . . the bastion and citadel. . . . .[2]

The word used in this inscription for citadel is *ḥiṣār*.

There are some things in this inscription which are not very clear, one being the statement that 'Ādil Khān was the son of 'Ādil Khān 'Ālī. The date falls four years within

---

[1] Firishtah tells us that a mud fort originally stood on the site.—Briggs' *Ferishtah*, Vol. I, p. 140.

[2] Where not otherwise stated, all translations of the Bījāpūr inscriptions occurring in this volume were made by the late Mr. E. Rehatsek of Bombay, and will be found *in extenso* in *Notes on the Buildings and other Antiquarian Remains in Bijapur*, by the author, published in 1890, as a Government Selection, at the Government Central Press, Bombay.

the reign of Ismā'īl, whose father was Yūsuf.[1] It will be noticed that "'Ādil Khān" is used and not "'Ādil Shāh". The portion of the walls in which this inscribed slab is built is shewn in Plate II.

There are two inscriptions, dated in *Hijrah* 945 and 951 respectively, upon the walls of the citadel gateway, both of which fall within the reign of Ibrāhīm I. There are two gates within a few yards of each other, the outer being protected by a flanking wall and barbican thrown across before it, the final exit being thus turned at right angles to this gate. The outer gate is shewn in Fig. 5. Inside, on a bastion between the entrances, is the first inscription, in beautifully formed letters. It contains the *bismillāh*[2] with the profession of faith, and the Shī'ah addition of the words "and 'Ali is the vicar of Allāh," which is very uncommon. It is also the *kalimah*[3] of the Khojahs. It then proceeds:

> In the days of justice of the exalted assembly of the Khān of high dignity 'Adil Shāh Ibrāhīm, may Allah perpetuate the days of his monarchy, this Burj Ilāhī [Divine Bastion] was built, 945. [A. D. 1538-39.]

The second is upon the barbican at the outer entrance, which, after the profession of faith, continues:

> Door. Work of Kurdā Khān Jita Gujarāti in the year 951. [A. D. 1544-45.][4]

Yet another inscription is found upon a large bastion of the walls south of the Chīnī Mahall, dated A. H. 94? [A. D. 153?], at the top of which is the word "Allāh", then the profession of faith, and below that:

> Abu-l-Muzaffar 'Ādil Shāh, Mulah Hārbūkzah built the citadel here. Khān 'Azīm Khān Gujarāti Kurdā [Kh]ān who came was here appointed. Date, the end of the month Rabī' the first, 94?

The third figure of the date is damaged but looks like a 2. This would bring it into the reign of Ibrāhīm I. But the title Abū-l-Muzaffar, in a few other instances in which it occurs, is applied by name to 'Ali I. The whole name, "Abū-l-Muzaffar Pādshāh 'Ali 'Ādili", stands by itself upon the walls of the Pānī Mahall. It occurs again in an inscription upon the Shāhpūr gateway as "Shāh-al-Muzaffar 'Ali 'Ādil Shāh"; and yet again upon the fort wall at Raichūr. But then, the title "Pādshāh" applied to him on the Pānī Mahall has been supposed to be the exclusive title of Muhammad, among the Bījāpūr kings, having been accorded him by Shāh Jahān as a favour.[5]

The word *hisār* for citadel, is still used in the last inscription. The term *'Ark-Qil'ah'* does not occur in any of the Bījāpūr lithic records.

---

[1] The following revised translation of this inscription has been kindly made for me by Dr. Horovitz, Epigraphist to Government of India. It removes the difficulty and gives a more suitable reading. It is as follows:

> The reason of writing the date was this that the humble Kashtan Rāi on account of besieging the aforesaid castle had been defeated on the 20th of the month of Jumādā-al-Ākhir of the year 928 Hijra. By the good luck of the favour of God and the blessing of the noble foot of saints, the cursed Kashtan, considering his defeat in the siege as his good fortune, took to flight on the day of Jumādā. In conformity with the order of His Exalted Majesty, the noble Khān of inaccessible rank, 'Adil Khān, son of 'Adil Khan Ghāzī (the champion of faith)—may his kingdom be perpetuated—the foundation of a tower and a castle was laid by the command of invisable lords.

[2] *Lit.* "In the name of God," an expression often used at the commencement of any undertaking.

[3] *Lit.* "The word". The Muhammadan profession of faith, viz., *Lā Ilāha illā'llāh: Muhammad Rasūlu'llāh.* "There is no deity but God: Muhammad is the Apostle of God." Compare with Deuteronomy, VI, 4. "The Lord our God is one Lord", or "Jehovah our Elohim is one Jehovah".

[4] Many inscriptions are only quotations from the Qurān, or are the *Bismillah* or *Kalimah*. Mention of such is often omitted as being of no special interest.

[5] The title was said to have been assumed by Bābar and was claimed as the exclusive prerogative of the Mughal emperors.

Another inscription, without a date, occurs upon the bastion just inside the south gateway of the citadel, one half of which consists of a well-known invocation to 'Alī, and the other of good wishes for 'Ādil Shāh. It reads thus :—

> Invoke 'Ali the displayer of miracles; thou wilt find him a help to thee in trouble; every care and every grief will be removed by thy aid O 'Ali, O 'Ali, O 'Ali. [Be] the world always under the command of the wish of 'Adil Shāh, the coinage of the state perpetually in the name of 'Ādil Shāh, felicity and conquest, and victory, and triumph and prosperity. May a cheerful heart constantly be the slave of 'Adil Shāh.

The inscriptions show that the walls of the citadel were put in hand before the outer defensive works of the gateway, and, perhaps, before the outer arched gateway. The only one at first was, probably, the inner one near the Hindu columns, represented now by no more than its skeleton of two upright jambs, apparently filched from some old temple, and a great beam thrown across over the top. What the original design was like cannot now be determined. The outer gateway was, no doubt, constructed some time afterwards as an additional safeguard; and, a few years later, the outermost flanking walls and barbicans were added to cover this gate. The courtyards, between these entrances, were well defended from loopholes and embrasures above; and ample guard-room accommodation was provided within these and upon the walls and bastions, with lofty look-outs to provide against sudden surprisals.

The citadel walls appear to have been very solidly built. The only portions remaining at present are those along the southern and south-eastern sides; the rest, with the exception of a small bit on the west near the Sāt Manzil, having been demolished, in recent years, in order to admit more air to the newly converted buildings within. At the same time the moat, which, up to then, contained water, was in parts filled in and drained to make the place more salubrious. Forty years ago the walls were almost entire, there being then but two entrances, the south gateway and one across the moat by a stone causeway on the west. The bastions are mostly round in plan, though some are polyhedrons, and project, in some instances, more than half their diameter from the walls. They are very massive, and are connected with curtain walls backed up by heavy ramparts thirty to forty feet high. The lops of the walls and bastions are crenellated with boldly designed embrasures and merlons *(kanguras)*. Upon the bastions, apparently at a later period, elevated gun platforms have been raised, and additional battlements have been built in coursed rubble over and above the original ones.

The following is a description of these walls, as they stood in the beginning of last century, given by Captain S. Sydenham :

> "The works of the citadel are composed of the same materials; it is regular and the defences consist of a rampart and fausse-braye flanked by towers and a wet ditch about 120 feet in breadth; the space between the rampart and the wall of the fausse-braye is very broad, the ditch entirely surrounds it; but the ramparts of the body of the place are not complete; there being about 3 furlongs in length on the north-face open. The circumference of the counterscarp of the ditch is about 5 furlongs. Its water is good and contains abundance of fine fish, but no alligators as has been stated by former writers. There is but one entrance into the place, which is through two gates; one of them, called the iron gate, is of wood cased with that metal." [1]

The 5 furlongs is here evidently a mistake for 1 mile and 5 furlongs, which is about the correct measure.

[1] *Asiatic Researches*, Quarto Ed., Vol. XIII, p. 433.

THE CITY WALLS.

The city has also been surrounded by strong fortified walls, which are now mostly in a very ruinous condition. There are, however, portions, here and there, which still remain in fairly good condition, and these are those parts which were the best built lengths originally. We are told that, when the walling in of the capital was undertaken by 'Ali 'Ādil Shāh I., after his return from the expedition against Vijayanagar, laden with spoils, the work was divided up amongst the nobles, each being responsible for the erection of the length allotted to him. Hence the great irregularity in the work. The general superintendence of the whole work was entrusted to Kishwar Khān. It is said to have been completed in the year A. H. 973 (A. D. 1565). The length of the walls is about six and a quarter miles, and it is made up of ninety-six bastions, not counting those that flank the gateways, with their connecting curtain walls, and five principal gates. The greatest length of curtain wall between any two bastions is about one hundred and thirty yards, some being as near together as fifty. The bastions are, as a rule, circular in plan, and, with the walls, rise to a height of thirty feet, the latter being about twenty feet thick. Beyond the wall is the ditch excavated in some places in the rock, the excavated material thus serving for the walls. This ditch or moat is from forty to fifty feet in breadth by nearly twenty feet in depth. The dimensions vary greatly at different points where the moat exists tolerably entire. Beyond the ditch, again, was a revetted counterscarp and covert way, only traces of which now remain. The walls have been built of stone laid in mortar, backed up with rammed earth between the outer and inner masonry casings or revetments. Along the top of the walls runs a broad platform, from bastion to bastion and over the gates ; and this is protected by a high battlemented breast-wall, which rises from the top of the curtain wall, provided with loopholes and embrasures.

Upon the curtain walls, in some places, have been mounted *jinjāls*, that is, long light field pieces carrying a ball from an inch to two inches in diameter, and working on a swivel. Upon the bastions were placed the heavy guns, and some of these have been built larger and loftier in order to carry specially large pieces of ordnance. Among these are the *burjs* or bastions carrying the great Malik-i-Maidān, the Lānḍā Qaṣṣāb and Muṣtafābād guns, the Sunda Burj, the 'Ali Burj, and the Farangi Burj. The gun platforms, constructed upon these, are curious and worth examination. In the centre of the paved platform is a small circular hole, to hold the pivot upon which the carriage revolved, and, at a distance from it, decided in each case by the length of the gun, are two opposite segments of a channelled ring, cut into the pavement, in which the wheels of the carriage travelled as the gun was swung round. Connecting the ends of these two segments, towards the back of the gun, is a heavy segmental recoil wall, built back at such a distance that the cascable of the gun very nearly touches it. When firing the gun, this space, between the two, was probably wedged up firmly in order to counteract the recoil of the gun, and prevent undue strain upon the carriage and its pivot. It appears that, in the original construction of these bastions, no cover was provided for the gunners, which would have interfered with the sweep of the gun ; but it has been subsequently added to some, if not all, by a low shelter wall built round the outer edge of the bastions, leaving embrasures at intervals large enough to fire through. Where these shelter walls exist, they are very light and flimsy, and could only provide protection against musket balls. The Farangi Burj, unlike the rest, has been built to accommodate several small pieces of cannon, large *jinjāls* in fact, one before each embrasure, mounted upon blocks of masonry, and each provided with a universal joint, so that it might be quickly turned about and pointed in any direction.

THE GUNS.

The principal bastions and guns will bear a few words of description.[1] The best known gun is, undoubtedly, the great Malik-i-Maidān or the "Monarch of the Field". This is not upon one of the ordinary bastions of the walls, but a special one built out from the curtain between two bastions on the western ramparts of the city, midway between the Makka and Shāhpūr gates. Next to the great iron gun, the Lanḍa Qaṣṣāb, this is the largest in Bījāpūr. It differs from this last, and most of the other guns, in that it is a casting in gun metal or some similar alloy.[2] It is more a huge howitzer than anything else, being a great thick dumpy piece with a calibre very large in proportion to its length, which spreads slightly from the powder chamber to the muzzle, allowing a very great amount of windage. It is said that ball was not usually fired from this gun, but rather grape-shot or slugs, in the shape, often, of bags of dumpy copper pice (coins) when nothing else was available. The state of the bore bears this out, as it is very much scored. Like Mons Meg, upon the plateau of the King's Bastion on the Castle Hill at Edinburgh, it has a smaller chamber for the powder, and this was no doubt intended to give the gun greater thickness where the greatest strength was required. The surface has been chased and polished after casting, the necessary excrescences of metal for this purpose being allowed for. The great muzzle has been fashioned into the shape of the head of a lion or dragon, with open jaws, through which the Monarch belched forth destruction ; and, beween the sharp curved fangs, is a small elephant, upon either side of the muzzle. The tip of the nose forms the foresight, and the small ears are drilled and thus converted into rings to attach tackle to.

There are three inscriptions upon the top of the gun. One records the name of the person who made it, namely, Muḥammad the son of Ḥasan Rūmi (Turk). Another gives the date of its casting as A. H. 956 (A. D. 1549) and reads :

Khān Murād, hast thou tried him apostle of Allāh? Year 956, Abū-l-Ghāzī Niẓām Shāh.

Khān Murād, mentioned here, is possibly the same man as the Khān Murād Khān in an inscription over the Shāhpūr gateway of twenty years later ; and, since the title of the Aḥmadnagar king is given, Abū-l-Ghāzī Niẓām Shāh, he must have transferred his services from Aḥmadnagar to Bījāpūr. He was, perhaps, an artillerist of repute. The third inscription is the longest, and was added by Aurangzeb when he conquered Bījāpūr in A. H. 1097 (A. D. 1685-86), recording that event, and giving the date in a chronogram : "He subdued the Monarch of the Plain." This chronogram gives 1096.[3]

The measurements of the gun have been often taken, and just as often have they varied. This is accounted for by its slight irregularity in shape, one side being longer than the other, and its diameter a trifle more one way than another. It measures 14 feet 4 inches long, with a maximum diameter of 4 feet 11 inches. Its bore, at the muzzle, is 2 feet 4 inches, and 2 feet 2 inches at the shoulder of the powder chamber. Its estimated

---

[1] Guns are mentioned in the time of Yūsuf 'Ādil Shāh. The Portuguese historian, Faria-e-Souza, tells us that when the Portuguese took Goa from that chief in A. D. 1510, they found vast quantities of cannon and military stores therein.—Briggs' *Ferishtah*, Vol. III, p. 508.

[2] An analysis, made a hundred years ago, by Dr. Thomson, shewed that it was composed of an alloy of 80·427 parts of copper to 19·573 parts of tin.—*Annals of Philosophy*, September 1813.

[3] Expressing dates in words was a favourite method. Each letter of the alphabet has a definite number allotted to it, and a sentence is composed in such a manner that the addition of the values of all the letters in it should give the date required. Skill is shown in constructing such a sentence as will have special reference to the event whose date is expressed.

weight is about 55 tons.[1] The Malik-i-Maidān was cast at Aḥmadnagar.[2] It is said to have been taken to the battlefield of Talikot (A. D. 1564), where it did considerable execution, perhaps more by its bark than its bite, in scaring and putting to flight Rāmrāj's elephants. Subsequently it was mounted upon the fort of Parandah, one of Niẕām S͟hāh's strongholds, fifty miles to the north-west of S͟holāpūr. But, after this place fell into the hands of Bījāpūr, the gun was brought away, in A. D. 1632, as a trophy of war, and was set up upon its present bastion. A larger and loftier cavalier was at a later date prepared for it, just above the one on which it rests, which is known as the S͟herzā Burj or Lion Bastion, either from the lions carved upon it, or from the muzzle of the gun being carved into the semblance of a lion's jaws. Upon the bastion is the following inscription, which gives us the date in a chronogram (the words in italics) A. H. 1069 (A. D. 1658) during the reign of 'Ali II. :

> In the time of the warrior sovereign 'Ali, surnamed 'Ādil,
> He who possesses by the gifts of Murtazā [*i. e.* 'Ali] evident victory
> By the ready, conspicuous effort of the S͟hāh, in five months was built
> Such a bastion of strong foundation, like a mountain preserved,
> An invisible herald from perfect joy the date of the year,
> *High became the S͟herzā bastion*, crowned from the upper sphere.

This inscription has reference to this particular turret, and not to the whole bastion which holds three gun platforms. The great bastion has its own inscription, on the outside wall, recording the fact that the *burj* which " became like a head and neck " (*i. e.* in plan, as it projects from the walls), was erected by Muḥammad S͟hāh and called the Muḥammad Burj. The date is given, but is in very small figures and hardly legible ; it might be read as 1042 (A. D. 1632). It mentions Amīr S͟hāh Afzal K͟hān Dabuls͟hahi.

Pietro Della Valle, the Italian, who travelled in India in 1623, that is, before the gun was brought to Bījāpūr, notices it in his account. He says :

" Of strange things they relate that *Nizam*-Sciah hath, I know not where in his country, a piece of Ordnance so vast, that they say it requires 15,000 pounds of Powder to charge it ; that the Ball it carries almost equals the height of a man ; that the metal of the piece is about two spans thick ; and that it requires I know not how many thousand oxen, beside elephants to move it ; which therefore is useless for war, and serves only for vain pomp. Nevertheless the King so esteems it that he keeps it continually covered with rich cloth of Gold, and once a year comes in person to do it reverence."[3]

It is still worshipped by the people, who smear the muzzle with red lead and oil, and present flowers to it.

This grand old gun was nearly meeting a sad fate as lately as 1854, when, by some misunderstanding, the " Monarch " was put up to auction and actually sold for its metal by the local subordinate magistrate, when it fetched one hundred and fifty rupees (about fifteen pounds). On reference to the Sātāra Commissioner the sale was cancelled and the gun saved. The Bombay Government in 1823 wished to send it to the king of England, and an Engineer was sent to examine it for the purpose ; but the state of the roads rendered the transporting of such a huge mass of metal to the coast almost insuperable.[4] Later it was

---

[1] The Bījāpūr Gazetteer says between 42 and 43, which is too little.

[2] At some place about two miles from the fort.

[3] *Travels of Pietro Della Valle in India*, edited by Edward Grey for the Hakluyt Society, Vol. I, p. 146.

[4] Grant Duff's *History of the Marattas*, Chap. II.

proposed to send it to the British Museum, but the Fates wisely ordered otherwise, and it still remains upon the walls it protected in days gone by. (Plates III and IV.)

All the guns of Bījāpūr have been dismounted and their carriages carried away, possibly by Aurangzeb, to prevent their being again turned upon him at any time. It is said that there were two guns cast in the same mould, the other, named the Kaṛak Bijlī or "Thunder and Lightning" having sunk in the Krishnā when being taken to or from the battle of Talikot.[1] Another account says that a larger gun than the Malik-i-Maidān was brought from Aḥmadnagar to Bījāpūr, and was placed upon the citadel wall behind the Chīnī Maḥall.[2] 'Ālamgir subsequently attempted to take it, so it is said, drawn by elephants, to Delhi, on a great truck with stone wheels, but it fell into the river at the junction of the Malprabhā and Krishnā (on the wrong side of Bījāpūr for Delhi !). It is also stated that at low water the gun appears above the surface, when a *jātrā* or fair is held annually in connection with it. The gun was called the Kaṛak Bijlī, which name is engraved on the muzzle. No one, now, seems to know anything about this.

Alarming stories used to be current in the town as to the terrible catastrophes that would happen, from the shock of the explosion alone, should the "Monarch" be fired. It was fired, however, by the Rājā of Sātāra, and later, on one or two occasions, by British officials ; but, though people left their houses, and even the town, when they heard of the intention, it went off with a mere puff, the only damage done being that to the window panes of the Civil Hospital right opposite it, as it was forgotten to throw the windows open before firing. The "Monarch" behaved better than "Muckle moo'd Meg" of Edinburgh, who burst herself when fired in 1682, in honor of the visit of the Duke of York.

The Laṇḍā Qaṣṣāb bastion, with its two guns, is situated about the middle of the south walls of the city, and upon it lies the greatest gun in Bījāpūr. In length and mass it is greater than the Malik-i-Maidān. It is made, like most of the iron guns of this period, by faggotting iron bars together. Wrought iron bars of square section, were laid horizontally about a core, and square section rings were slipped on over these, one at a time, each being welded with the last while white hot. As they shrank in cooling, they bound the bars firmly together thus forming the cylindrical bore of the gun. At the breech, in most cases, another layer of short bars and rings was added to strengthen the piece at the point of explosion ; whilst, at the muzzle, a few extra rings were slipped on to improve the appearance and give it a lip. This gun measures 21 feet 7 inches long ; it has a diameter at the breech of 4 feet 4 inches, while that of the muzzle is 4 feet 5 inches ; its calibre is 1 foot 7½ inches, length of bore 18 feet 7½ inches, and estimated weight about 47 tons. Lying beside this gun is a small one, which looks like a long gun cut down ; it was probably an attempt at a mortar (Plate IV).

A little distance away, to the south-east from this bastion, some mounds may be seen, which are said to indicate the position on which Aurangzeb posted his batteries when he breached the walls on this side. This particular bastion shows many shot marks, one ball having struck the muzzle of the big gun, leaving a deep dent.

---

[1] In the *Peshwa's Diaries* occurs this entry : "1764-65.—a cannon called "Sharp Lightning" lying at Vījāpūr [Bījāpūr] was ordered to be brought to Poona." This probably refers to the Malik-i-Maidān, the two names having got mixed up.

[2] Probably upon the great bastion with the inscription of Abū-l-Muẓaffar 'Ādil Shāh already noticed. Curiously, I found an old Persian MS. map at Bījāpūr, upon which a gun is shewn as being upon this bastion. There is none there now.

Upon the bastion is an inscription, but it is too much damaged to allow of a translation being made. It contains no date. In the first line occurs the name 'Ali. But upon the inner side of the wall, a little to the west of this bastion, is an inscription which tells us that in the reign of the exalted sovereign, the Pādshāh, equal in dignity to Solomon, 'Ali II. 'Ādil Shāh Ghāzi, in the year 1073 (A. D. 1662), by the efforts of the servants of the palace completed the wished-for work. Still further along westward, on the fourth *burj* from the Lānḍā Qaṣṣāb, is another inscription which records the construction of the bastion by Ni'mat Khān Himmat in A. H. 1056 (A. D. 1646) during Muḥammad Shāh's reign. If, as we are told, 'Ali I. originally built the walls around the city, these must refer to repairs or reconstructions. A little way east of the Lānḍā Qaṣṣāb bastion, over a small closed-up postern, is an inscription dated A. H. 976 (A. D. 1568-69), which seems to refer to the closing up of this exit by Shah 'Ādil Shāh.

Passing round the city walls, eastwards from the Lānḍā Qaṣṣāb, and omitting the gates which will be separately described, we come to a large *burj*, just beyond the Fatḥ gate, known as the Farangi or Tābūt *burj*, which has an inscription upon it with an outline drawing of a *tābūt*. The inscription is much decayed, but it seems that the bastion was constructed by order of 'Ali 'Ādil Shāh. There is a date, or figures which look like one, but it is 100, which is unsatisfactory. It is an interesting piece of work in its way, and is supposed to have been erected by a Farangi, or foreigner, a Portuguese general, who took service with 'Ali 'Ādil Shāh I., about 1576. He is supposed to be referred to in the inscriptions on the gun turrets upon the bastions of the Makka and Fatḥ gateways, which are called in the inscription the Farangishāhi bastions. Another *burj* has a curious double arrangement for a battery of small guns or *jinjāls*. Further on, again, is a fine *burj*, with an inscription dated A. H. 1072, built by Manjete Shāh in the time of 'Ali 'Ādil Shāh II. On the first bastion south of the Allāhpūr gate is a large gun, round the muzzle of which is the following inscription :—

Fig. 6. Old guns such as were used in Bījāpūr.

The command of high import was published,
To Ṣandal, who is small of the servants,
If there be a gunner in Muṣṭafābād,
Send him quickly, for it is the order of the Shāh.
In the blessed month Jumādā the second,
His majesty the just Shāh departed.
If thou desirest the date of that year, by work
It is augmented under the victory of four armies.

The Ṣandal mentioned here is probably the Malik Ṣandal mentioned in the inscription in mosque No. 74, in the north-west corner of the Langar Bāzār. The chronogram is rather obscure. If it means that the equivalent of the word "work" has to be deducted from "victory of four armies" then the result becomes 1006 (A. D. 1597), during the reign of Ibrāhīm II.[1]

About five hundred yards, due north of the Gol Gumbaz, is a large bastion which goes by the name of the 'Ali Burj, upon which lies another large iron gun. Nothing seems to be known about it, and there is nothing either in the gun or the bastion calling for special notice. The second bastion north of the Shāhpūr gate, at the north-west corner of the city walls, is a very large one; it is called the Sūnda Burj. Upon it also, is a long iron gun. Finally, there is the great cavalier, known as the Ḥaidar Burj, situated, not upon the line of the walls, but in a solitary position by itself inside the town, in the north-western quarter, and upon the highest ground. It is by far the loftiest gun platform in Bījāpūr, and is a very conspicuous object for miles around. It is also called the Uprī or Uplī (the lofty) Burj. In plan it is oval, or nearly circular, and rises to a height of about eighty feet. A narrow staircase ascends round the southern and eastern sides to the top, and, built into the wall of the *burj*, on the stairway, near the top, is a tablet bearing a Persian inscription, which records the building of the tower by Ḥaidar Khān, a general who served under 'Ali I. and Ibrāhīm II. He is, no doubt, the same man who built the Ḥaidariyyah *masjid*, near the Baṛī Kamān, in A. D. 1583. This inscription is also dated in A. H. 992 (A. D. 1583), the chronogram giving the date, saying: "This bastion is in the name of Ḥaidar." Lying, dismounted, upon the top, are two iron guns, the larger one being the longest piece of ordnance in Bījāpūr. It measures 30 feet 7 inches in length, is 3 feet 2 inches diameter at the breech, and has a bore of 12 inches in diameter, while the other gun is 19 feet 10 inches long with a bore of 8 inches. Both are constructed in the usual faggotting method of long bars with rings shrunk over them. The longer one goes by the name of the Lambcharri or "Far-flier". There is little doubt but that the tower was specially built for this "Long-Tom", since it was felt that to mount it upon the low walls of the city would have been to cripple its capability. Many wonder how these great guns were placed upon the tower. They could have been dragged up a great inclined plain to the top, but a very much simple method, and very likely that adopted, would have been to lay the guns upon the site selected for the tower, and to raise them foot by foot with the masonry as it rose. The tower shows signs of having been fired at from the west, but being very near the Malik-i-Maidān, missiles directed against that gun may also have struck it. Being the highest tower in the city it very probably flew the 'Ādil Shāhi standard.

THE CITY GATES.

There are five principal gates to the city. The Makka gate on the west, the Shāhpūr gate at the north-west corner of the walls, the Bahmanī gate on the north, the Allāhpūr gate on the east, and the Fatḥ or Mangoli gate on the south. In addition to these there are other smaller ones, some being but breaches in the walls necessitated in later times by local exigencies. The principal one of these is the Pādshāhpūr gate, a short distance north of the Allāhpūr gate; and these two, together with two late breaches in the walls on this side,

[1] I have a note upon this, but upon what authority I do not remember, to the effect that this gun was brought from Murtaza Bāgh (Ahmadnagar) by Malik Ṣandal (the lesser) in A. H. 1042 (A. D. 1632). This is the date of the transfer of the Malik-i-Maidān to Bījāpūr.

through which roads pass, make four exits within six hundred yards. The Pādshāhpūr gate, said to have been inserted by Muḥammad Shāh, is now in disuse. Another is the Zuhrapūr exit—a breach in the walls leading out of the west end of Bījāpūr into the suburb of Zuhrapūr; while, just beyond it, is the Fatke gate, being also a breach as its name indicates. There are numerous *diddis* or small posterns, leading out into the ditch, such as the Sarvad *diddi* in the south-west corner of the walls, just where the Begam *talāo* aqueduct enters the city.

The main gateways are built, more or less, upon the same plan. They are well protected by flanking bastions, double gates, and covered approaches. The Makka gate, which is so called on account of its being on the west or Makka side of the town, has, subsequently to its erection, been further strengthened and fortified, upon its inner side, and has thus been converted into a small stronghold, safe against enemies within and without. It is said to have been still further added to by the Peshwā's government, probably as a better protection for their small garrison and revenue offices. The British, upon taking over the country, also located their local offices in this place, until later conversion of some of the old buildings in the citadel provided them with better accommodation. It still remains closed up. Upon the west face of the east wall, inside the gateway, is a beautiful inscription in four lines which runs as follows :—

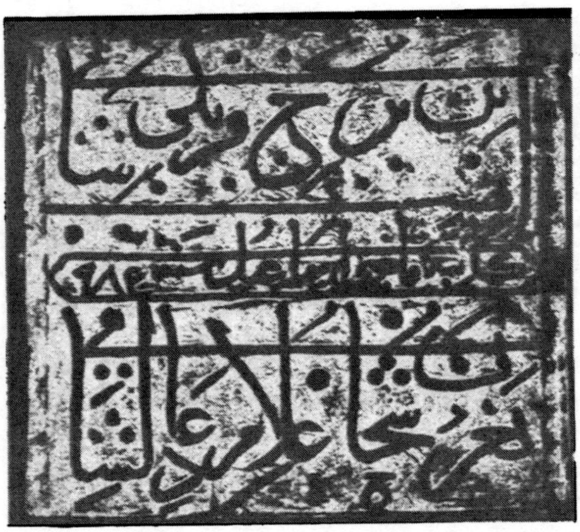

In the reign of Shāh 'Adil Shāh Ghāzi,
Muḥammad Shāh, the justice dispensing Shāh,
By order of the Khān Khānān, Khān Muḥammad,
Whose order is current in the seven regions,
Malik Sandar, on whom, from the exalted Dīvān,
His victory-boding title was bestowed,
Has, for warding off the rebellious Yājūj,
Made a breastwork like the rampart of Alexander.

Year 1066. [A. D. 1655-56.]

Fig. 7. Inscription on the south bastion of the Makka gateway.

It was a very curious irony of fate which ordained that Khān Muḥammad, who, in the inscription, is said to have erected this bastion against the rebellious, should himself, a few years later, be assassinated as a rebel on the roadway beneath this very tablet he had set up.[1]

It is questionable whether the Malik Sandar in this inscription is the same Malik Ṣandal of the inscription of the Ibrāhīm Rauza, the mosque in the Langar bāzār, and the Muṣṭafābād gun. If he is the same, and this is simply a mis-spelling of his name, he must have been an old man at this time.

[1] Not near the Bahmani gate as Meadows Taylor states. *Architecture at Beejapoor* by Jas. Fergusson and Meadows Taylor, p. 59.

Upon a gun turret in each of the northern and southern bastions is an inscription identical in wording, which reads:

> Built was this *burj* [named] Farangīshāhi
> By Baghrash Khān Ghulām 'Adilshāhi.
> The writer of this was Qāzī Ismā'il, year 984.
> [A. D. 1576-77.]

Upon the south turret was an iron gun with a ring of small inscribed circles upon the muzzle. But this, with others, has been removed and set up in the gun trophy in front of the museum at the Gol Gumbaz.

The Fatḥ gate or 'Gate of Victory', was so named by Aurangzeb when he conquered Bījāpūr, and through it entered the city in triumph. It was previously known as the Mangoli gate, after a village of that name to which it led. Above the gateway was a short inscription, in ornamental characters, dated, at the top, A. H. 984 (A. D. 1576-77), but containing nothing of interest.[1] But upon the *burj*, above the gateway, is another inscription which is identical with that on the turrets above the Makka gateway, except that the writer's name is omitted. The date at the bottom is A. H. 984. It is thus evident that defensive works upon these gateways were being carried out at the same time, probably original construction, during the reign of 'Ali I. At the museum is a gun which is said to have been found near this gateway, having been dropped when Aurangzeb's troops poured into the city. Thence it was taken to the Makka gate, and afterwards adorned the terrace of Khān Muḥammad's tomb. It is an ornamental piece of work, being of cast iron inlaid with brass in a scroll pattern.

Above the Allāhpūr gate is a small inscription, the middle part of which is abraded. On the right side the words "by the grace of Allāh" may be made out. On the left side the date A. H. 1088 (A. D. 1677) is given, which falls within the reign of Sikandar. Comparing the masonry of this outer gate (Plate V) with that of the inner and adjacent walls, it seems clear that this is a re-erection. It leads out to the Allāhpūr village, hence its name.

The Shāhpūr gate has three inscriptions upon it. The oldest, dated A. H. 978 (A. D. 1570-71), is over the inner gateway. It reads :—

> In the days of the Sultanate of the just Sultān
> Shadow of Allāh and Shāh-al-Muzaffar 'Ali 'Adil
> Shāh, may Allāh perpetuate his kingdom and his power.
> By the effort of the great Khān Murād Khān Ghāzi
> Amīr Jumlah in 978.
> [A. D. 1570-71.]

Over the outer gateway is another which runs thus :—

> By the gift of grace from Allāh the divine King, the always victorious and conquering Sultān Muḥammad 'Ādil Shāh the powerful [is] engaged in bestowing Shāhanshāhi [imperial] enlightened mercies and favours. It was named Aḥmad Burj Pādshāhi A. H. 1053. [A. D. 1648-49.]

Upon a turret, above the north bastion, is a short ornamental inscription, more like a monogram, which gives the name of the bastion as the Aḥmad Burj, with the same date as in the last inscription. Who the Aḥmad was, whom it is called after, is not clear.

---

[1] This slab was taken by the Executive Engineer to the Museum.

BĪJĀPŪR ARCHITECTURE.

ON the break up of the Bahmanī kingdom, the 'Ādil Shāhi family of Bījāpūr, one of the minor states which rose out of the ruin of the former, came rapidly to the front as the most potent factor in the Dakhan ; their advance being marked not only by their superiority in arms over their neighbours, but also in the arts of peace. They were a race of builders, and left behind them more monuments of note than the rest of the Dakhan kingdoms put together. Muḥammadan architecture had already got a start in this part of India under the Bahmanī kings, just at the time that local Hindu architecture was on the decline ; but it was little more than a start, and their public buildings and other memorials were few indeed. The extensive city of Bījāpūr, under the 'Ādil Shāhis, soon became too small for its aspirations, and overflowed for miles to the east and the west of its walls.

The Bahmanīs, no doubt, imported artizans from the north to erect the few great monuments whose ruins we still see at Gulburgah and Bīdar, and it is likely the Bījāpūr kings borrowed men from those places to build their lines of fortifications, and early rubble and plaster palaces and mosques. But later, as the state grew richer, there is abundant evidence to shew that first class architects were induced to come south from Northern India ; while the masked Hindu forms in the Ibrāhīm Rauza plainly indicate that the help of the local Hindu architect was not altogether despised. There is no such thing as a single Bījāpūr style, for there were, at least, two principal classes of work—that of the plainer rubble and plaster buildings, simple and often heavy in their outlines, and that of the lighter quasi-Hindu construction in cutstone and abundant decorative details, such as the Ibrāhīm Rauza and the Mihtar Maḥall. The baser work at Bījāpūr does not always indicate an early age or later decadence, but rather the use of cheap labour, and inferior architects—shoddy buildings, in fact, which are found at all times, even contemporary with the best work.

For some time after Yūsuf 'Ādil Shāh had thrown off his allegiance to Bīdar, he and his immediate successors had enough to do to maintain their newly acquired status among the chiefs of the Dakhan : all their time and funds must have been devoted to this purpose.

But when once firmly established, especially after the return of 'Ali I. from the defeat of Rāmrāj, attention was more seriously focussed upon the defences and architectural adornment of the city. The real building period of Bījāpūr did not commence until 'Ali 'Ādil Shāh I. ascended the *masnad*. It flourished from the laying of the foundation stone of the great Jāmi' Masjid, about 1537, to the death of 'Ali II. in 1672—a hundred and thirty-five years. 'Ali I. was a great patron of the arts, and welcomed learned men and artists to his capital. The first building of importance that was put in hand was the great Jāmi' Masjid, which has remained intact to the present day—a monument at once worthy of the best traditions of the 'Ādil Shāhis. In this mosque we have the style which is chiefly used in Bījāpūr, coming upon us in its full development, in its purest and best form. It is, therefore, evident that this style and its exponents were imported, and that subsequent buildings of this class were built upon the lines laid down by these men by their descendants and local builders who copied them. It is a fact that no subsequent building is equal to this one for its perfect proportions.

The long reign of his successor, Ibrāhīm II. was a remarkably busy one in building construction, notwithstanding the frequent military expeditions that called away the king and his nobles from the city for long periods at a time. The work during this king's reign is chiefly characterised by the lavish use of delicate decoration, in which the influence of the Hindu workman is very apparent. Sulṭān Muḥammad seems to have concentrated almost the whole of his attention upon his own colossal sepulchre, the great Gol Gumbaz. 'Ali II. did little beyond commencing his own mausoleum, which, had he lived long enough to finish it, would have been an ornament to the city.

The architectural buildings of Bījāpūr comprise mosques, tombs and palaces, the first two classes of buildings predominating. It was safe to put money and work into these; for, being almost surrounded by other Muḥammadan states, there was little fear of violence being done to these religious buildings. With palaces, it was otherwise. No sanctity surrounded them, and they were thus open to destruction at the hands of enemies, even those of the faith. So we find that few of any architectural merit were ever raised, those, whose ruins we now see, being built of rubble and plaster. A certain amount of architectural display was lavished upon some of the larger tanks and reservoirs.

It is unnecessary, at this point, to go into details with regard to peculiarities of construction and decoration, as this is all treated in full in the separate descriptions of the buildings which follow. But it may be as well to say, at once, that the type of arch used so universally in Bījāpūr, and which has been supposed to be peculiar to the 'Ādil Shāhi buildings, is by no means confined to them. It is seen plentifully used among the monuments of the north of India. Excepting the early mosques, constructed from Hindu material, Fergusson wrote:

> "There are no others at Beejapoor, which, in so far as local peculiarities are concerned, might not have been found at Agra or Delhi, and indeed in Persia, or anywhere else. They have peculiarities of their own, it is true, which will be pointed out hereafter, but they do not arise from the local situation of the city in the Deccan, so much as from the idiosyncrasy of the people to whom they belong, and the circumstances under which they were erected. . . . . On the other hand there is nothing in Hindostan which can compare for grandeur of conception with the tomb of Mahmood, nor any so elaborately rich in ornamental detail as the group of buildings comprised in the Ibrahim Roza. The tombs of Humaioon and Akbar will not bear comparison with them. Some will, no doubt, be

inclined to think that the Taje Mahal at Agra is superior to anything in the south; but it is difficult to institute any very satisfactory comparison between it and them. The white marble of the Taje, and its inlaying of precious stones, are most important adjuncts, but hardly legitimate circumstances to take into consideration in criticising an architectural design. The situation, too, of the Taje on the banks of the Jumna far surpasses that of any building at Beejapoor, and it retains its gardens and its range of marble fountains, which every Roza had, but only very few indeed now possess; all these add immensely to the charming effect of the Taje Mahal as it now stands, but must not be allowed to mislead us in judging of the comparative merits of its designs. With the same advantages the architect of the Gol Gumuz would certainly have produced a far grander building, and the architect of the Ibrahim Roza one more picturesquely magnificent, either, in all probability, much more impressive than the pride of the northern capital. Indeed, for certain qualities, the buildings at Beejapoor stand quite alone among the examples of Saracenic art, and these qualities, if not the very highest, rank very high among the art principles of architectural design."[1]

The builders at Bījāpūr were greatly handicapped by the limited area from which they were able to draw their material, which was necessarily contained within the confines of the state. The result of this is very apparent today; for, whereas the surface of even the most ornamental stone-work is, as a rule, fresh looking and crisp, yet the blocks themselves, especially those used as brackets or cantilevers, have developed cracks throughout their masses which have threatened the very stability of the buildings in which they have been built. The local trap was used, and this is a very poor material, indeed, for anything beyond rubble construction, being very brittle and friable. Most of the damage that has overtaken these monuments has been caused by the cracking and snapping of brackets, tie-beams, and cornice slabs. About the time of the building of the Ibrāhīm Rauza, stone was frequently used after the style of wooden construction, in open defiance altogether of its suitability for that kind of work. The designs of those great overhanging cornices, with their deep brackets and running tie-beams, would have been more appropriately carried out in wood. The balconied windows of the Mihtar Maḥall are essentially wooden in construction. Yet, in spite of this, and even of the cracked condition of the masonry, much of it still stands today in fairly good condition.

The peculiarities in doming in Bījāpūr, the decorative minarets, constructed for ornamental purposes and not for use as those of Northern India were, and the rich cornices, which more or less characterise the Bījāpūr buildings, are discussed at length in the accounts of the buildings which follow. One device which was perfected and more extensively used at Bījāpūr, in the construction of domes, than, perhaps anywhere else, was the happy idea of the pendentives which completely solved their problem of stability in a very graceful and beautiful manner. This, too, is fully described further on.

---

[1] *Architecture at Beejapoor*, by Fergusson and Taylor, p. 85.

THE MONUMENTS OF BĪJĀPŪR.

EARLY BUILDINGS.

THE earliest Muḥammadan remains at Bījāpūr are, no doubt, the two tall clumsy-looking *mīnārs* attached to the corners of the eastern end of the corridor round the courtyard of the Makka *masjid* in the citadel. Close by is buried a *pīr* or saint Mhābri Khandait, who is said to have built a mosque here about the end of the thirteenth century. It was only after the inroads of Malik Kāfūr, in the beginning of the fourteenth century, that the Muḥammadans became sufficiently masters of the country to break up with impunity, Hindu temples for materials with which to construct their own mosques; before that time, the few followers of Islām, who may have penetrated into these districts, were there on sufferance, and, if they built at all, did so with their own material. So we find that these towers are built of rough simple masonry, and, probably, by unskilled labour. Instead of the fine cut-stone brackets found in later buildings, wood was here used, supporting wooden balconies or galleries, pieces of which still remain.

OLD HINDU COLUMNS.

Of Bījāpūr, before the advent of the Muḥammadans, there is very little now remaining; and we could expect but little. In the first place, we have no records to shew that it was ever a place of any great importance in Hindu times, more than the headquarters of a local district officer under the Western Chalukyas—pretty much, in fact, what it is now under the British—and, in the second place, wherever the Muḥammadans settled down to found a new centre, under their own government, they invariably, at the outset, demolished all idolatrous shrines, and gloried in erecting their own mosques upon the very sites, and with the material of whatever temples they found upon the spot.[1] This they did at Delhi, Aḥmadābād

[1] This practice appears to have been followed long before the time of Muḥammad, for did not Gideon destroy the altar of Baal and build one to Jehovah in its place out of the material (*Judges* VI, 25)? The Hindus, on their part, never missed an opportunity of retaliating in the same spirit. Even in Bījāpūr itself there is a small mosque in the New Bāzār (No. 7 on the map) which has been converted into a Hindu temple, in which are a *liṅga*, *Nandi*, and snake stone.

Māṇḍū, Bīdar, and many other places. At the last place the chronogram, composed to record the date of one of the old mosques, is in the words "Temple converted into a mosque by the grace of God."[1] Bījāpūr did not escape this general practice at the hands of the Muḥmmadans; but whether, in the case of Bījāpūr, they found its ancient fanes still in use or already ruined, cannot be definitely settled. From the fact that several of the old Hindu pillars, standing at the south entrance to the citadel, have cross-lined diagrams roughly scored upon their sides, upon which to play games akin to draughts, it is evident that these particular columns must have been lying prone upon the ground for some considerable time, uncared for, before being utilised in the gateway. Moreover, had the pillars been taken from standing temples they would have had their own capitals in every case, which would have saved much subsequent trouble in piecing and patching to bring them to uniform heights. The re-erection of this material was carried out during the early occupation of the place by the Muḥmmadans, either under the Bahmanī government or that of the 'Ādil Shāhis.

The columns in the gateway, which had been arranged, with others on the opposite side of the road, to form guardrooms, now stand upon a high plinth, roofless and desolate, like so many nine-pins (Plate VI). They are not of the best class of Chālukyan pillars; they lack the more graceful proportions of the usual tenth and eleventh century work, and there is clumsiness and want of delicacy about the proportions of the circular discs of the capitals, and the mouldings are neither so varied or so rich. The paucity of decorative images, so characteristic of the best work, is very marked, and where they are introduced on the central square panels of some of the pillars, they are very poor and coarse. There is a well-turned pillar, of better workmanship, lying in a shed at the south entrance to the Āthār Maḥall. Others found lying about the place have been gathered together at the museum at the Naqqārkhāna of the Gol Gumbaz. One of these seems to have formed part of a very tall square column which was probably set up before some temple.[2] This was found lying outside the south-east gateway of the citadel. The upper square block is a separate stone, which appears to have formed part of the pillar, and is so shewn in the plate. It might be of any age from the tenth to the thirteenth century. It is most certainly not, as one writer supposes, "not later than the seventh century".[3]

CHĀLUKYAN INSCRIPTIONS.

Built in, low down, on the south side of the east face of the inner gateway of the citadel, close by these columns, was a large well-inscribed slab, in old Kanarese characters, which has been already mentioned in the historical chapter. It is a record of the time of the Western Chālukyan king Bhuvanaikamalla, or Someśvara II., and is dated in *Śaka* 996 (A. D. 1074-75),[4] which states that the temple of Ṣrī Svayambhu-Siddeśvara was erected at that time in the town of Vijayapura. The gateway into which this was built, is made up of temple material, but rebuilt. The slab was thus not in its original position, and may not have

---

[1] *A Guide to Bidar,* by Nawab Framurz Jung Bahādur, p. 15.

[2] A volume upon Chālukyan remains, dealing with this class of work, is in preparation.

[3] *Indian Antiquary,* Vol. VII, p. 121.

[4] *Indian Antiquary,* Vol. X, p. 126.

been built in as part of the temple to which it refers. Such slabs, in the Kanarese districts, are, more often than not, set up apart from the actual walls of the temple, generally somewhere in the courtyard. In the forty-second line of the inscription, a later record begins, but which is apparently unfinished, appertaining to the time of Tribhuvanamalla or Vikramāditya VI.; but it contains no historical information. The columns, we have been describing above, have, upon their shafts, short Kanarese inscriptions ranging in date between *Śaka-Samvat* 1144 and 1180 (A. D. 1222 and 1258), during the period that this district was under the sway of the Devagiri-Yādava dynasty, which shew that they belonged to a temple dedicated to Svayambhū-Śivalinga. It, therefore, seems plain enough that there was such a place here as Vijayapura, Bījāpūr being the Muḥammadan pronunciation and spelling of the same name. It is curious, therefore, that it is not mentioned in the Muḥammadan account, already referred to, where seven villages are named which were absorbed in planning out the city of Bījāpūr. It might, though, admit of a simple explanation, namely, that Vijayapura was the central spot upon which Yūsuf, Ismā'īl, and Ibrāhīm I. resided within the Ārk-qil'ah, and that the other seven villages were absorbed when 'Ali I. enclosed the greater area of his new city.

KARĪM-UD-DĪN'S MOSQUE.

A stone's throw from this gateway, to the north-west, is the earliest dated mosque in Bījāpūr (Plates VII and VIII). It is, save the surrounding wall, wholly made up of pillars, beams and slabs taken from old Hindu shrines. The entrance porch to the enclosure is, in fact, part of a Hindu temple *in situ*—the hall or *maṇḍapa*, with its pilasters and niches, but now wanting its roof. The shrine, which was a continuation on the west side, has been entirely cleared away, and a through passage thus gained to the courtyard within. The inner doorway, flanked with perforated screen panels, has been so inserted by the Muḥammadans. The space between these panels and the doorway beyond was the antechamber to the original temple.

Across the west side of the courtyard, within, is the mosque, made up, as already shown, of pillars of Hindu temples of many patterns and varying heights, brought to one uniform level with odd pieces, over which are laid the beams and slabs of the roof. This chamber measures 85 feet 6 inches from north to south by 51 feet from east to west. As in the mosques of the trabeate style in Gujarāt, the central portion of the roof is elevated above the rest, the extra height being gained by piling one pillar upon another. This does not constitute a second storey; it rather corresponds to the clerestory of our churches, or that part of the nave which rises above the roof of the side aisles, and through the walls of which light is admitted. This arrangement is very necessary in mosques of this construction in order to admit more light into the interior, which would otherwise be very dark towards the back owing to the low elevation, the great expanse of floor space within, and the very poor light which filters through the few small perforated windows which sometimes pierce the walls. It also relieves, very effectively, the otherwise monotonous effect of a great flat roof, and adds a certain amount of dignity to the general design. It is the only mosque in Bījāpūr in this style. It is unnecessary here to go into the peculiarities of this method of construction, since similar buildings have been fully described and illustrated in Dr. Burgess' volumes on the Muḥammadan architecture of Aḥmadābād, and the Muḥammadan architecture of Broach, Cambay, etc., already published. It may be stated that there is nothing to shew in the pillars, or other parts of the building, that they belonged to a Jaina temple, as has sometimes been stated.

There is an inscription upon the face of a pillar, inside the mosque, which tells us, in old Kanarese, that Malik Karīm-ud-dīn erected the upper part of the mosque in the *Śaka* year 1242 (A. D. 1320), and that the architect, Revoya of Salhasdage, carried out the work, or, as it is put, built the mosque. This may record the erection of the whole building or only the addition of the clerestory; it is not very clear. It would have been quite possible, even for the Hindus, when in power, to have suffered an early colony of Muḥammadans to use up old material from ruined and disused temples, since they do not set so much store upon desecrated temple material as the Muḥammadans themselves do upon every stone of even a dilapidated and utterly ruined mosque. The material once consecrated to God's service can never again be alienated or otherwise used. The Hindus use many of their own ruined shrines for the vilest and most shameful purposes,[1] and do not hesitate to sell them to any contractor for road metal. Karīm-ud-dīn was the son of Malik Kāfūr, one of the ablest generals of the emperor 'Alā-ud-dīn of Delhi, who conducted several successful campaigns against the Hindu kingdoms of the south during the early years of the fourteenth century. It is said that he settled at Bījāpūr for some time, and on his death his son Karīm-ud-dīn became governor of the place. Around the *miḥrāb,* or central prayer niche in the back wall, are inscribed portions of the Qurān, which give the full text of four verses, 256, 257, 258 and 259 of chapter II, and 9, 10 and 11 of chapter LXII, being the last three verses of the chapter. It was possibly to this mosque—the "grand mosque in the citadel"—that Yūsuf went in state to introduce the Shī'ah faith into Bījāpūr.

Fig. 8. Pillars in Karīm-ud-dīn's Mosque.

[1] See *Annual Report* of the Archaeological Survey of India for 1907-08, p. 189.

by having the *khuṭbah* read in the names of the twelve *imāms* for the first time in Hindustān.[1]

This building, or at least some portion of it, has been called an *agrāhāra* or Brahmanical college; but this is altogether wrong, for, as I have alteady said, it is, save for that portion forming the entrance to the courtyard, a purely Muḥammadan building erected from a miscellaneous lot of material obtained from one or more old temples.[2]

In the courtyard is a tomb which is said to be that of a son of the *pīr* Mhābri Khandait,[3] who was slain some twenty years before the erection of this mosque. It is also said that the mound is the burial place of several Muḥammadans who fell in a mêlée with the Hindus, when the former first settled here, and who thus became *shahīds* or martyrs.

KHWĀJAH JAHĀN'S MOSQUE.

Four hundred yards due north of the last mosque, is another similarly constructed of old pillars, but it is not so large a building, nor has it the central clerestory rising from the roof. The bases of the pillars are embedded in the floor; or rather, perhaps, the stone floor has been added after the completion of the building, thus burying the bases. It will be seen in the photograph (Plate VII) how additional blocks have been inserted in the shafts to bring them to one level. In the *Bombay Gazetteer* it is stated that this building was erected by order of Khwājah Jahān, wazīr of the Bahmanī kingdom, probably about A. D. 1488, but no authority is quoted for this statement. This is possibly Khwājah Jahān, father of Nūr Khān, who succeeded him in the title and was known for long years afterwards as Khwājah Jahān Dakhanī, governor of Parandah. The father, at the time of Yūsuf's death, was governor of Sholāpūr. By whomsoever built, it was very likely a private chapel attached to a residence occupying the site of the 'Adālat Maḥall (now the Collector's residence), and was perhaps erected during the time of the Bahmanī governors of Bījāpūr.

---

[1] Briggs' *Ferishtah*, Vol. III, p. 23.

[2] In the work *The Architecture at Beejapoor*, written by James Fergusson and Meadows Taylor, published in 1866, two photos are published of this building, taken from different points of view and have been described as two separate buildings. This blunder has been referred to by subsequent writers, amongst them Mr. Sinclair, Bo. C. S., in the *Indian Antiquary*, Vol. VII, p. 121.

[3] Who lies buried just beside the Makka Masjid, on the east.

probably had a projecting wooden eave or cornice along the top of the façade. There are, inside, three shallow flat niches in the back wall, the central one of which served as a *miḥrāb* or *qiblah*.

Somewhat similar buildings, of, perhaps, the same period, are those called Hamza Husain's Masjid and the ruined mosque close to the Jahāz Maḥall (nos. 131 and 135 on the map). In the former a small domed *c͟hhatri* rises upon the roof straight above the central arch.

Over a ruined gateway, quite close beside Āsen Beg's mosque (no. 127 on the map) is a slab bearing the following inscription :—

> Allāh, who be praised and exalted, has said :—[Qurān, ch. IX, part I of v. 18.] Verily this edifice of the mosque has been made a *waqf* [pious endowment] by order—in the government of the exalted assembly and inaccessible dignity, may Allāh complete their glory—of Ibn or Bin 'Adil K͟hān to be perpetual by order of his government. It has been made a *waqf sharʿī* [*waqf* according to the provisions of the law] by Malik Amīn-ul-Mulk G͟hāzī K͟hān [with] one house containing six contiguous shops, arranged, near the Atin darwāzah Dehli on the greatest mosque opposite to his own house, which [is the] Akar k͟hānah with nine shops. The expense of the edifice of the mosque and of that one house is to remain fixed [in the] way [*i. e.* for the service of God] ; and whoever ruins this vow-house is to be under the curse of Allāh the Most High. Written by the Ḥāfiẓ [memoriser of the Qurān] Niẓām-ud-dīn in the year 943. [A. D. 1536-37.]

THE DAKHANĪ 'ĪDGĀH.

An early and very inelegant looking building is the Dakhanī 'Īdgāh, situated upon high ground in the north-west quarter of the city near the Ḥaidar Burj. It is generally the practice to build *'īdgāhs* outside the town limits upon high ground, if possible, on the west. In this case, therefore, it may be inferred that the limits of Bījāpūr city, as it existed when this was built, did not embrace this ground. A later *'īdgāh*, ascribed to Aurangzeb, was built outside the present town walls, on the west, beyond the Malik-i-Maidān bastion. An *'īdgāh*, unlike a mosque, which is used for daily worship, is intended only for the two religious occasions of the *'īds* or festivals of *'Īd-ul-fiṭr* and the *Baqar 'Īd*. This building has generally been ascribed to Yūsuf 'Ādil S͟hāh, but an inscription upon the face of it tells us that it was built by K͟hwājah Najjār G͟haflat (?) in A. H. 945 (A. D. 1538), during the reign of Ibrāhīm I. In the inscription the building is called a *namāzgāh* (place for prayer).

An *'īdgāh* usually consists of a short length of walling, at right angles to the *qiblah* or direction of Makka, flanked by a *mīnār* or bastion at each end, and having a *mimbar*, or pulpit steps, alongside a niche or *miḥrāb* occupying the centre of the wall on the side away from Makka, so that the worshipper may face Makka as he kneels before it. Out in front of this is a large platform, in the open air, where worshippers assemble. This *'īdgāh*, being a very large one, with an extraordinary thickness of wall, a terrace runs along the top to rooms under the domes of each of the bastions or towers, to which access

Fig. 10. The Dakhanī 'Īdgāh.

is gained by a staircase, through the wall, in continuation of the pulpit steps. Upon the wall, above the central *miḥrāb* or niche, has been placed a small dome.

IBRĀHĪM'S OLD JĀMI' MASJID AND IKHLĀṢ KHĀN'S MOSQUE.

There are two old mosques in the south-west quarter of the city which are worthy of attention on account of their peculiar characteristics (Plates IX—XII). The one is known as Ibrāhīm's, and sometimes 'Ali's, old Jāmi' Masjid, and the other, near the Fatḥ gate, as Ikhlāṣ Khān's mosque. The most notable feature of these is the tall *mīnārs* over the central piers of the façade. We have already noticed the sky-line of the façade, between the corner *mīnārs*, interrupted by a central *chhatri* over the apex of the middle arch, in the end of the account of Āsen Beg's mosque. Here, however, are two, one rising from above each of the piers of the central arch. It seems to have been felt that some central tall feature was necessary to accentuate the importance of the buildings, as well as to improve away the otherwise monotonous appearance of a straight-lined low sky-line when no dome was used. The absence of the dome is peculiar, and there seems to be no reason for it, unless it be that there were no skilled masons at hand to construct it. But this could hardly be the reason, for the masons who built the facade arches, and the pendentives within, were surely capable of constructing a small dome.

Moreover, in 'Ain-ul-Mulk's tomb, described further on, we find a perfect dome, while the mosque attached to it, like this one, has a flat roof without one. It was, after all, perhaps, but a fancy. The desire for extra elevation over the central part of a flat-roofed mosque without a dome, is shewn very well in the small Damri Masjid near the fort of Aḥmadnagar where a light lofty arch ring has been thrown across between the two central *mīnārs*, thus simulating the outline of a dome. But in this case, as in the later mosques of Bījāpūr, where intermediate *mīnārs* or *chhatris* were introduced, they were smaller than, and subordinate to, the outside corner ones. The presence of a lofty central dome did away with the necessity for height in the central *mīnārs*.

It will be observed in these two mosques that the arches of the façades are a very great advance upon those of Āsen Beg's. Not only is the segmental portion of the arch carried further up, but the lines are turned up at the points by way of ornament. But what strikes one, as much as anything, in Ibrāhīm's Jāmi' Masjid is the rather clumsy appearance of the façade, owing to the stumpy short shafts of the arch piers. They look as if they had been cut down or that their lower halves had been sunk in the floor. What would have been an otherwise elegant façade has thus been completely spoiled. The reason for this was, no doubt, the desire to get as much light into the mosque as possible, using as large a span of arch as permitted, while, at the same time, economising in the material and work required for a loftier building, which the more fitting proportions of the arches demanded. This defect is not quite so apparent in Ikhlāṣ Khān's mosque, where the proportions of height to width are more pleasing. The latter building is an advance on the former in many respects, even to the apology for a dome—the little two-storeyed kiosk erected on the roof above the *miḥrāb* niche. The *mīnārs* are so broken down and dilapidated that it is not easy to judge of the general appearance of this bundle of chimney-like excrescences upon the roof—six *mīnārs* and the attenuated kiosk, or seven vertical pillars crowded into so small a space. The corner ones were possibly low *chhatris*, similar to those on Āsen Beg's mosque, but still the three very tall objects in the middle, all of the same height, was a mistake.

In the decoration of the façade there is considerable advance in that of Ikhlāṣ Khān over that of the old Jāmi' Masjid. The bracketting of the cornice—the only feature in unplastered cut-stone upon the building—is rich, yet with but very little additional labour; the rest of the decoration, which is entirely in plaster, is more pretentious. The curious bracket design supporting the decorative discs in the spandrils of the arches, which we shall notice again further on, is used both within and without Ikhlāṣ Khān's, but is not seen in the Jāmi' Masjid. This is one of the most frequently occurring ornamental designs in Bījāpūr. This plaster ornament became a great feature in these brick and rubble buildings before Ibrāhīm II. set the fashion of the more elaborate and enduring work in cut and carved stone. There are many such buildings, now, alas !, in irretrievable ruin, scattered about amidst the débris of the city, serving the base purposes, where sufficiently intact, of squalid dwellings, stables, or store-houses.

In Ikhlāṣ Khān's mosque double arching has been used in the façade, thus still further closing up the entrances and shutting out much light ; but since it is a very shallow building this does not matter so much. In the space between the two arches is a moulded frame with rectangular zigzag corners—a very neat method of adapting the straight lines to the curves of the arches. The central inner arch has its intrados cusped, more after the style of Mughal work. These arches may be a later addition to provide support for the upper original ones, which, owing to poor masonry, were beginning to give way. The slabs of the cornices, or overhanging eaves, were too valuable to escape the hands of the despoiler.

There is an old mosque on the outskirts of Dargāhpūr, near the Amīn Dargāh, which is very like Ikhlāṣ Khān's, having large brick *mīnārs* rising over the central piers of the façade, as well as smaller ones over the corners. It is known as the 'Elephant-Slayer's Mosque', because that, during a quarrel with the *mālik* of the Sonahrī Masjid, the *mālik* of this one killed his elephant.

It does not always follow, of course, that because tradition has connected a man's name with a building, as in this case of Ikhlāṣ Khān's, that he ever had anything to do with it; or even, if he were connected with it at all, that he necessarily built it. An ancestor may have constructed it; but he, being the last known, or the most illustrious member of the family, has been more specially remembered; or, as an old building, it may have come into his possession. I say this, because the time of the only Ikhlāṣ Khān we know of seems rather too late for the erection of this mosque. The great Jāmi' Masjid, would, at his time, have been built or nearly completed.

This Ikhlāṣ Khān is first heard of as a Bījāpūr noble in connection with one of Afzal Khān's expeditions against Quṭb Shāh of Golkondah during the minority of Ibrāhīm II.[1] Kishwar Khān was prime minister or *wazīr* at Bījāpūr at the time, and, when he fell into disgrace, Ikhlāṣ Khān joined with the other nobles in driving him out of the kingdom. On the release of Chāṇd Bībī from Sātāra he was appointed to the charge of the young king and his education, and soon gained full control of all state matters, civil and military. Upon 'Ain-ul-Mulk being appointed *peshwā* and getting the upper hand, Ikhlāṣ Khān was for a time imprisoned, but was eventually released and put into possession of the high office of *vakīl*. Quarrels between Ikhlāṣ Khān and another noble, Ḥamīd Khān, led to skirmishes in the city between their factions, which were carried on with bloodshed for two months, when, losing favour, he was requested to make the journey to Makka.[2] On arrival at the fort of Miraj, or Murtazābād, as it was then called, he was imprisoned and blinded, and died in 1597. He was an Abyssinian, and was known as Ikhlāṣ Khān Ḥabshī *alias* Bade Khān.

RANGĪN MASJID.

Of the same style of work as the preceding, though without any date or clue thereto, is the little mosque known as the Rangīn or Coloured Masjid (no. 216 on the map), about three to four hundred yards east of the hamlet of Shāhpeth, so called on account of the traces of some painted decoration which embellished its walls and ceiling. The front of this little mosque was very tastefully decorated with raised stucco ornament; and the arches, being rather of the ogee type, improve the general appearance. The medallions in the spandrils of the arches, and the surface ornament upon the *mīnārs*, are very neat. Judging from the few traces that remain, blue and majenta appear to have been the prevailing colours used in the interior decoration; and, a few years ago, some scraps of gilding were still quite bright and untarnished. Over the *miḥrāb* is an inscription in plaster, and others adorn the façade and other parts of the mosque, all of them being extracts from the Qurān. A glance at the photograph of this

[1] Not the Afzal Khān murdered by Śivāji, but a predecessor in the title, who also met his death at the hand of the assassin.

[2] A polite way of dismissing a noble and telling him his services were no longer required.

building (Plate XIII) shews how rapidly the disintegration of these old buildings is progressing. Above the roof will be seen three small *mīnārs*—one over the south-west corner, and two over the *miḥrāb*—which were standing when the mosque was photographed in 1888, but which had fallen before it was again photographed in 1905. I have selected the later photograph for illustration, as it is better in many respects than the earlier one. This multiplicity of *mīnārs* upon the roof, with no dome, characterised the last buildings described, but, in other respects, especially in ornamental detail, there is as much advance in this example on I<u>kh</u>lāṣ <u>Kh</u>ān's, as there is in I<u>kh</u>lāṣ <u>Kh</u>ān's on the old Jāmi' Masjid. The stone cornice is more elaborate, with deeper brackets; but, as yet, we do not find, what was so universal after the elaborate stone-work of the Ibrāhīm Rauza was introduced, namely, the intermediate larger and deeper brackets, usually placed above the centre of each pier and at the ends. The ordinary brackets, here and in I<u>kh</u>lāṣ <u>Kh</u>ān's, are arranged symmetrically with regard to the piers, but they are not so in Ibrāhīm's old Jāmi' Masjid. The *kanguras*, or merlons along the roof, are far more decorative; but it is impossible to compare the richness of the surface ornament around the arches, since it has been entirely destroyed, and the side arches look as if they had been plainly replastered.

Fig. 11. Interior of Mosque No. 213.

The *miḥrāb* is here a full-sized niche, occupying most of the wall space under the arched recess in the middle of the back wall. In plan, it consists of five sides of an octagon, and thus forms a very considerable alcove. There is an inscription, in plaster, above the *miḥrāb*, consisting of an extract from the Qurān.

MOSQUE No. 213.

About a hundred and fifty yards to the east by north from the Rangīn Masjid is another small mosque (no. 213 on the plan) of the same style, having four *mīnārs* upon the roof, and all the three arches of the façade of the ogee type. The only features of special note about the building are the pretty fan, or cockle-shell, pattern pendentives,[1] which are a very light and graceful variety of this very characteristic expedient. The intersecting or crossing of the mouldings of the arch rings, below the pendentives, is noteworthy. It is here the only arrangement possible to lead the lines of the arch rings down to the twelve-sided columns, which, with the ogee arch and cockle-shell pendentives, form a very happy combination (Fig. 11).

[1] Pendentives are described in the account of the Gol Gumbaz, further on.

Upon the face of the mosque are some inscriptions, but none of any historical interest. They are merely extracts from the Quran and pious expressions, the letters of which are interlaced and symmetrically reversed to form evenly balanced ornamental designs.

MOSQUE No. 207.

This is a small mosque, close beside the Executive Engineer's residence, on the roadside, and a little over a hundred yards east of the milestone. It was, in its day, a very ornamental little *masjid,* but it is, now, sadly dilapidated. The façade, *kanguras,* and *minārs* have been covered with delicate stucco ornament; the *kanguras,* or battlementing, along the top, being of a more ornamental style than elsewhere. There is not the usual sunk *miḥrāb* niche here, but two small shallow niches, side by side, under the central wall arch. The forward central dome of the ceiling, which is fluted, is decorated with ornament in each flute. There appears to be an inscription above the *miḥrāb,* but buried beneath plaster.

'AIN-UL-MULK'S MOSQUE AND TOMB.

Of the same type as the Rangīn Masjid is that which stands beside 'Ain-ul-Mulk's tomb, and which is situated about a mile and a half to the east of Bījāpūr (Plates XIII and XIV). The tomb is a massive square building, surmounted by a particularly well proportioned dome, and stands out as a very conspicuous object upon the wide stretch of barren plain. The mosque, no doubt, belongs to the tomb, although its sides are not parallel with those of the latter, being set at a slight angle to them. It has been a very ornate building, though now much the worse for years of neglect; but it is even now as good an example of the richly decorated plaster buildings as may be found in Bījāpūr. Not only is the façade enriched with delicate surface tracery, but it is lavishly, and yet not excessively, used in the decorative treatment of the walls, arches, and ceilings within. The ornament is rich and lace-like, and has been applied with that due restraint and consideration for contrasting effects with plain surfaces that mark the architect as a man of refined taste. Discs or medallions, which are the elaboration of the rosette or lotus, with censers and chains, and the lotus bud, are among the more favourite forms used, and with most excellent and chaste effect. Ornamental Arabic or Persian writing, in the form of select extracts from the Qurān, lends its beautiful and appropriate forms of interlacing letters to the general scheme. In such very damaged condition are these buildings that it is not possible to fully appreciate their *tout ensemble* as they left the builders' hands. They were, perhaps, at their best fifty to a hundred years later, when the elements had mellowed the surface tints of the plaster, and the appearance of raw newness had worn off. We cannot say what the pillars were like, or the lower parts of the walls where the plaster has been stripped away; but there is little doubt that the pillars were sparingly decorated, probably by nothing more than a delicately fretted fillet or two around their capitals, under the springing of the arches. The *kanguras* or merlons of the parapet, around the edge of the roof, are not only, like those of the Rangīn Masjid, of a very elaborate outline, but they have also been covered with surface tracery in stucco.

Though the plaster decoration is so very pleasing, the general outlines of the building are not so. In the proportions of the arches there is a slight improvement upon the last examples considered, in that the height, compared with the span, is greater, and the pillars of the façade are not quite so squat. Yet, even more so than in those, there is an unpleasant heaviness in the appearance of the masonry at the springing of the arches just above the pillars. This would, in great measure, have been corrected had the pillar shafts been at least twice their present height. The illustration (Plate XIII) gives one the impression that half the height of the pillars is sunk in the floor. Then there is great weakness and a want felt in the finish of the roof. These tiny *mīnārs* or pillarettes at the corners are not enough. Had a well-proportioned *mīnār* risen from the middle of each of

Fig. 12. Plaster tracery on the mosque at 'Ain-ul-Mulk's tomb.

these little foursquare clusters, such as we find on the mosque of the Ibrāhīm Rauza, the appearance of the building would have gained very much thereby. The jamming of a little minaret, with mouldings, in between two halves of a *kangura*, is very clumsy. This minaret should have been raised upon a square pedestal, to either side of which the halves of the *kangura* would have been better joined.

The same type of cornice and eave-slabs is used here as in the Rangīn and preceding mosques, but the cornice is placed higher above the arches, and nearer the roof line, and it is questionable whether with any better effect. The brackets are all of uniform depth, and are spaced symmetrically with the vertical lines of the piers below. The transverse ties between the brackets, stringing them together, do not, in most of these earlier mosques, as in the later ones, help to support the eave-slabs above.

At first sight it seems difficult to believe that the great tomb of 'Ain-ul-Mulk, standing on the east of the mosque, was built at the same time and by the same architect. Yet the fact that the mosque, the proper complement to the tomb, stands in its proper position, symmetrically placed, with reference to the tomb, and upon the same high platform, leaves little doubt but that such was the case. Moreover, within the tomb, upon the walls, is more of that fine lace-like tracery in plaster which adorns the mosque. The tomb, certainly, has the air of a later building. The dome, as already noticed, is a particularly fine one, which is in good proportion with the cubical mass of the building below it; and the little corner *chhatris* are just sufficient to work off, gracefully, the otherwise awkward corners of the square terrace around its base. In the base of the dome, on the western side, is a window, a very unusual feature in Indian Saracenic domes. The stucco ornament on the walls within, takes the form of great flat lozenge-shaped pendants or censers hanging by chains upon the face of each wall (Plate XV). The exterior does not seem to have had any plaster ornament used upon it. It will be noticed that the cornice has here dwindled down to a mere shallow corbel table, and is not the prominent feature it usually is upon these buildings. Suspended from the dome, inside, was a long chain, of which Meadows Taylor wrote:

> "Part of a gold chain still hangs from the roof of which pieces have been shot away by local marksmen from time to time, and only a small portion remains."

The building is seen to best advantage from a distance. It has been used by the neighbouring villagers as a cattle-shed.

This tomb is ascribed to 'Ain-ul-Mulk Kanāni, one of the nobles of Ibrāhīm I., who rebelled against that king and was killed in A. D. 1556. He seized upon certain districts near his *jāgīr*, or estate, on the coast, and, being attacked by the king, fled for protection to the country of Nizām Shāh. The latter, unwilling that this rebel should be the cause of trouble between him and the 'Ādil Shāh, had him arrested and executed.[1]

There was another noble in the time of king Ibrāhīm II., holding the same title, who, strange to say, was also a rebel against his king, and who met a similar fate near Belgaum. He figures more largely in Bījāpūr story than the former, having been a leading spirit in the movement to depose king Ibrāhīm in favour of his younger brother Ismā'īl.

TOMB OF 'ALI 'ĀDIL SHĀH I.

The earliest royal tomb to be constructed in Bījāpūr was that of 'Ali 'Ādil Shāh I. (A. D. 1557—1580). He seems to have been a man with larger ideas than his predecessors which a long purse, well filled from the loot of Vijayanagar, enabled him to carry out. The state was becoming more consolidated, the king felt secure upon his throne, and he realized that, whatever his fathers had been, he was no longer a mere soldier of fortune, but the responsible ruler of a newly created state. Bījāpūr was not only his inheritance, but it was also his home; so, unlike them, who were sufficiently attached to the old associations of Gogī to have their bones carried there for interment in the ancestral vault, he prepared his own tomb at his own new capital (Plates XIV and XVII). Comparing it with the great Jāmi' Masjid, which he began, it is evident he thought more of his religion than he did of his own glorification, for the tomb is but a poor mean edifice. It is situated in the fields in the south-west quarter

[1] Briggs gives the name as "Seif-ood-Deen Ein-ool-Moolk Geelany". The name in the text is that given in the *Basātīn-i-Salātīn*.

of the city. It is a low, almost square structure, each of its four walls being pierced by five arches, the two end ones being wider than the others, and corresponding to the width of a verandah which runs round the central sepulchral chamber. There is very little about the building that calls for remark save its severe plainness. The outside walls, from the ground line to the *chhajja* or cornice, does not appear to have been plastered, and the dressing and size of the masonry precludes the idea of there having been any intention to cover it; but the two lines of upper walling are of rougher finish and smaller masonry, and was no doubt plastered or intended to be. In the inner chamber are four graves—two of adults, male and female, and two of children. The exterior of the walls of this chamber has been painted, but it has so weathered that little of it can now be seen. Over the northern doorway are painted inscriptions containing the Shī'ah profession of faith, the throne verse, and the words "Allāh and Muḥammad (his) apostle", but neither the names of the occupants of the graves, nor a date. A staircase leads up to the roof from the south end of the east face of the inner wall.

Close to 'Ali's mausoleum, on the south side, are a number of small graves and tombs, which Meadows Taylor describes as those of the ladies of the royal *harīm*.[1] But this is altogether conjectural, since it is really not known whose they are; and the chief one among them, the beautifully carved and dressed greenstone tomb, upon a high basement, is, by its shape, seen to be that of a man (Plate XCVIII).

THE IBRĀHĪMPŪR MOSQUE.

The mosque at the village of Ibrāhīmpūr, about a mile outside the Fatḥ gate to the south-east, is a solid, heavy-looking structure (Plate XVI). Its three façade arches do not look lofty enough for good proportion, there being too much depth and weight of masonry above them. In the mosque at Shāhpūr (Plate LXVI), described further on, we find the same great depth of masonry above the arches, but in that case it is broken up very pleasingly by a bold and beautiful cornice. In this mosque the cornice is a very poor one, and does not arrest the eye and divert it from the heavy masonry. This would not have looked so bad had the parapet and walling above the cornice not been so deep. Like the 'Aināpūr mosque, this one stands upon a high basement, with a high platform before it. It is said to have been built by Ibrāhīm 'Ādil Shāh I. in A. D. 1526.

THE GAGAN MAḤALL.

The Gagan Maḥall, or 'The Sky [kissing] Palace' (Hall of Assembly), situated in the citadel, is ascribed to 'Ali 'Ādil Shāh I., and is said to have been built about A. D. 1561 (Plates XVI, XVII and XIX). It is notable for the immense arch spanning the whole front of the *darbār* hall, which, with a tall narrow one flanking it on either side, forms the façade of the building. It is now roofless, and is naught but a vast empty shell of masonry, its cracked and ruined walls being in a very tottering and unsafe condition. It seems to have been intended, before the other palaces were built, to serve the twofold purpose of a royal residence and council chamber. The private apartments were on the first floor, above the great hall of assembly.

[1] *The Architecture at Beejapoor*, by Taylor and Fergusson, p. 77.

and its wooden floor was supported in front by two massive wooden pillars, such as are in use in the Āt͟hār Maḥall. Projecting above were probably balconies, from which the ladies of the royal household could see, through suspended screens, all that was passing in the hall below, or upon the esplanade, or Fatḥ Maidān, out in front of the great arch. The front of this uppe gallery or hall, immediately above the great hall of assembly, does not seem to have been carried forward to abut upon the inner side of the great arch; it was of the same size as the lower hall, which, save for the two great pillars, was fully open in front, and extended only to the edge of the raised floor. But the side chambers, above, did run forward, on either flank, right up to the great arched façade, the upper portion of the two tall narrow arches forming windows into these. From windows or balconies on the inner sides of these forward chambers, good views could have been had of the interior of the great hall below, right back to the throne seat itself. Staircases ascend to these upper apartments through the thickness of the back wall, and one staircase descends to the outhouses and kitchens on the west of the palace.

The great arched façade now stands out alone from the rest of the building, the cross arches and vaulted roofing, which connected it with the main block, having fallen. This was probably due to the sinking of the foundation of the back wall, and consequent canting over of the main block of building; the façade arches refusing to yield, the two parted company, with the result that the intermediate ceiling and transverse arches fell. In the Sangat Maḥall at Torweh, four miles west of Bījāpūr, we have a duplicate of this building, though not quite so large, the roof of which was in great part remaining when I first visited it; and a study of this building throws considerable light upon the construction of the roofing of the Gagan Maḥall (Plates LXIII and LXIV). All the timber-work, which must have been very heavy and valuable, was cleared away by the Marāṭhās, the beams and brackets being ruthlessly torn from the walls.

The main architectural feature of this palace is its great central arch, which has a span of sixty feet nine inches. It was most desirable to have a clear, open front before the *darbār* hall, unobstructed by piers or masonry of any kind, in order that the king and his nobles might have an uninterrupted view of the plain before the palace upon which tournaments, duels, and military displays were frequently held. With this end in view the architect made his span equal to the full breadth of the hall.[1] It was a bold, but not altogether successful venture from an architectural point of view, for the result is that the noble effect of the façade is rather marred by the squat proportions of the arch; it wants more height in proportion to its width. This is a common fault with the arches of the early mosques that we have been studying. On the other hand the side arches are stretched out to far too great a height. These defects were to a great extent remedied in the later building, the Ānand Maḥall, close by, where, moreover, greater dignity was imparted to the building by setting it upon a much higher basement (Plate LV).

There was a great deal of woodwork about this palace. The ceiling of the great hall was entirely of wood, and heavy wooden beams supported the upper terraced roof above the halls, as in the Āt͟hār Maḥall. The windows had wooden frames, with projecting balconies and eaves boards, all elaborately carved. Some idea of the style of these may be gleaned

[1] This is not the largest arch at Bījāpūr; there is a still greater one under the viaduct connecting the citadel walls with the Āt͟hār Maḥall, and spanning the old moat (Plate LXXIV).

from the accompanying illustrations of some few bits of this old work on Plates XVIII and XXIV. The interior woodwork, such as the ceilings and pillars, was, no doubt, richly painted and gilded, more especially in the later days of the building.

Meadows Taylor, in his *Tara* and *Noble Queen,* paints some very pretty word pictures of some of the scenes which were enacted within and without this building. Since he lived a hundred years nearer to the time of his stories, and had a greater acquaintance than any other writer with the private and public life of Dakhan courts of his own time, when customs and costumes were in nowise changed since the 'Ādil Shāhi period, his pictures, though perhaps painted in rather more vivid colours than were natural, give a very good idea of events in those stirring times. Writing of a scene in this same hall of assembly he says:

"The king had early taken his seat. The musnud, or royal throne, was under the centre of the balcony before mentioned, upon a dais, raised a step above the general floor of the hall. There was no decoration visible upon it; and it consisted of a wide cushion and pillows, covered with white muslin, supported at the back and sides by a railing of wood, covered with plates of gold, which, indeed, appeared as if of solid gold. On the right hand of the king, who was dressed in simple white muslin, with a single gold ornament in his turban, sat the Peer Bundagee Sahib, the religious instructor we have before mentioned; and at the back of the rail the Secretary, with two young nobles, whose hereditary office it was to wave over the king the jewelled morchas or fans of peacock feathers.

"Farther again behind, among the arches, closing up the entrance to the cloisters, and leaning against the pillars, were servants bearing the king's weapons, the aftabgeeree, or sunshades, the royal umbrella, and the private guard of slaves, mostly Nubian eunuchs.

"Like the monarch's seat, the whole of the floor was covered by quilted cotton carpets, over which white muslin was spread; so that, with the exception of here and there a coloured scarf or waistbelt, and an occasional turban ornament, the whole of the persons seated wore the same character of dress as the king, with little variation. In some respects, the assembly had a monotonous appearance; but, on the other hand, the effect was chaste and solemn, and agreed with the plain undecorated character of the building.

"The privileged attendants, however, who were allowed entrance with their masters, and who stood in files behind them against the wall, were dressed in the brightest and gayest colours which could be devised. Here were tunics of satin and cloth-of-gold, brocaded turbans and scarfs of the richest materials mingled together in the greatest profusion; and this brilliant array, in which all hues seemed to blend with a strangely gorgeous harmony, formed a powerful background in relief of the white dresses, and white coverings of the floor.

"Then beyond, the eye followed the graceful outline of the vast arch against a deep blue sky flecked with white clouds. Below, it rested upon the plain, where, in the quivering heat, which gave a tremulous movement to the atmosphere, stood the serried masses of royal troops and sowarees, caparisoned elephants ard led horses; litters and their bearers—all in the glowing colours which we have already seen from the Queen's balcony; and with bright arms and armour, which flashed and glinted in a thousand sparkles as the wearers moved.[1]

"It was a sight at once gorgeous and impressive in itself; the costumes and banners of the ranks of infantry, interspersed with cavalry—Dekhanies, Arabs, Persians, Oozbaks, Circassians, Tartars of many tribes, Georgians, Turks, and many other foreigners; while a strong division of Beydurs, in their peculiar costume of conical leather caps and leather drawers, which has been described on a former occasion, were by no means the least conspicuous or remarkable of the motley assemblage."[2]

---

[1] *Tara,* 2nd Ed. 1874, pp. 252-253.

[2] *Noble Queen,* 1882 Ed., p. 156.

In this hall were enacted many of the most momentous deeds recorded in Bījāpūr history. It was here that the noble queen Chānd Bībī sat for many years at the helm of state, guiding its barque through the troubled waters of intrigue and party faction—the noblest example of Indian womanhood. It was from within these walls that the glory of the 'Ādil Shāhis departed for ever, when the Emperor Aurangzeb, after his capture of the city, commanded its unfortunate king, Sikandar, the last of his line, to appear before him in silver chains, while he, at the same time, received the submission of its nobles.

What a contrast to its present state. The silent hall and roofless walls now stand, from year end to year end, in their splendid ruin, hardly disturbed by a sound save the cooing of pigeons by day or the hoot of the solitary owl by night. The glory of those days lies now in the dust, and is represented only by the broken arch, the ruinous graveyard, the gaping tomb, and the crumbling wall, which oblivion is fast claiming for her own, and which Nature, with her thorns and weeds and jungle, is fast covering up.

THE JĀMI' MASJID.

The earliest building of importance, put up in Bījāpūr, was the great Jāmi' Masjid or public mosque of assembly, where the *khuṭbah* or Friday sermon was delivered, and which is also called the Jum'āh or "Friday" mosque on that account (Plates XX—XXIII). 'Ali 'Ādil Shāh I., on his return from the ever memorable expedition of the four confederate armies against the forces of Rāmrāj, his coffers overflowing with the spoils of war, and his head full of new plans for the better defence and adornment of his capital, naturally, as a good Muslim, first turned his attention to the erection of a suitable place of worship for the ever-increasing population of the city—one that should be worthy of his capital and state. It thus became a permanent memorial of the great victory of Islām over the vast infidel kingdom of the south. Later kings thought more of their own glory than that of Allāh, and vied with each other in leaving memorials of their own selves, which should hand down their names to posterity. 'Ali, satisfied with his own simple tomb, seems to have resisted this temptation.

It is evident that up to this time Bījāpūr possessed no architects of any account, so it was necessary for the king to summon abler men from elsewhere. Certain it is, that the man who designed the great Jāmi' Masjid was a man of more than ordinary ability, and possessed of high ideas. Nothing, on anything like the same scale of magnificence, had, up to this time, been attempted within the city, nor, for that matter, in the Dakhan. The only other great mosque in Western India with which this one can be compared is the Jāmi' Masjid at Aḥmadābād, built a hundred years previously; but this, with its forest of tall, thin pillars and smaller detail, lacks the peculiar dignity and sublimity of that of Bījāpūr, with its great solid square piers and splendid arches—restful massiveness rather than a bewildering accumulation of attenuated details. The interior, save for the gorgeously decorated central *miḥrāb,* which was not part of the original design, is severely plain: and here is a quiet simplicity about it which adds much to the impressive solemnity of the place. An old writer says of it: "The sacred grandeur, united with simplicity, that is so striking in this building, appears to us as better calculated to inspire the devotee with sensations suitable to the purpose of prayer, than the eye-distracting elegance of some of the magnificent temples of Christianity." [1]

[1] Moore's *Narrative of the Operations of Captain Little's Detachment,* 1794, p. 318.

The mosque is situated about the middle of the south-east quarter of the town, and stands upon the south side of the road leading from the Allāhpūr gate to the citadel. Including the great open courtyard, embraced between its two wings, it occupies the greatest area of any building in Bījāpūr—about 91,000 square feet to the bases of the towers at the ends of the wings, beyond which is a further and later extension up to the eastern gateway, bringing the total area up to 116,300 square feet. The main building—the mosque proper—is built across the west end of the great court. The massive square piers, which support the vaulted roof, divide the length of the façade into nine bays, and the depth of the building into five, which gives a total of forty-five bays in the body of the mosque; but nine of these, in the centre, are absorbed by the great square open space beneath the great dome (Plate XXII); that is, four central piers being absent, the great bay, so formed, is enclosed by the surrounding twelve piers, over which, and rising high above the flat roof outside, hangs the dome. Unlike the mosques and tombs of Gujarāt, which have a main dome surrounded by subsidiary ones above the roof, or a number of equal-sized ones, corresponding to the number of bays in the chamber below, the mosques at Bījāpūr, save in the solitary instance of the Nau Gumbaz, have but one exterior dome. Though each bay, within, has a domical ceiling, these are embedded in the thickness of the flat roof and do not rise above it. This is so in the case of the Jāmi' Masjid, and these smaller domical ceilings are therefore very flat, but have a very graceful section.

The great dome, to Western eyes, accustomed to hemispherical curves, is the best proportioned dome in Bījāpūr; but it is not the usual Saracenic dome, which swells out to much more than a hemisphere with a narrow or constricted base, producing a bulbous outline. In fact, the idea of the bulb, or rather bud, is brought out very strikingly in these domes, the row of petals around the base or neck giving the whole a more natural appearance (Plate XX). It is still more apparent in the finials of many of the minarets, such as those at the Ibrāhīm Rauza. The idea is further elaborated in the dome and finials of the Anḍā Masjid, where the separating petals of the bud are indicated by the corrugation or ribbing of the surface. The general appearance of the great dome of the Jāmi' Masjid would, perhaps, have been improved, had it been raised by a cylindrical drum some four or five feet, or even more, out of the great square upon which it rests. Most of the ornamental petals, too, are hidden behind the *kanguras* along the edge of the square roof.

As is the case with all the larger Bījāpūr domes, they are more or less lost, internally, in their own gloom, being lighted only by reflected light from the floor and inner surfaces of the piers below. Of this particular dome the late Mr. James Fergusson wrote: "If he (the architect) had had the courage to pierce the niches at the base of his dome, and make them into windows, he probably would have had the credit of designing the most graceful building of its class in existence." [1]

The façade of the mosque is noticeable for the absence of *mīnārs* or *kanguras*. Since they are present upon the upper terrace around the base of the dome, there can be little doubt but that it was intended to have them also above the main façade. That the building was left unfinished is clearly shewn by the bases of the octagonal buttresses or *mīnārs* at

---

[1] *History of Indian and Eastern Architecture*, Revised Ed., 1910, Vol. II, p. 271.

the eastern ends of the two wings of the corridors, on the north and south sides of the great courtyard; these points were to have been joined across by an eastern wall. This unfinished work, not including the *mīnārs,* was carried out later by Aurangzeb, who further extended the courtyard some ninety-five feet, and built a great gateway on this side. He also, it is said, caused the floor of the mosque to be marked out, in black lines upon its polished plaster, into small compartments or *muṣallās,* each of which was to accommodate one worshipper at prayers: they were the pews, in fact. Altogether there are over 2,250 such spaces in the body of the mosque alone, the wings or corridors not being so marked. For use on special occasions the mosque was provided with lengths of prayer carpets divided into similar spaces, the *qiblah* being woven in the design. These are known by the Persian name of *jā-i-namāz* (Plate XXIV).

As for architectural ornament, the building is comparatively free of it, and where it has been used, it has been applied with judgment and care—just sufficient to accentuate the particular member to which it is applied—and the choice of positions for such decoration has been well considered. The central arch of the façade, for instance, has been very prettily cusped around from springing to apex, while the flat spandrils and surface immediately above the crown, have been further enriched with delicate lace-like patterns in plaster tracery. This emphasises the central archway, which stands straight before the central *miḥrāb* or prayer niche, while the side arches are very plain, having but the narrowest embroidered band of stucco around their arch-rings. The walls, piers, arches, and domical ceilings, within, are covered with a coat of the finest white plaster, which, with age, has assumed a softer and mellowed creamy tint. High up in the back wall and the walls of the wings, is a row of small windows filled with geometric lattice in perforated stone, but which, owing to the small interstices in the patterns, and the thickness of the slabs, admit but a very subdued light; it, perhaps, serves better the purpose of ventilation. A few coloured tiles have been very sparingly used as borders around the arches of the central open space under the dome.

Before the great central *miḥrāb,* or prayer niche, hangs a heavy curtain, and when this is drawn aside a sight of gorgeous colouring is revealed (Plate I, Frontispiece). The whole front and recess is covered with rich gilding upon a coloured ground. There are representations of tombs and minarets, censers and chains, niches containing books, vases with flowers, and the whole is interspersed with bands and medallions bearing decorative inscriptions. Among the latter are these:

> "Place no trust in life: it is but brief."
> "There is no rest in this transitory world."
> "The world is very pleasing to the senses."
> "Life is the best of all gifts, but it is not lasting."
> "Malik Yāqūt,[1] a servant of the mosque, and the slave of Sulṭān Muḥammad, completed the mosque."
> "This gilding and ornamental work was done by order of the Sulṭān Muḥammad 'Ādil Shāh, A. H. 1045." [A. D. 1636.]

On an old native manuscript plan of the city the date of the mosque is recorded as A. H. 985 (A. D. 1576). As the mosque was commenced, and, no doubt, in great part

[1] Yāqūt Dābulī was an Abyssinian slave. His tomb and mosque are at the north-east corner of the citadel, and his *maḥall* or palace is said to have been that across the road, which has been used as a travellers' bungalow (297 on the plan of city).

finished, by 'Ali I., it will be seen that the decoration of the *miḥrāb* was no part of the original design. The colouring of it was conceived by Sulṭān Muḥammad and carried out under his orders. It is possible that the structure and shape of the *miḥrāb* was also altered at the same time, for the *Basātīn-i-Salāṭīn* says he broke the arch *(kamān)* and rebuilt and coloured it, and tells us it was done by Malik Yāqūt Dābulī. That Muḥammad was very partial to painted mural decoration is evident from his adorning the walls of the Āthār Maḥall; and the frescoes in the water pavilion at Kumatgī, described further on, were probably of his time. He also gilded and painted the walls of the Sāt Manzil or Seven-storeyed Palace, said to have been the special apartments of his favourite mistress Rambhā. Surface colour decoration was used in the tombs of 'Ali I. and Ibrāhīm II., but it was chiefly confined to geometric patterns and conventional foliage. It was not until the time of Muḥammad, when the prohibition against it was disregarded, that figure painting was introduced into Muḥammadan buildings at Bījāpūr.

The bracketted cornice and eaves had been very much damaged, it is said, by lightning, but have lately been repaired. It will be noticed here that the monotony of a whole long row of brackets of exactly the same size, set close together, is relieved by double or deeper brackets above the centre of each pier. This, a small thing in itself, makes a very great difference in the general effect. It seems to have been intended that the cornice and brackets should run round the whole length of the wings as well, but, beyond one or two brackets, turning the corner at each end of the façade, it was not carried on.

Standing out before the central arch of the façade, and between it and the cistern, is a small platform, ascended by steps, from the top of which the *muaẕẕin* called the *aẕān* or summons to prayer.[1] The cistern is a plain square reservoir which has had a fountain in the middle fed by water brought through earthern pipes from the Baṛī Bāurī, near the walls to the south of the Jāmi' Masjid. Its purpose was for the ceremonial washing of the hands and feet before going into the mosque to pray.

The exterior of the walls of the building, other than the façade, which, owing to the nature of the requirements of a mosque, have no special features about them, do not readily lend themselves to architectural treatment. They have, however, been very cleverly relieved of much of their monotonous bare areas by an arched corridor running round the whole length of the back and wings (Plate XX). This, with a similar row of blind recessed arches along on the ground floor level beneath it, very agreeably converts what would otherwise have been a painfully blank range of uninteresting masonry into a satisfactory setting to the great dome and terrace above, being in thorough keeping with the character of the latter. The back walls of Gujarāt mosques were sometimes very ornate, owing to the decorated buttresses which projected behind every *miḥrāb,* and the pretty perforated windows between them. In Bījāpūr little attention was paid to these features, and it was unusual to have more than one buttress standing out from the back wall—that behind the central and only *miḥrāb*.

The dome is surmounted by a tall, graceful finial finished off with a metal crescent. This symbol is not, as many suppose, a Muḥammadan religious symbol; in fact it is almost unknown in the East. It is the national symbol of Turkey, adopted by the Turks

[1] "The callers to prayer may expect Paradise, and whoever serves in the office for seven years shall be saved from hell fire." *Mishkāt*, Book IV, Ch vi.

after their conquest of Byzantium, and is used on all the public buildings at Bījāpūr on account of its dynasty claiming descent from the Ottoman Sultāns of Turkey. In Gujarāt the *pippala* leaf is the symbol which tips the finials of old Muḥammadan buildings, while in Māṇḍū, the Mālwā Sultāns had a three-pointed symbol not unlike a *triśūla,* the central point being shorter than the outer ones.

KISHWAR KHĀN'S TOMB.

The tomb of Kishwar Khān is a small building, situated close to the south-east corner of the Nau Bāgh, and not far to the south-east of the "Two Sisters". It is unfinished, its brick dome not having been carried up beyond the ring of leaves around its neck. There is some very fair plaster ornament on the arch rings, with bands of ornamental inscription. Within the building is a much-damaged brick and plaster grave placed to the east of the centre. Over the south doorway of the tomb are inscriptions in plaster containing the *bismillāh* formula and sundry extracts from the Qurān. This tomb is said to have been built about A. D. 1600.

Fig. 13 Kishwar Khān's Tomb.

It is not very clear to which Kishwar Khān we should ascribe this building. There were two Kishwar Khāns of note, father and son. The father was Khwājah Kamāl Lāri, son of Asad Khān Lāri, who was given the title by Ibrāhīm I., when he was governing the district of Hukeri and other *parganahs.* He favoured the succession of 'Ali I. to the throne, and assisted him thereto; and it was in Kishwar Khān's garden, on or near the site of the suburb of Shāhpūr, that 'Ali halted, on his return from confinement at Miraj, to receive the acclamation of the nobles before entering the capital. After serving the state as a military commander for some time, he was eventually deserted by the other nobles when defending the fort of Dhārūr against the Aḥmadnagar troops, and was killed. His head was paraded by Niẓām Shāh before his troops and subsequently delivered over with the body to Kishwar Khān's negro slave Yāqūt, who is said to have taken the remains to Bījāpūr for burial. He, it was, who was entrusted by 'Ali with the oversight of the construction of the walls of the city. If this were his mausoleum, and he had been buried in it, we should expect to find his grave occupying the centre of the chamber, but it appears to be vacant. His son Hāji Kishwar Khān followed him in the title, rose to eminence in the state under the young king Ibrāhīm II., imprisoned the queen Chānd Bībī in Sātāra fort, disgusted the nobles, and met with the same fate as his father He had compassed the death of Muṣtafā Khān Ardistāni, and, when himself obliged to fly from the kingdom, was murdered by a dependant of Muṣtafā Khān in Golkonda territory. Dying so far from home, he probably lies in an unknown grave where he fell. And this would agree better with the state of this tomb as we find it. As the elder Kishwar Khān had a garden, and presumbly a palace, out of the city by Shāhpūr, it would be natural to seek there for his tomb; but the *Basātīn-i-Salāṭīn* tells us that his body was buried in a garden in the city. There is nothing, however, said about the body of the son having been brought back to Bījāpūr for burial.

MOSQUE AND TOMB OF HAZRAT SAYYID 'ALI SHAHĪD PĪR.

A mosque of an unusual form of construction is that of Hazrat Sayyid 'Ali Shahīd, situated in the fields at a little distance to the south-east of the Mihtar Maḥall. The particular feature in which it differs from most of the mosques is the roof, which is here a long arched or wagon-vaulted roof, rising to a long top ridge parallel to the face of the building. With the exception of a smaller mosque, more rudely constructed, to the west of this one, there is no other example of this style of roofing in Bījāpūr. This variety of wagon-vault occurs, often enough, as roofing for a single bay of a ceiling, where the principal bays are domed, but not, except in these cases, as one vaulted roof covering the entire mosque. In these smaller examples it is more or less a flat vault, without a central ridge line, whereas in this mosque it has a steep rise and a central ridge line running along the whole length of the building. In other words, the cross section simply presents a Gothic arch, and this section is the same from end to end (Plates XXV—XXIX). The longitudinal section has a rectangular outline, no curves, whatever, being seen.

The plan of the mosque, omitting the *miḥrāb* buttress, is square, measuring 35′ 6″ each way, upon which it would have been easy enough to construct a groined roof, but a true groined roof is never found in Bījāpūr, save, perhaps, in very small bays in a larger ceiling. The *miḥrāb* is unusual in several ways. In plan it is a nine-sided recess, two sides in the front being open into the body of the mosque. Odd-sided *miḥrāb* niches are usual, but not generally so deep as this, where it becomes almost a separate chamber. Again, there is a doorway leading out through one of the sides of the *miḥrāb,* which is most unusual and inexplicable. One might suggest a dozen different reasons for it, but they would be, at the best, but hypothetical. Another interesting feature, which we also find in other mosques, is the very tall narrow chimney-like vault over the *miḥrāb* recess, which is well seen in the cross section (Plate XXIX). It is so deep that, looking up into it from inside, little can be seen for the gloom with which it is filled. Here is a clear case for double doming, for a lower interior shell, thrown across about halfway up, would have corrected this defect, presuming that the elongation of the vault cylinder was necessary to provide a conspicuous external feature.

In the longitudinal section is seen the neat and rather elegant panelling of the vaulted ceiling. It reminds one much of similar panelling in the vaulted ceilings of the chancels of mediæval Christian churches, and specimens of these, in ruins, are seen at Bassein, which were built by the Portuguese when they settled there. The ceiling is divided into three sections by arch rings round the vault, corresponding to the two piers in the façade, the panelling in the centre one being richer than that of the side bays. The front of the *miḥrāb* was originally richly decorated with coloured tile work, but all within reach of the outstretched arm has been broken away and carried off. An inscription in the same work runs across over the top of the *miḥrāb* arch, but it gives us no information whatever, being nothing but extracts from the Qurān. The letters are white on a blue ground.

The façade of the mosque is very pleasing from the effect obtained by the introduction of a great number of receding lines of moulding round the arches, giving them a deep-set appearance; and these lines are carried down the piers. The outer ring of arch moulding is cusped, and the spandrils are ornamented with beautifully designed medallions in stucco. Altogether this is a very successful little building of its class, and it is well and solidly built. The drawings and photographs illustrate it fully.

Hazrat Sayyid 'Ali Shahīd, after whom the mosque is called, was one of Bījāpūr's saints in the time of the king 'Ali I., who is said to have constructed the mosque to his memory. It is related that he became a *shahīd* or martyr by being killed in battle in the country of "Raylan". On the north-east of the mosque is a substantially built gateway, which was intended to lead into a courtyard before the mosque, opposite to which is a roughly-built three-arched *sarāi* or rest-house. Without the gate is a much damaged tombstone over the grave of 'Ali Shahīd.

THE SĀT MANZIL.

The pile of apartments known as the Sāt Manzil, or Seven-storeyed Palace, stands a little way to the south-west of the Gagan Maḥall, at the corner of a range of buildings enclosing a great quadrangle known as the Granary (Plates XIX, XXVI, and XXX). At present it rises to a height of five storeys, or ninety-seven feet over all, but a narrow staircase rises from the fifth to a sixth, which does not now exist. It is possible there may have been a still higher terrace above this again, but, if so, it must have been but a very small one. In the original building there were possibly but three storeys; the row of *kanguras* round the walls, seen in the photograph between the third and fourth storeys, seems to indicate the line of the original terrace roof, over which were subsequently added the additional storeys. It is said to have been built by Ibrāhīm II., in 1583, as a palace, but, if this were so, it must have been far more extensive than it is at present for its accommodation, as a glance at the plans of four of its floors shew, is very limited (Plate XXX). We must, I think, consider it as an adjunct to the whole of the palace buildings rather than a separate one in itself, and part of the group represented by the ranges around the quadrangle, and the Chīnī Maḥall at the south end. The latter perhaps was the principal building in the group, containing, as it did, a very fine *darbār* hall, which, in the converted building, is still used as such on public occasions. The Sāt Manzil block certainly extended somewhat further upon the south side, and still further along the walls to the north. A passage along the terrace above the range of rooms on the west side of the quadrangle, very likely connected this with the Chīnī Maḥall.

The building was evidently erected for pleasure and for royal baths rather than for business purposes, as may be gathered from the free use of ornamental bath cisterns in the various rooms, and the presence of water pipes, laid from storey to storey through the masonry. This lavish distribution of water and bathing cisterns is a peculiar feature of this class of buildings, other examples of which are Mubārak Khān's Maḥall, in the south-east of the city, close to the walls, and the water pavilions at Kumatgī, twelve miles east of Bījāpūr. In the Sāt Manzil we find cisterns upon the different floors; and, like the buildings just mentioned, the walls were subsequently painted with human figures and other objects. Mr. James Bird wrote, about 1844, after visiting the city:

"The walls were formerly covered with fresco paintings and portraits of people belonging to the court, most of which are now defaced. I observed, however, an elegant portrait of a Mahomedan priest, whose features were Turkish, and complexion very fair. There is also a drawing of Mahomed [Captain Sydenham says 'Adil Shāh] the sixth king, in company with his favourite dancing girl Rambhā. He is seated on a cushion, near which are laid his sehtar, a basket of flowers and a Persian book. The expression on his countenance is that of good nature, and much kindness of disposition—virtues for which he is yet celebrated among the people, and has been frequently praised by historians." [1]

Traces of two of the figures still remained, a few years ago, on the north wall of the first floor, and the imaginative mind detected in these the outlines of Rambhā and the Sulṭān himself. The walls are said to have been beautifully gilded until the Raja of Sātara ordered it to be scraped off, thinking thereby to reap a rich harvest of the precious metal. As was the case with the Gagan Maḥall, all its woodwork was carried away. It is certainly by no means a handsome building now, being without definite form or design, and would have been passed over in this monograph with scant notice were it not for its intimate associations with many of the most interesting events in Bījāpūr story. The richly-carved window frames and screens, with their deep weather boards and bracketting, when they existed, must have improved the appearance considerably; and it would then have been, if not elegant, yet a very picturesque pile. Beside the extensive views of the city and country around, obtained from the upper terraces, it formed a splendid coign of vantage for the inmates of the palace. This was a very desirable thing to have in those days of unrest, when the king's life was never safe from the evil machinations of intriguing ministers, who could surround the palace or citadel with troops at any moment.

Immediately in front of the Sāt Manzil, on the north side, is a neat little structure called a *jalamaṇdir* or water pavilion. It stands in the middle of a small reservoir, which had been filled in with earth and lost sight of for many years, until it was recently re-excavated and the whole fabric put in repair. Locally, the Hindus looked upon it as a *rath* or sacred car, having its wheels buried in the ground. Such a *rath,* indeed, made in stone, stands among the famous ruins of Vijayanagar. There is another *jalamaṇdir,* though not so big or fine as this, and which is falling to decay, in the fields a short distance to the south-east of Muṣṭafā Khān's Mosque. The presence of this one would indicate the existence here of secluded courts and gardens within the palace precincts set apart for the use of the *zanānah.* It is manifestly later work than the Sāt Manzil and partakes more of the style of work of the reign of Ibrāhīm II.

---

[1] *Journ. Bombay Branch of the Royal Asiatic Society,* Vol. I, p. 375.

Unlike the Kamatgī and Mubārak Khān pavilions, this one does not appear to have had pipes laid through its masonry for a water display. It was, no doubt, intended as a pleasant place to sit in and while away an hour; and, as there is a doorway on the north side, in the place of the three lancet windows on the others, there must have been some means of access, such as a light wooden gangway, thrown across to it from some part of the palace buildings which stood on the north side of it. The pavilion was further decorated with coloured tiles in bands on each face, but these have all been picked out.

Fig. 14. The Jalamaṇḍir, restored.

To the east of the Sāt Manzil, and near the road, passing north and south through the citadel, is a very ruinous block of small apartments which must originally have formed part of the great group of palace buildings (No. 282 on the plan). It has, very erroneously, been called the old mint, but there is nothing whatever about it to lead one to suppose that it could ever have been used for such a purpose. The mint was located close to the Mihtar Maḥall, on its west side, where the garden at the back of the houses, is still called the Ṭaksāl-kā-Bāgh or Mint Garden.[1] These rooms have rather the character of bathing apartments. The upper floor is now cut off from the lower by the disappearance of the staircase. Although the dismantled and ruined aspect of its exterior promises nothing of interest within, yet a climb into its upper storey, over the broken masonry, amply repays the trouble, for here we find some of the best and most chaste designs in plaster to be found in Bījāpūr. As we have already seen, many of the buildings of the city contained a very great deal of this beautiful surface tracery, but, owing to its friable nature, and the exposed positions in which much of it was used, very little of it now remains, and that little in a deplorably damaged state. It is, then, a pleasure to find a

[1] Dr. James Bird says (*Journ. Bom. Br. R. A. S.*, Vol. I, p. 376) that "eastward from the citadel along the Jāmi Masjid road, between the citadel and Mehtar Mahal was the Khizanah bazar or Treasury Market". This would, no doubt, have been so called after the Mint or Treasury which was located here. Captain Sydenham writes (*Asiatic Researches*, Quarto Ed., Vol. XIII, p. 444), more than a hundred years ago: "In a handsome street leading from the eastern gateway of the citadel to the Jāmi Masjid, are the remains of a grand state prison and a mint."

few beautiful examples almost intact. The domical ceilings of many of the Bījāpūr buildings have been decorated with plaster ornament, but very few, at all, approach the excellence of design and good taste displayed in these. The harsh black and white line work, as reproduced in the accompanying plates, do not give one an adequate idea of the beautiful effect produced by the soft lights and shadows on the creamy plaster. (Plates XXX, XXXIII—XXXV.)

In working out these patterns, it would seem that the workman laid on the plaster in flat masses, varying from three-eighths to three-quarters of an inch in thickness, and, while moist, carved out the interstices, leaving the design in relief. Some parts, such as the bossed centres and ribs of the designs, stand out considerably higher.

Standing off the south-east corner of the Gagan Maḥall, and almost touching it, is a little square building now used as the station church. It is an old ruin converted to its present use, but what it was originally it is impossible to say. Within it were some more of these beautiful plaster ceilings, but these retained much of the gorgeous colouring with which the patterns were picked out. On the conversion of the building, the Executive Engineer restored this colouring as nearly as he could match the old. This building is seen in Plate II, in the foreground on the left.

The Chīnī Maḥall, now converted into public offices, and referred to in a previous chapter, occupies the south end of the great quadrangle, at the north-west corner of which the Sāt Manzil stands. It was in the clearances, carried out here, that great quantities of old broken china were found—fragments of plates, bowls, candlesticks, hookah bowls, cups, and other articles. This ware was imported into Bījāpūr from China and Persia. Much of it remained in the possession of old Muḥammadan families at Bījāpūr until some thirty or forty years ago since which time it has been almost wholly cleared out by enterprising visitors and local officials. The articles on Plate XXXII give a good idea of this ware. It was about here that the great iron grille was excavated, formed of perforated wrought iron of considerable thickness, shown in Fig. 15. It measures four feet five inches, by two feet ten inches, and has been used, for many years, as a screen in the station church, mounted in a heavy wooden frame.

Fig. 15. Wrought iron grille excavated near the Chīnī Maḥall.

THE CHHOṬA ĀTHĀR.

There is a small mosque situated in the New Bāzār, about two hundred and fifty yards east of the Dakhanī 'Īdgāh and close to Sikandar 'Ādil Shāh's grave, which is remarkable for the amount of stucco ornament, such as has just been described, which covers the walls, ceiling, and part of the façade. Other than this, there is nothing of note about the building. It is known as the Chhoṭa Āthār, but, for what reason, no one seems to know. It has a very flat wagon-vaulted ceiling of a kind frequently met with in Bījāpūr. As has already been explained, the ornament is obtained by cutting out the interstices of the design from the flat coating of plaster on the walls. These designs appear to have been thrown into stronger relief by the sunk surfaces being blackened, but it is very doubtful whether this was any improvement upon the natural shadows of the soft creamy-tinted plaster (Plates XXXV and XXXVI).

THE ḤAIDARIYYAH MASJID.

Taking the buildings, as near as it is possible, in their chronological order, the Ḥaidariyyah Masjid, close beside the Baṛī Kamān or Great Arch of Muṣtafā Khān, on the road between the citadel and the Jāmi' Masjid, should come immediately after the Sāt Manzil, if, indeed, it should not precede it. An inscription over the entrance doorway tells us that the mosque was built by Ḥaidar Khān Ibn Jamīl in the year A. H. 991 (A. D. 1583), during the reign of Ibrāhīm II. It runs thus :

> In the reign of the just Sulṭān Ibrāhīm 'Ādil Shāh was built the blessed mosque, named Ḥaidariyyah after Ḥaidar Khān Ibn Jamīl in the year 991.

Ḥaidar Khān was one of king Ibrāhīm's generals, to whom was entrusted the erection of the great cavalier or gun tower known as the Ḥaidar or Uplī Burj [1] near the Dakhanī 'Īdgāh, and who was mixed up in the quarrel and subsequent tumult between the adherents of Ḥamīd Khān and Ikhlāṣ Khān. He was one of Dilāwar Khān's party, and was dismissed his post of Qil'adār by Ikhlāṣ Khān while the former was with the troops in the field (Plate XXV).

Save for its connection with a noted character in Bījāpūr history, and the fact of it being a dated building, the mosque has nothing about it worthy of special attention. It was probably Ḥaidar Khān's own private chapel, and was possibly attached to his own dwelling, which may have stood near here. The design of its façade is almost identical with that of the Ibrāhīmpūr mosque, ascribed to Ibrāhīm I., outside the city walls on the south, and is of the early type of building with rather squat piers and arches which are too wide for their height. If anything, the proportions are better in the Ḥaidariyyah Masjid. The Ibrāhīmpūr mosque has a dome which this one has not ; in both, the arches are slightly ogee, turning up at the crowns rather more in the later than in the earlier building.

MALIKAH JAHĀN BEGAM'S MOSQUE.

We now arrive at a period, during the long reign of the luxurious king Ibrāhīm II., when a more elaborate style of work was introduced into his capital. Discarding the plaster and concrete buildings of his predecessors, he launched out into the free use of sculptured stone-work, in which his masons seem to have revelled. Restricted, as good Muslims, to geometric designs and conventionalized forms of foliage, they excelled in these, and evolved the most complicated, and, withal, pleasing combinations. They impressed into their service even the Qurān itself, whose texts they reproduced in elaborate

[1] This has already been described in the general description of the city.

interlacing of Arabic letters, which lend themselves so well to decorative effect (Plates XXXVII, XXXVIII and XL).

One of the first mosques in this style to claim our attention is that called after Malikah Jahān Begam, or the Zanjīrī Masjid, as it has also been called, on account of the small stone chains which once adorned its cornice. There is no inscription in or about the mosque, but the building of it is attributed to Ibrāhīm II. who is said to have built it about A. D. 1586 in honour of his wife Malikah Jahān, daughter of Qulī Quṭb Shāh, and we may well believe that she was as beautiful among the maidens of her princely house as this little gem is amongst the mosques of the city. The amount of delicate work compressed within the space between the arches and the dome is marvellous, and it is distributed and assigned to the various parts with the greatest taste and judgment. The richness of the fretted sky-line, the minute tracery of the little kiosks, the serrated and foliated fringe of the eave slabs of the cornice, and the wonderful beauty and elaboration of the brackets which support them, combine to form such a profusion of loveliness as is not surpassed elsewhere in Bījāpūr.

Again we find here, as in the Jāmi' Masjid, the accentuation of the central arch of the façade by its cusped contour. Stucco ornament still enters into the general scheme of decoration. The spandrils of the arches have all had a thin coat of plaster, on which were medallion ornaments, but these latter have disappeared leaving only the marks of their outlines; and this plaster, with the arches, piers, and lower portions of the minarets, have all been covered with undesirable whitewash. The leaves round the dome have also been minutely worked in plaster ornament. The dome rises over the central bay before the *miḥrāb*, and the ceiling, within, is carried up to the full height of the dome; and thus, instead of being a finely-designed feature in keeping with the rest of the building, it is enveloped in darkness—it is a veritable black hole. This is, indeed, an unpardonable fault, for the remedy for it is so simple, namely, double doming, a device not altogether unknown to Muslim architects.[1]

The minarets are very graceful. Unlike those of Gujarāt, which are larger in plan, and contain a spiral staircase within them, leading to the various balconies from which to call the people to prayer, these, in Bījāpūr, are mere ornamental appendages, and are in keeping with the lighter style of work and the more ornamental bulbous dome. The leaf and bud enter largely into their decorative details, the latter as a crowning member and the former engirdling the shaft at different points. The *mīnārs*, as well as the great dome, were surmounted by metal finials and crescents, but only the supporting pegs for these now remain.

A great deal has been done to this building in the way of repairs, and most of the beautiful cornice, which had been badly damaged, has been renewed, together with portions of the perforated parapet. The hanging stone chains, described further on, in connection with the Kālī Masjid at Lakshmeśwar, which hung from between the brackets under the cornice, have all disappeared (see Figs. 16 and 17).

---

[1] A good illustration of double doming, in a ruined mosque at Bagdad, may be seen in an illustration opposite page 130 in a little book called *The Euphrates and the Tigris*, 1884. T. Nelson and Sons, London.

THE KĀLĪ MASJID AT LAKSHMEŚWAR.

In some of the outlying provinces of the Bījāpūr kingdom were erected, especially at the headquarters of local governors, buildings in nowise inferior in point of design and finish to those at the capital. At Lakshmeśwar, in the Dhārwār District, a town now under the rule of the Miraj State, is a very good example of the style of work we have been considering, and, probably, of about the same date, called the Kālī Masjid or 'Black Mosque'. It is a trifle heavier, in appearance, than Malikah Jahān's, but this is rather due to the square outline of the façade, it being higher in proportion to its width. For delicacy of work, however, it is not one whit behind the Bījāpūr example (Plate XLI). In this we see these curious stone chains which were so largely used for decorative effect, hanging from every conceivable point (see Fig. 16). Before these were so damaged, by swinging to the winds of centuries, and being further mutilated by the hand of man, the little building must have looked like a creation in silver filigree work rather than a substantial fabric in stone. These chains are always cut out of single slabs of stone, having all their links, in many cases double or in pairs, free and flexible. They generally had a globular pendant at the end, carved as a perforated hollow ball with a smaller ball inside. The chain shewn in Fig. 16 was drawn from a chain hanging with others, in a tomb at Rauza, near Aurangābād, and it is almost identical with some of those still hanging under the deep cornice of the Lakshmeśwar mosque. Fig. 17 is a restored elevation of the north *mīnār* of this mosque shewing the chains as they existed originally.

Fig. 16. Stone chain pendent from a tomb at Rauza, near Daulatābād.

Fig. 17. One of the minarets of the Kālī Masjid at Lakshmeśwar, restored.

There is no doubt such additions contributed very much to the prettiness of these buildings, giving them a fairy-like look, more appropriate to an 'Arabian Nights' setting, than as everyday houses of prayer for battle-scarred veterans and rough and rude soldiery But no doubt the spirit of those men was the grand spirit of sacrifice—the spirit that prompted king David to exclaim at Araunah: "Neither will I offer unto the Lord my God of that which doth cost me nothing."[1]

[1] In *Architecture at Beejapoor,* by Fergusson and Taylor, the Lakshmeśwar mosque is described as being at Adoni, in the Raichūr District, as far away from Bijāpūr in an easterly direction as Lakshmeśwar is in a southerly. It is compared with the Andā Masjid (Mosque in the Fort), and both are said to be of the time of Aurangzeb, which is altogether wrong. The latter, indeed, has its date upon it—A. D. 1608, before Aurangzeb was born.

THE BUKHĀRĪ MASJID.

The Bukhārī Masjid, which is somewhat of the same style as those we have been considering, is a small building which stands close beside the Post Office, having, itself, been for some twenty years occupied for that purpose. It has, of late, been reclaimed and restored to its original condition, its windows, doors, and partition walls having been removed. Nothing is known of its origin. It is a very neat and compact little building, is carefully finished, and has a well-designed cornice whose brackets are beautifully carved, but the slabs, above, have been badly smashed up. Within, about the arches, is some pretty stucco work (Plate XLII).

In front of the *masjid* there is a gateway and row of arches, meant, possibly, for a rest-house or *sarāi*, and it is very likely that these, with the walls, now demolished, enclosed a courtyard around the building. Above this gateway is an inscription to the following effect:

> Allāh, Muḥammad! May Allāh, who be exalted, be pleased with Abū Bakr, ‘Umar, and ‘Uthmān and ‘Ali, and with all the rest of the companions [of the Prophet].

When the *masjid* was first taken up for use as a post office in 1882, the owner of the land adjoining, named Muḥyu-d-dīn *walad* Burhān Ṣāḥib Bukhārī, laid claim to it and asked for Rs. 53,000 as compensation. The matter went before the Court when, about 1884 or 1885, it was compounded for Rs. 786-4-0, the claimant to retain the gateway and arches, which latter he appears to have sold subsequently for Rs. 200. The mosque, no doubt, takes its name from this man.

THE IBRĀHĪM RAUZA.

As the group of buildings, collectively known as the Ibrāhīm Rauza,[1] must have been in progress during the greater part of the reign of Ibrāhīm II., it may be as well to take it up at this point. It is, without doubt, the *magnum opus* of the ‘Ādil Shāhis. Fergusson declares it to be "a group as rich and as picturesque as any in India, and far excelling anything of the sort on this side of the Hellespont,"[2] which "is more remarkable for the profusion and richness of its ornamental details than for either its dimensions or the elegance and propriety of its general form . . . . . The two [the tomb and the mosque] must, however, be taken together as parts of one composition; and with their gateways, their terraces, and their external colonnades, they make up a group of gorgeous, but it must be confessed somewhat barbaric, splendour, that it would be difficult to match in any part of the world."[3] (Plates XLII—LIV.)

This magnificent group is situated at a short distance to the west of the city, out and beyond the Makka gate. Upon a high terrace, within a great square enclosure, are two large buildings, facing one another, with a square reservoir and fountain between them; while surrounding this platform upon three sides, and within the great enclosure walls, is a

---

[1] Rauza, a garden. Originally the garden in which is situated the tomb of the Prophet at Madinah. The name is also applied to the tomb itself by some writers.

[2] *History of Indian and Eastern Architecture*, Revised Ed., 1910, Vol. II, p. 273.

[3] *Architecture at Beejapoor*, by Fergusson and Taylor, pp. 89-90.

level green sward, which, at one time, was a royal garden. The building standing on the east side of the terrace is the mausoleum of king Ibrāhīm II. and certain members of his family (Plate XLIII). From the inscriptions upon it we gather that it was primarily erected as the mausoleum and memorial of his queen Tāj Sulṭāna, but the king, dying before her, was first interred within it.[1] There is nothing to indicate whose the individual tombs are in the sepulchral chamber, except that the men's tombs are distinguished from those of the ladies by the arched ridge stones along the top, the ladies' tombs being quite flat.[2] The tombs are arranged in a row from east to west; and, as the third one from the

Fig. 18. The graves in the Ibrāhīm Rauza.

east is the largest, and is a man's tomb, we may presume it is that of Ibrāhīm, and that, naturally, one of the women's tombs, on either side of him, is the grave of Tāj Sulṭāna. Tradition gives the following order from east to west: (1) Tāj Sulṭāna[3]; (2) Haji Badī' Ṣāḥiba, Ibrāhīm's mother; (3) Ibrāhīm Jagat Gīr, himself; (4) Zuhrah Sulṭāna, his daughter; (5) Darvesh Pādshāh, his son; and (6) Sulṭān Sulaimān, another son.[4]

The building on the west side of the terrace, facing the mausoleum, is the mosque—the usual adjunct to a tomb (Plate XLIII). But while we find it the more important of the two buildings, architecturally, in Gujarāt, in Bījāpūr it is usually a subsidiary structure, except, as in this case, where, for the sake of the general balance and symmetry of the whole composition, it is the counterpart of the tomb in size and its main outlines.

---

[1] The building, in old writings, is also called the mausoleum of Zuhrah Sulṭāna, his daughter, after whom the adjacent suburb was, and still is, called Zuhrahpūr.

[2] This ridge stone is said to represent a *qalamdān* or pen box, indicating a lettered person, and hence, in those days, a man Graves are placed north and south, so that the body with its head to the north, may lie with the face turned round towards Makka.

[3] Or Jahān Begam, daughter of Abd-ur-Raḥmān, and mother of Muḥammad Shāh.

[4] In Moor's *Narrative of the Operations of Captain Little's Detachment*, the order is given as follows: Eastern grave that of Hāji Badī' Ṣāḥiba; second, Tāj Sulṭāna; third, Ibrāhīm; fourth Zuhrah, who died at six years of age; fifth, Zuhrah's brother, the king's youngest son, Burhān Shāh; and sixth, the king's eldest son. This is, perhaps, the more correct order.

The conception, design, and profusion of the richest decorative details mark these buildings as the culminating point of the style we have been considering in connection with Malikah Jahān's and the Lakshmeśwar mosques. The heavy and congested masses of small and dainty detail of the later Chālukyan temples may well be compared with the more elegant and lighter distribution of the almost equally fine work upon these buildings. The lovely setting of the Tāj Maḥall at Agra, amongst green trees and water, which imparts to its *tout ensemble* half its charm, shews what we lose here by the absence of the garden, and the splash of its fountains and rills of running water. Some day, when funds permit, it may be possible to restore all this, when the Ibrāhīm Rauza will be to the Dakhan what the Tāj Maḥall is to northern India—one of the most lovely and delightful dreams of architectural beauty.

The sepulchral chamber in the mausoleum is 39 feet 10 inches square. In the middle of each of its four sides is a doorway, and on either side of each of these is a three-light shuttered window with an arched fan-light above, the latter being filled with beautiful perforated stone tracery (Plate XLVI). The whole fan-light, which measures, in each case, 5 feet, is filled with interlaced Arabic letters, the perforations or interstices between these forming the lights. The letters, which are so entangled, and in some cases drawn out, in order to distribute them evenly over the area of the window, form sentences which it is exceedingly difficult to unravel. They contain extracts from the Qurān. These with the open door—for the lower windows are seldom opened—let into the room a subdued light which is just sufficient to reveal a most remarkable flat stone ceiling. Each of the more important buildings at Bījāpūr has some noticeable feature peculiar to itself, either of constructive skill or in decoration. This flat ceiling must surely have been the *chef d'œuvre* of the architect of the Ibrāhīm Rauza. It is practically a hanging ceiling (Plate LII). The whole span is the size of the room, namely, 39 feet 10 inches square, of which a margin all round, 7 feet 7 inches wide, is coved downwards to meet the walls. The flat central space is 24 feet square. Upon closely examining this, it is found to be composed of slabs of stone set edge to edge, with no apparent support. There are certainly two deep ribs, or beams, running across both ways, but these are entirely decorative and are made up of separate stones, and do not, in any way, support the slabs in the nine bays into which they divide the ceiling. This has been a most daring piece of work—or so it appears to those used to western methods—carried out in open defiance of the ordinary rules of construction; but the result shews that, whatever we may say against it, the architect knew what he was doing, and had as full confidence in his workmen and materials as he had in himself. It has stood the best test that any work can stand—the test of time. South of the walls of the town there is an old tomb, surmounted by half a ruined dome, parts of which overhang without support, and has done so since it was partly shot away by a cannon ball during the siege of Aurangzeb. The whole secret of the durability of the masonry of those days is the great strength and tenacity of the mortar. This is the secret, too, of this flat ceiling. At the north-east corner of the Tāj Bāurī is a partly destroyed dome (Fig. 28). It is rather a flat one, but it is constructed in the same manner as this, with a lining of flat slabs, which, by themselves, could not possibly stand. They are nothing more than the lining of a concrete ceiling, which stands, of itself, as a great strong shell, the sheer adhesive strength of the mortar keeping the slabs where they are. It was possible, as is seen in the upstair corridor of the tomb, that, although the ceiling as a whole may remain intact, there was the danger of individual stones dropping out, and this, to some extent, has been guarded against by rabetting the edges, and, in many cases, fastening adjacent stones together with iron clamps. The slabs of the ceilings of the corridors are supported in the same way, and they may all be examined from below and above, staircases leading to the upper chambers, through the thickness of the walls, from behind the east and west doorways. Above this great flat ceiling, the upper surface of the concrete shell forms the floor to a large chamber immediately under the main dome. In fact, this great flat ceiling is, practically, an instance of double doming, which we have already pointed out as the only practical remedy for those high, dark, gloomy domed ceilings so frequently met with in Bījāpūr.

The exterior walls of the sepulchral chamber are most elaborately decorated with shallow surface tracery of arabesque and interlaced writing from the Qurān, the whole text of which is said to be inscribed upon the four walls (Plate L). The effect has been further heightened with colour, but this has weathered badly. Captain Sykes, who was in Bījāpūr in 1818, says the carved letters were gilt, and the ground azure, and the gilding and colour were even then preserved in some places, the brilliancy of the azure being remarkable.[1]

The doors are of teak, are divided into carved panels with Arabic writing, and are furnished with deep rails and styles carrying gilt iron bosses. The photograph (Plate XLVII) shews the west door, with its surrounding work upon the walls, in which it will be seen how well its design harmonises with the latter. The sentences upon the eight little square panels are as follows: "Allāh is one." "Allāh is present." "He succeeded him for good." "My helper is Allāh." "Muḥammad and his family." "Allāh is witness." "And all his companions." "Indication of Allāh." Immediately around the door, the inscription, in six compartments, reads thus:

> And who is he whose affairs change and he remains?
> And thou hast no advantage in a palace thou hast built in vain
> We shall be judged according to our sins as thou art aware.
> According to thy dignity will be established that which is forgiven
> In Paradise; and to the obdurate man—to thee—its grapes will be hidden.
> They hope for them; and he is hoping and fearing.

The very free use of Arabic or Persian characters in the designing of decorative detail is also well shewn in the plate, noticeable among the panels and bands being the discs in the spandrils above the door, where the writing, by reduplication and reversal, has been reduced almost to geometric patterns. Upon the bands, between the patterns, may be seen the remains of painted flower ornament. Further illustration of the abundant use, and with the most excellent taste, of Persian writing may be noticed in Plates XLV and L where it is seen covering great areas of the walls, and is formed by the skilful manipulation of the letters into rich and singular ornament. Again, in Plate XLV, painted portions of the walls can be seen, but it is exceedingly doubtful whether all this painting and gilding was an improvement at all, masking and confusing, as it must have done to a very great extent, the delicate surface tracery of the stone. It added, no doubt, an air of barbaric

---

[1] *Transactions of the Literary Society, Bombay*, Vol. III, p. 58.

splendour to the place, which must have pleased the prodigal tastes of king Ibrāhīm. Above the doorway, in Plate XLVII, is seen that peculiar bracket ornament supporting the discs, the two together looking very like a bracket lamp and globe. It is found as a constantly occurring combination upon most of the buildings of Bījāpūr, and, where used in the spandrils of arches, it relieves the otherwise stiffness of appearance that the discs would have had by themselves.

The square pillars, which form the outer support of the mezzanine gallery within the mausoleum, are very Hindu in style, having little that is Saracenic about them. This likeness to Hindu forms is brought out more in the photograph (Plate XLV) than in the drawing (Plate LI), where the narrow neck of the capital is better seen. Compare the elevations of the pillar from the Ibrāhīm Rauza, on Plate LI, with the second one from the left on Plate VI, upper illustration. The ceilings between these pillars and the walls, which is beneath the mezzanine gallery, is covered with shallow surface carving including geometric, lotus, key, spiral, and intricate knot designs. The arches, in the outer verandah, are additions, made a good many years ago, when the whole fabric was put in repair.

Both the tomb and the mosque, opposite it, are noted for their deep rich cornices and graceful minarets; and the amount of labour expended upon these has been unstinted. These cornices, like those of many other buildings in the city, have suffered very greatly; but they have lately been repaired, or rather restored, for it was found impossible to repair them in the ordinary sense, since they were found to be cracked through and through, hardly a bracket being entire. The least movement, in taking out damaged parts, threatened to bring down the whole mass, so nothing was left to be done but to dismantle the damaged parts very carefully, fragment by fragment, and reconstruct in new material. The main cause of this wholesale damage has been the poor quality of the stone used. The Bījāpūr builders must have been restricted in their choice of quarries to the small circumscribed area of the state itself. They often quarried upon the same site on which they were building, the quarry hole, with a little further dressing down, serving the purpose, afterwards, of a well or reservoir. The local amygdaloidal trap and basalt is full of seams and cracks, and is not fit for lengths upon which any leverage is brought to bear, and very long slabs were required in the under bracketting to support the great flat top slabs, which project a great distance from the walls. The little lotus buds, depending from the points of the brackets, in their long lines and clusters, give the impression of countless petrified drops of rainwater. Between the brackets may be seen a few remains of those wonderful stone chains, already described. The fascicular grouping of miniature *mīnārs* around the bases of the minarets is very pleasing; and the perforated parapets, round the tops of the buildings, look, at a distance, like a deep fringe of lace.

Originally the *mimbar*, or pulpit steps of the mosque, was surmounted by an ornamental representation of a miniature mosque or kiosk, but Aurangzeb, considering this unorthodox, ordered it to be removed.[1] Parts of this canopy were lying about in the courtyard until recently, when the stones were removed to the local museum.

Among the principal inscriptions, which give us any information, upon the walls of the mausoleum—for it is upon this building alone that we find them—are the following:

---

[1] *Journal of the Bombay Branch of the Royal Asiatic Society*, Vol. I, p. 388.

Around the south door, on the inside band, in six compartments :

By handsome efforts this work of the Rauzah
Malik Ṣandal established in buildings;
He called it the Rauzah Tāj Sulṭān
Eternal [this line is not very clear].
The expense was one and a half lakh *hūn*,
But nine hundred more were added thereto.

Around the south door, on the outside band, in six compartments :

I asked the *pīr* of wisdom for the date,
He said *Tāj Sulṭān, dweller in Paradise.*
Dignified like Zubaidah and exalted like Bilqīs,
Kind and affable in behaviour, the diadem [*tāj*] of modesty;
When from this earthly abode she passed away
To the abode of the realm of Paradise she departed.

In the above the words in italics, or rather, the Persian equivalent words *Tāj Sulṭān ahl-i-jannat*, form the chronogram which gives us the date A. H. 1043 (A. D. 1633) as the date of the death of Tāj Sulṭāna, the wife of Ibrāhīm II., who died some seven years after the king.

Between the above two bands of inscription is a triangular inscription in the top of the arch which reads :

When the Shāh was in the rose garden of paradise, in its eternity, I asked the *pīr* of wisdom [for the date]; he said:—*The place with the guide.* Year 1037. [A. D. 1627-28.]

This inscription records the date of the king's death. The *Basātīn-i-Salāṭīn* tells us he died on the 10th Muḥarram, 1037.

Around the north door, on the outside band, in six compartments :

The king allied to the sphere called for the date of it :—
This heart-rejoicing edifice is commemorated as Tāj Sulṭān
[Two lines not clear]
A garden and a Paradise is this Rauzah in freshness, carrying off the ball,
Each column thereof in gracefulness, strength, from the garden of purity.

The translation is not very satisfactory, and may be due to an imperfect estampage being submitted to Mr. Rehatsek, the translator. A free translation of the inscription is given in the Bombay Gazetteer, Bījāpūr volume, as follows :

"Heaven stood astonished at the elevation of this building, and it might be said when its head rose from the earth that another heaven was erected. The garden of Paradise has borrowed its beauty from this garden and every column here is graceful as the cyprus tree in the garden of purity. An angel from heaven announced the date of the structure by saying 'This building which makes the heart glad is the memorial of Tāj Sulṭāna'."

The rest of the inscriptions contain nothing of any importance. It is clear from those given above that the building was erected to the glory and memory of Tāj Sulṭāna. It was, thus, completed some years before the Tāj Maḥall at Agra was commenced.

The architect of this magnificent pile—the creator of all this fretted loveliness—was Malik Ṣandal, of whom we should have liked to have known more. One might well ask how men could evolve such grand conceptions, and translate them into stone in those rude old times. "How? Because in those rude old times, as we are pleased to call them, there were men like simple old Thomas Peyton of Ely, who, having food and raiment, were therewith content; men who lived for the joy and glory of their work and did not regard their art as a means of livelihood, so much as an end to live for; men who were so stupid, so far astray, that to sacrifice the joy of living for a mountain of coin seemed to them *propter vitam vivendi perdere causas.*"[1]

MALIK ṢANDAL'S MOSQUE.

Malik Ṣandal's name is preserved in an inscription in the *miḥrāb* of a small plain mosque, of no architectural account, situated in the Langar Bāzār, close to Ki<u>sh</u>war <u>Kh</u>ān's tomb (No. 74 on the plan). He was, as we have just seen, the architect of the Ibrāhīm Rauza. The building has been used by some Muḥammadans as a dwelling. The inscription reads:

When Malik Ṣandal built this mosque he prepared the date only by *divine effusion.*

The italicised words give a date 1024 (A. H. 1614), thirteen years before the death of Ibrāhīm II., and probably during the period in which the Ibrāhīm Rauza was under construction. The lower portion of the inscription is but an extract from the Quran. It is quite possible that Malik Ṣandal's house stood near this mosque, which was his own private chapel for himself and household.

As already stated, his name is connected by tradition with a small mean group of buildings close to the Bu<u>kh</u>ārī Masjid (No. 5 on the plan). There is here a small mosque, and a little pavilion over a tomb, said to be that of his mother or wife, in the middle of the courtyard. Surrounding these are rooms forming rest-houses. It has been said by some that the great architect himself lies here in the grave in the open; but this is probably a mistake, since the weight of evidence, such as it is, goes in favour of Tikota, 15 miles west of Bījāpūr, being his last resting place. It was probably his *in'ām* village to which he retired in his old age. There is at this place a ruined tomb and mosque which are supposed to be his. A few years ago, it is said, the roof of the mosque was dismantled at the instigation of a *yogi*, who was well paid, in order to get at hidden treasure alleged to be buried in it. None was found, nor was the *yogi.*

The name Malik Ṣandal often crops up in inscriptions and tradition. First, there was a slave of Dil<u>sh</u>āh Āg<u>h</u>a, in Ismā'īl's reign. It occurs in the inscriptions on the mosque just mentioned and the Ibrāhīm Rauza. In an inscription on the Makka gateway is the name, but spelt with "S" instead of "Ṣ". On the Muṣṭafābād gun we find the name Ṣandal without the "Malik", and we are told that the Tāj Bāurī or great tank near the Makka gateway, was constructed by him. The earliest date for him, in the Bījāpūr inscriptions, is A. D. 1614, while the latest, on the Makka gateway, is A. D. 1655, a period covering forty-one years. Firi<u>sh</u>tah tells us that the eunuch Malik Ṣandal, and other officers under Malik 'Ambar, the Abyssinian noble who was practically governing a portion of the Aḥmadnagar territory, deserted to Murtazā Niẓām <u>Sh</u>āh II. Subsequently, he and other officers fled from the Aḥmadnagar kingdom and entered the service of Bījāpūr. This

[1] Extract from "Who Owns the Churches" by the Rev. Dr. Jessop, in the *Nineteenth Century* for August, 1888.

was about A. D. 1602. The stray references to him that we have, seem to point to him as being rather a man of war than a man of peaceful employment. Can it be that, after all, he is not the architect of the Ibrāhīm Rauza, but simply a minister of works under whose control the buildings were erected? In this case, we know nothing whatever of the real architect whose name has dropped into the limbo of oblivion.

THE ĀNAṆD MAḤALL.

In order to keep as far as possible to some sort of chronological sequence in describing these buildings, it is necessary here, to go back to one of the plainer buildings—the Ānaṇd Maḥall, or 'Palace of Pleasure', which is situated in the citadel, close to the Gagan Maḥall, on the east. It is said to have been built by Ibrāhīm II. in A. D. 1589. The *Basātīn-i-Salāṭīn* states that it was built for dancing and singing; and, certainly, the great central hall, as seen in the photograph of the building before conversion to its present use, bears out this statement. When the general conversions of the buildings in the citadel took place this was transformed into a joint residence for the Assistant Collector and the Judge. A glance at the two photographs (Plate LV) will show how difficult a matter it is to adapt old world arrangements to modern requirements. The result in this case is a rabbit-warren of passages and awkward little compartments, in which one might almost lose oneself. Small rooms, and unsatisfactory lighting and ventilation, make it anything but a desirable modern abode. The only feature remaining, more or less intact, of the original edifice, is the great central façade with the entrance hall. The former is modelled upon the lines of the Gagan Maḥall, but with the addition of a lofty basement upon which the palace stands, and which gives more dignity to its frontage. In the photograph taken before the alterations, will be seen the holes and slots in the masonry above the great arches, showing where a wooden cornice existed, with heavy projecting eavesboards. Underneath the hall, and in the basement, are store and servants' rooms; and these must, with their general untidiness, have constituted a decided disfigurement. Immediately behind the palace are some small subsidiary buildings, among them being a small mosque, or private chapel, with a short inscription in its *miḥrāb*.

It was to the newly-completed Ānaṇd Maḥall that king Ibrāhīm II. rode in great state when he entered the city on the 14th Muḥarram, 1004 (A. D. 1591), amidst general rejoicings at his signal victory over Ibrāhīm Niẓām Shāh. On that occasion the city was splendidly arrayed, without regard to expense, in honour of its sovereign; the road from the Allāhpūr gate to the citadel being hung with rich brocades and other precious hangings—no cheap bunting—while, at night, the whole place was brilliantly illuminated. We are told that the king, being pleased with all arrangements and with the Ānaṇd Maḥall itself, praised the latter, and distributed largesses to the people. It was in the Ānaṇd Maḥall that 'Ali II., as an infant, was brought up by Hājī Badī' Ṣāḥiba, queen of Sulṭān Muḥammad.

THE ANḌĀ MASJID.

A curious little building is the Anḍā Masjid [1] which stands upon the east side of the road running from the citadel to the Lāṇḍā Qaṣṣāb bastion, and not far from the former

[1] So called on account of its egg-shaped dome, *anḍā* meaning an egg.

(Plates LVI—LVIII). It is a two-storeyed building, but not a two-storeyed mosque, the upper floor, alone, being a prayer chamber, while the ground floor is a hall or rest-house. The reason for placing this mosque upon an upper storey is not apparent, unless it was that the buildings around it were too congested to afford space for both a mosque and *sarāi* otherwise. Or it may have been but a whim and nothing more. The upper terrace certainly provided a very pleasant lounge after prayers, whence views of the town could be had, and greater privacy was ensured to those in the mosque at their devotions. There is no *mimbar*, or pulpit, in the mosque, and this may give us a clue to the true reason for its elevated position. Women's mosques have no pulpit, for the reason that no man can enter them to address the worshippers. This was so in the case of the Makka Masjid in the citadel. The apartment below, closed as it could be by a single door, the staircase through the wall to the upper terrace, and a low parapet around the latter, would be all that was required to afford the necessary privacy. The façade of this mosque is made up of three equal-sized arches, which enhances the general appearance very much indeed; but we could have wished for a slightly larger and more elevated dome. The central ceiling, within, is carried up into the dome. The mosque is about the best built of any in Bījāpūr, and the surface of the stone is all but polished, having probably been rubbed down with sand and water, so as to efface all tool marks. The joints of the masonry are so fine that the edge of a sheet of note paper could barely be inserted within them; the courses are kept as near as possible horizontal with vertical joints; and the weathering of three hundred years seems hardly to have left its impress upon it. The ornament is sparingly and discreetly applied, and its general appearance is greatly improved by the numerous offsets and recessed angles in the perpendicular lines. The front seems not to have been quite finished, the two large lower brackets, under the cornice, one on the face of each pier, have not been inserted, but the corbels and slots have been made for them. Along the top of the south end of the terrace is what appears to be the first course of a parapet or screen wall. In the back wall of the mosque is a large central *miḥrāb*, and a small niche in each of the side bays. Some of the bands of ornament about the *miḥrāb* are also unfinished. Around the inside walls is a pretty horizontal string-course of *pān* or leaf ornament.

The dome is of the ribbed melon-shaped variety, which occurs on two or three buildings at Bījāpūr, and the bud finials of the *mīnārs* are also ribbed. These *mīnārs* rise from each of the four corners of the roof, and also, in a group of four, above the *miḥrāb* at the back. This arrangement reminds us somewhat of the Rangīn Masjid already described (Plate XIII). It is hardly an improvement to the building, as it crowds too much on to the dome. The latter would have been better had it been higher. A handsome perforated parapet, forming a lace-like fringe, adorns the crest of the building. A plain horizontal string-course, on the outside of the walls, separates the upper from the lower storey, and while the upper is very ornate, the lower is severely plain. The ground floor, as we have seen, was intended either as a *sarāi* or rest-house, or a retreat for *pardah* women, if the building was really a women's mosque.

The only two-storeyed mosque at Bījāpūr, having a prayer-chamber both above and below, is that attached to Afzal Khān's cenotaph to the west of the town, and close to the village of Afzalpūr or Takki.

A long inscription, around the entrance doorway, tells us that the mosque was built by I'tibār Khān in A. D. 1608. He was one of the nobles of Ibrāhīm II. and Sulṭān Muḥammad, and is mentioned in connection with the first campaign of Muḥammad Shāh against Niẓām Shāh, when he was taken prisoner by the latter king, who, however, treated him generously and released him. He was one of the officers sent against Shāhjī when the conduct of the latter fell under suspicion. Unfortunately, we know no more of him. As the inscription is rather a characteristic one, laden as it is with the usual hyperbole which delighted the heart of the scribes of those days, it is given at length. It runs:

In the reign of the Shāhanshāh of the period
There is a master of those who are eloquent.
The melody of David has found life in the body
Where can the praise of the Shāh have a tongue?
The high mosque has been completed.
In such a period it will be a memorial.
The year-date of that noble place
I sought from intellect, how can it remain concealed?
The year thousand and seventeen more [A. D. 1608-09]
Is the year-date of that place.
As at the sight of the rise of this cupola.
The cupola of the sky is in lamentation [from grief at the rivalry].
Of the Shāh-Khān God is the guardian.
This prayer is the orison of every tongue.
The architect of this paradise-like mosque
Is His Excellency I'tibār Khān;
Any one has seen few mosques of this fashion.
A fashion of this kind is heart-ravishing.

MAUSOLEUM OF SHAIKH ḤAMĪD QĀDIRĪ AND LAṬĪFULLĀH QĀDIRI.

In the south-west corner of the city, nearly four hundred yards west of the tomb of 'Ali 'Ādil Shāh I., is a mausoleum which covers the remains of two local saints named Ḥazrat Shaikh Ḥamīd Qādirī and his brother Ḥazrat Shaikh Laṭīfullāh Qādirī, who died in the years A. H. 1011 (A. D. 1602) and A. H. 1021 (A. D. 1612) respectively (Plate LIX). It is recorded that the building was erected by Fāṭimah Sulṭāna widow (?) of 'Ali 'Ādil Shāh. In Fāṭimah's well, close by, which goes by the name of the Gumat Bāurī, just in front of the mosque attached to this tomb, is an inscription which tells us that, in the Sultanate of Shāh 'Ali 'Ādil Shāh, this "*bairi*" was constructed by the pardoned Sittī Fāṭimah Salmānsittī, in the year A. H. 970 (A. D. 1562), as a pious endowment. It seems likely that the same Fāṭimah is referred to in both cases. If these dates are correct, she must have been an old lady when she built the mausoleum over these two saints. And this is perhaps the reason why we find the tomb left unfinished, she having died before its completion.

The building has been a very well-designed one, and would have looked particularly well had it been finished. It consists of a central sepulchral chamber, surrounded by a verandah or side aisles, part, only, of which was erected. Here, we have, again, one of those very lofty domes, which, were it not for two little clerestory openings which allow a soft subdued light into the dome, would have been lost in darkness ; and here, again, was a good case for double doming. The interior of the dome is fluted ; and still remaining within it, are some horizontal wooden tie-beams used for constructional purposes, but not removed. There are here no regular pendentives ; the four corners of the chamber being cut off by corner arches, the walls are reduced, above, to an octagon, and these were further turned into a sixteen-sided figure under the dome. The ceilings of the side aisles were to have been flat, slightly coved at the margins. Within the tomb chamber are two graves, while over the north doorway is an inscription containing nothing more than an extract from the Qurān.

Adjoining the tomb, at its north-east corner, is a well-constructed mosque, which, probably, was built in connection with the tomb. Within, it is very similar to that of Malikah Jahān Begam, but, from without, it has not much appearance. The *mīnārs* have gone, and the cornice, which is very plain, is damaged. Within the *miḥrāb* or prayer niche, is an inscription which contains the *bismillāh* formula, with the short profession of faith ; and, in a frame around this, an extract from the Qurān.

Out in front of the mosque is an old much-ruined step-well, used for irrigation purposes, known as the Gumat Bāurī, in the wall of which, on the left of the staircase when descending, is a long inscription which tells us that the well was constructed by Sittī Fāṭimah Salmānsittī in the year A. H. 970 (A. D. 1562). It reads thus :

On the top :

"O Allāh ! O Muḥammad ! O 'Alī !"

Then :

"Allāh has said." [The Qurān, ch. II, v. 263, in full].

Then :

In the period of the Sulṭān in the country, protector of the religion of Allāh, warrior in the path of Allāh the Victor, his majesty Shāh 'Ali 'Adil Shāh, may Allāh perpetuate his monarchy and his sultanate, this *bairi* was constructed in the path of Allāh by the pardoned Sittī Fāṭimah Salmānsittī ; her possession in both worlds are high degrees . . . . . in the year 970 on the 20th day of the month Zulḥijjah and this edifice in *waqf* [pious endowment], whoever prohibits or becomes a prohibitor . . . . . will have no share in the intercession of his majesty the Apostle. [The rest consists of minatory expressions.]

The saints buried in the mausoleum, or at least one of them, was, probably, the religious preceptor and private chaplain to the queen Fāṭimah ; who, as a pious and meritorious act, started to erect the building for them within her own private garden. This south-west quarter of the city seems to have been chiefly used as gardens and graveyards ; and, the depth of soil being favourable, the little English graveyard is also situated close by. Queen Fāṭimah is, perhaps, resting beside her husband, in his own mausoleum, some three hundred yards to the north of this.

On the east side of the saints' tomb are two small tombs in line, the first of which is unfinished, but which looks as if intended to have a pyramidal roof, one or two examples of which we find at Bījāpūr. The pyramidal form is seen in the roof of the Nau Gumbaz, between the domes. Whether, when used as the only dome over a tomb, it has any special significance is uncertain. There is a larger tomb than this one, near the large tomb on the west of the Ḥāfiz Bāgh at Junnar, which has one of these pyramidal roofs.

A third small tomb stands about a hundred yards away to the north-east of this group, in which is some curious pot and flower ornament in stucco in the octagon under the dome (Plate XXIX).

BĀTULA KHĀN'S MOSQUE.

Situated by the roadside, almost midway between the Mihtar Maḥall and the Jāmi' Masjid, stand a mosque and gateway, in much the same relation to each other as in the case of the former building and its gateway, which goes by the name of Bātula Khān's mosque; but who Bātula Khān was, does not seem to be known. Perhaps, it is merely the name of some late owner of the land on which the building stands. The mosque has been used for some time as a Kanarese school, with the inevitable disfiguring additions of partition walls, and inserted doors and barred windows. The masonry of this building is very good indeed, quite equal to that of the Anḍā Masjid. The courses are quite horizontal. The arches, in the three-arched façade, are of the ogee type, being turned up at the crowns, which is more ornamental, and less severe, than those of the usual Bījāpūr pattern. The central one has those recessed mouldings seen in the mosque of 'Ali Shahīd Pīr, though not to the same extent.

But the most peculiar feature in the building is its ceiling, which is somewhat similar in arrangement to that in the tomb of 'Ali 'Ādil Shāh I. (Plate LVIII). Two transverse cross-arches divide the interior into three equal bays, each of which is a long rectangle. Therefore, in order to fit in a circular dome into the middle of these, two smaller transverse arches, resting upon the haunches of the greater arches, are thrown across to divide the long rectangle into three parts, forming a small square bay in the middle for the dome and a narrow bay on each side of this which is wagon-vaulted. The whole arrangement is clumsy in the extreme. The only advantage that it has is that it obviates the use of pillars within the mosque, two of which would have been needed, had the ceilings and roof been worked out in the ordinary way.

The gateway at the north-east corner of the mosque, and at right angles to it, is a very much less imposing structure than that of the Mihtar Maḥall. It is not near so lofty, nor is it decorated like it. The masonry is very bad, and it does not look as if it were built by the same builders as erected the mosque.

Within the enclosure is a high masonry platform with the tombstone of a male upon it, which may be that of the builder of the mosque, and, in the south-west corner, is a small grave of a European child who died at Bījāpūr.

PĀR KHĀN'S MOSQUE.

A small mosque on the south of the road, five hundred yards inside the Allāhpūr gate, is worth a passing notice. It is called after Pār Khān, a Paṭhān, but who he was is not known; it may be, as in many similar cases, the name of some person who, in late years, owned the ground upon which the mosque happened to stand. It is a neat building, having two slender *mīnārs*, and a good but damaged cornice. Of the three arches in the façade, the central one is cusped. The style of work is that of Jahān Begam's. A gateway, with two *mīnārs*, facing the road, and at right angles to the mosque, likens the buildings, in general arrangement, to the Mihtar Maḥall and Bātula Khān's mosque, which two are upon the same road, which in those times was the principal thoroughfare in the city.

MOSQUE No. 231.

A mosque which, in the arrangement of its roofing and ceiling, resembles Bātula Khān's is that marked 231 on the plan of the city, and situated on the waste land, about five hundred yards to the north-west of the Gol Gumbaz. It is a well-built, substantial building. The central domed ceiling is ornamented with spiral ribbing (see Plate LVII), and the dome over the *miḥrāb,* as in the other mosque, runs away up high, inside, chimney-like, into darkness. The plan of the *miḥrāb* in Bātula Khān's mosque is bounded by seven sides of a nine-sided polygon, whereas, in this, it is bounded by five sides of a seven-sided figure. A further likeness is in the shape of the arches, which are slightly ogee. The building has had a pretty cornice, but it is greatly destroyed. There is some pretty plaster work in the medallions on the façade. The building is much damaged.

HĀJĪ ḤASAN'S TOMB.

Hājī Ḥasan's tomb is a square building in the Darsi Bāzār, on the south of the road, about midway between the Jāmi' Masjid and the Allāhpūr gate, and near the point where that road is met by that running north and south from the Gol Gumbaz. Around the four sides of the building are rows of little windows with wooden shutters, the doorway being, as usual, on the south side. The manner in which the dome is carried up from the square is worth notice. The usual buttresses or piers, within, which are usually provided to stiffen the walls for the cross-arching and pendentives, do not exist here. About the octagon there are three tiers of arched recesses, one above the other, sixteen in each. These have been decorated with painted borders and representations of foliage, but it is very coarsely executed. Within the building are three tombs, the central one being that of a male—Hājī Ḥasan, who died in A. H. 1024 (A. D. 1614). On his left is the tomb of a female, while the one on the other side has been destroyed.

Of this tomb, which he wrongly calls that of the Begam Ṣāḥib,[1] Fergusson says it is "most graceful in design. The attic of sixteen sides, by which the dome is raised out of the square in which it stands, is a very happy expedient, and its form is singularly graceful and appropriate to a composition of this sort."

NAURASPŪR.

The reign of king Ibrāhīm II. was a very busy period for the architect and builder, for not only were the splendid group of the Ibrāhīm Rauza and many fine buildings within the city walls raised, but an altogether new city was projected and commenced at Torweh, a few miles to the west of Bījāpūr. The walls and bastions of the capital had hardly been finished, and were still brand new from the mason's hands, when a strange whim possessed the king to change his seat of government to a new spot which was to be called

[1] *Architecture at Beejapoor,* by Furgusson and Meadows Taylor, p. 92, Pl. 68.

Nauraspūr,[1] and which was to eclipse all other cities in splendour. Perhaps, after all, the scheme was not such a strange one as it appeared. The water supply of Bījāpūr, within the walls, was very limited and the population depended mostly upon water brought in by pipes and aqueducts from outside, which sources could easily have been cut off by an enemy investing the town. It will be seen from the map that the new site included within its walls a stream whose bed traversed the site from side to side, through the middle. The damming up of this stream would produce a great sheet of water, which in time of siege would last the town and garrison for a very long time, and be protected from the enemy. Besides this, its useful purpose, it would have formed a lovely neighbourhood, some two and a half miles long, for the erection of palaces along the margins of the lakes so formed. All this may have been in Ibrāhīm's mind. The stream was, in after years, dammed up, further along, to form the great Rāmling tank to the north-east of the site.

In A. H. 1008 (A. D. 1599), we are told, Ibrāhīm summoned masons and other artizans from all quarters, and placed Nawāb Shabāz Khān[2] in charge of the work. Twenty thousand workmen are said to have been engaged. Nobles, ministers, and rich merchants were induced to build; and, it is said, each vied with the other in trying to produce a residence better than his neighbour's, and thus many fine *maḥalls* were erected and adorned with gilding and other decoration. Tradition says the astrologers interfered and declared that evil would come upon the kingdom if the capital were removed to a new site, so the scheme was abandoned. The more likely reason for its relinquishment is, perhaps, the following. In 1624, when Ibrāhīm was at war with Niẓām Shāh, the latter sent an army under Malik 'Ambar against Bījāpūr. The walls of Nauraspūr, not being completed, Ibrāhīm withdrew within the old city, and left the new one to the mercy of the enemy, who finding it unprotected, with its walls unfinished, completely wrecked it. Ibrāhīm was too disheartened to continue the project, and, as Malik 'Ambar died in the following year, Ibrāhīm was cheated of his longed-for vengeance. Up to the time of its destruction the new city had been more or less populated.[3]

All that is now left are the ruins of the great wall[4] surrounding more than half the circuit of the selected site, from which it may be seen (see map) that the new city, if completed, would have been more than half as large again as Bījāpūr. About the centre of this, near the village of Torweh, within a high walled enclosure, are the remains of the Nauras or Sangat Maḥall, and, beside it, is the Nari Maḥall. Beyond this is the Tagani and other mosques, tombs, and buildings of sorts.

The Nauras Maḥall is a duplicate, on a slightly smaller scale, of the Gagan Maḥall in the citadel of Bījāpūr. It is in ruins, having suffered like the other buildings which originally

---

[1] A legend in the *Basātīn-i-Salāṭīn* is to the effect that, when the city was being laid out, a man from Torweh brought a vessel full of wine and presented it to king Ibrāhīm, who was so pleased with its delicious taste and fragrance, that he exclaimed, "Today, I have had a new enjoyment," using the word *naurasīdah*, meaning 'newly obtained'. These words were looked upon as very auspicious and the city was called, on that account, Nauraspūr. Another derivation of the word is from *nau*, 'new,' *ras*, 'juice,' and *pur*, a 'city,' *i.e.* the city of the new wine. But it is, perhaps, more likely to have been derived from *nauras*, 'new obtained' or 'newly founded' with no connection with the wine story. It has also been called Naurozpūr, from the festival of the *nauroz*. Whatever the origin of the name, it very soon became popular, and the word *nauras* became quite the fashion. We are told that all government works were named after it; a royal seal, bearing the word *nauras* was prepared; copper coins were stamped with the word and were called *Ibrāhīm Nauras*; and two palaces were called respectively Maḥall Nauras and Maḥbūb Naurasī. The poet 'Abdul Qādir assumed the title of Naurasi; certain singers were called *laskar nauras*; and Firishtah called his own historical account of the 'Ādil Shāhis the Nauras Nāmā

[2] His tomb is the twelve-pillared one near the *sarāi* (Jail) at Shāhpūr.

[3] Compare the attempt to move this capital with the more disastrous and terrible scheme of Muhammad Tughlaq, who, two hundred and fifty years before, attempted to move his capital and all its inhabitants from Delhi to Daulatābād.

[4] The outer casing of the wall, only, had been built, the earthen ramp, or hearting, and inner retaining wall had not been added.

had much wood-work about them. It is a lonely but pretty spot, surrounded by cultivated plots, forests of prickly-pear, and heaps of ruins (Plates LXII—LXIV).

There appears to have been, at one time, a great broad road running straight from this towards Bījāpūr, known as the grand bāzār of Muḥammad Shāh. It can be distinctly traced, for some distance, from near the Sangat or Nauras Maḥall to the Motī Gumbaz.

THE MIHTAR MAḤALL.

The Mihtar Maḥall is one of the show buildings of Bījāpūr. It stands upon the south side of the road, between the Jāmi' Masjid and the citadel gateway, being nearer the latter. It is a building of no exceptional design, yet, nevertheless, the clever treatment of its parts and its decorative detail, make it one of the prettiest structures in Bījāpūr (Plates LXII—LXXI). Though called a *maḥall,* or palace, it is really a gateway to the inner courtyard of a mosque, which, itself, would have attracted considerable attention had it not been so eclipsed by its annexe. It is, however, a little more than a mere gateway, for it has upper rooms and balconies above the entrance, where men might assemble and spend an hour lounging in the bays of the windows, and enjoy the pleasant views of the city. Unfortunately it has no inscriptions about it to tell us who built it. But though history is silent, tradition is not so, and the following stories, accounting for its origin, claim credence in the town. One ascribes it to a sweeper *(mihtar)*, who was unexpectedly enriched by the king in fulfilment of a vow, and who, not knowing what to do with so much wealth, built this *maḥall,* which was on this account called the Mihtar or Sweeper's Maḥall. Another credits one Mihtar Gada, a *faqīr* or mendicant, in the time of Ibrāhīm II., with the building of it, but both stories are equally improbable. They both leave out of account the mosque to which the gate is but an adjunct. Perhaps, after all, the term *mihtar* was not originally applied to it at all, but at a later date, when it simply meant the 'superior' maḥall, and was given to it on account of its delicate beauty.[1] It is more likely that the mosque and gateway were originally called after him who built them. Then, as it was private property, and the great door was usually closed to the public, the mosque was lost sight of, and the gateway was raised to the dignity of a *maḥall.*

On the Anḍā Masjid, already described, and which is of the same style of work, though less profusely decorated, we have the date A. D. 1608. On the little pavilion, or Pānī Maḥall, on the bastion in front of the 'Arsh Maḥall, which is covered with precisely the same kind of surface decoration as is used on the face of the Mihtar Maḥall, is found the date, twice over, A. D. 1669. The masonry is of the same class as that of the other two buildings. Moreover, the traditional accounts place the erection in the reign of Ibrāhīm II. If we place it at about A. D. 1620, we cannot be far out.

The general outline of the gateway is that of a tall square tower, 24 feet each way in plan, surmounted by two slender minarets at its upper forward corners, which run down the corners of the building, as buttresses, to the basement level. The total height to the tops

---

[1] On an old MS. map the building is called the *chhajja* (balcony) of Mihtar Gada Vazir (minister), but no such name occurs in Bījāpūr history.

of the minarets is about 66 feet. The main entrance runs through the centre of the ground floor, admittance being obtained through a doorway provided with a great heavy pair of doors. Above this is the first floor—a square room with a large bay or balcony window projecting from each of its four sides—while over this again is an open terrace protected by a high wall all round, with a little five-light projecting window in front.

The most striking feature about this building is these balcony windows. For pure gracefulness and delicacy of treatment, there is nothing to surpass them in Bījāpūr. The projecting seat of the window is supported beneath by deep bracketting, ornamented with rows of hanging buds or drops, which remind one of the same arrangement under the cornices of the Ibrāhīm Rauza mosque, the brackets being tied together by transverse tie pieces in ascending tiers. The balcony parapet, under the lights, with its lotus panels, is carried across the face of the building, thus serving its purpose to two little side windows. From this rise three lancet-shaped lights in the front and one at each end; and from the mullions, between these, project a row of richly wrought stone struts or brackets supporting a deep overhanging cornice. These brackets are exceedingly thin, long slabs of stone, perforated and worked over with beautiful arabesque patterns. They are such as one would expect to find in woodwork, and look far too frail to be wrought in brittle stone; but they have, nevertheless, lasted remarkably well through all these years. The hanging fringe to the cornice above has now disappeared, but a small portion of it was still there not so many years ago, as may be seen in the photograph (Fig. 19). Not the least pleasing feature is the lace-like parapet which runs along the very top of the building, between the *mīnārs*. Nearly the whole of this has been lately restored, a small piece only of the original having been left on the roof. It is about the richest designed parapet in Bījāpur. Fig. 20 is a portion of this photographed from a fallen slab.

Fig. 19. Balcony window in the Mihtar Mahall.

Captain Sykes tells us that, like the Kālī Masjid at Lakshmeśwar, already described, "from the angles of the building hang massy stone chains, which must have been cut out of solid blocks, as there are no joining in the links."[1] These have

[1] *Trans. Lit. Society of Bombay*, Vol. III, p. 59.

all disappeared since his time, but a glance at the photograph of the Kālī Masjid (Plate XLI) will give some idea of the appearence of this building when all its chains were present. They may not be what we should call legitimate architectural decoration, yet there is little doubt they did enhance the delicate beauty of these dainty little buildings.

Fig. 20. A portion of the roof parapet from the Mihtar Maḥall.

Passing within, we enter a chamber, through the centre of which, between the two raised platforms for the use of the *chaukidārs* or janitors, is the passage to the inner court. The most noteworthy thing in this room is the very curiously designed ceiling. This, like that in the upper floor, is constructed on the same principles as the great flat ceiling of the sepulchral chamber in the Ibrāhīm Rauza. The ground floor ceiling is coved at the sides, while the upper one is quite flat, being divided into nine panels, each prettily carved, by deep square stone beams. The old wooden doorway is worth inspection, with its heavy massive framing, and quaint iron bosses and nail heads (Plates LXVII and LXXI). Some similar ironwork very prettily perforated, may be seen on the door of the tomb of Shāh Karīm, near the south-east corner of the Jāmi' Masjid. The masonry of the gateway is superior to that of the mosque.

The mosque, within, is a neat little building. It possessed a very fine cornice and brackets, and has a rich parapet along the top. The minarets, however, are not quite in keeping with the rest. They are very primitive looking and inelegant, and compare very unfavourably with those of the gateway, being nothing more than tall tapering round shafts, with a ring of leaves about half way up to break the monotony of their outline.[1] They are not even surmounted by the usual bulbous finial, but are plainly rounded off with a very small ball and trident. This latter is an unusual device. Being rather shaky they were taken down some years ago and rebuilt. When this was done, the damaged remains of pretty trellis-work collars, round the minaret buttresses below, seen in the photograph on Plate LXII, were not reproduced, and are now lost. The masonry of this building is fair, but not nearly so good as that of the Anḍā Masjid. The mosque has many points of resemblance to that of Malikah Jahān. It has been decorated with those curious stone chains, but they have disappeared, leaving only the engaged links to shew where they had been. There is no dome over the mosque, the roof being flat.

Fergusson, in drawing attention to the essentially wooden character of the decoration on the Mihtar Maḥall, writes :

---

[1] Similar *mīnārs* are found on mosque No. 119.

"We find the same balconies used at the present day; and in any city between Benares and Boorhanpoor similar objects might be found with almost identical details, but always constructed in wood . . . . It is clear, however, that the Moslems could have had very little experience in building in stone, when this work was undertaken, and as little knowledge of their own style as then practised at Agra and Delhi. They must also have been actuated by a wonderful aversion to anything savouring of Hinduism, when they designed a building so original as this, and so manifestly unlike anything to be found in the country in which they had settled. . . . . . Here, fortunately they are perpetuated in stone; and for minute elegance of finish and beauty of drawing, are quite equal, if not indeed superior, to anything found at Cairo, or in any western style. The details of the Alhambra might almost be styled vulgar in comparison."[1]

He, however, is not quite correct in saying the Moslem was averse to anything savouring of Hinduism, for we have already seen how well they adapted Hindu forms to their pillars in the Ibrāhīm Rauza, and most of the Gujarāt Muḥammadan architecture is essentially Hindu in style.

THE SHĀHPŪR MOSQUES.

Away out beyond Shāhpūr and the Amīn Dargāh are many mosques and other buildings dotted over the country side, which indicate the great size of this north-west suburb in its palmy days. From among these, three are selected for description and illustration. The first (Plate LXVI) is a particularly fine example. A very noticeable feature in this is the great depth of façade above the three arches. And, yet, unlike the older Ibrāhīmpūr mosque, already described, it does not obtrude itself upon the eye, owing to the bold and beautiful cornice which breaks up the depth so very pleasingly. In the Ibrāhīmpūr building (Plate XVI), the cornice, being a poor one with no striking parts about it, does not count for much, and is only so much more heavy masonry helping to crush in the low arches below. The construction and details of this Shāhpūr example are much on the same lines as in Jahān Begam's Mosque, but the smaller tall dome, with a much more constricted neck, points to a rather later date for it.

Another mosque, almost a duplicate of the last (No. 329 on plan), was built, no doubt, at about the same time (Plate LXXII). Before it stands a well-built and richly ornamented mausoleum. The holes in the dome are probably due to birds picking out the softer filling-in of scaffolding holes in order to build their nests. The green parrot is the most destructive bird in this way.

A very interesting mosque is that known as the Sonahrī Masjid (Plate LXXII), standing about half-a-mile due east of the Amīn Dargāh. It is almost a replica, on a smaller scale, of the mosque of the Ibrāhīm Rauza. Being smaller, it has three arches, instead of five, in its façade; but, in other respects, the various features, and even the ornamental detail, are the same. It has been much damaged, and the fallen *mīnār*, at the south end of the façade, broke away much of the cornice when it fell. The back *mīnār* at the opposite corner of the building has also gone, together with the two little *chhatrīs* or kiosks over the central piers of the façade; and the miniature *mīnārs* at the corners of the upper terrace, around the base of the dome, have been destroyed. It will be noticed

[1] *Architecture at Beejapoor*, by Fergusson and Taylor, p. 87.

that the lace-like fringe along the roof, over the cornice, which, unfortunately, has almost all disappeared, is identical in pattern with that of the Ibrāhīm Rauza Mosque, and this is a feature which usually varies with each building. Even the plainer *kangura* battlementing, in continuation, round the sides, is also of the same pattern in both. The cluster of miniature *mīnārs,* around the minaret above the cornice, is also copied ; and, as an addition, it is repeated as a pretty lace-like collar round the *mīnār* piers below, just as we have seen it in the case of the Mihtar Maḥall and the Jahān Begam's Mosques. These three mosques —the Ibrāhīm Rauza, Malikah Jahān's, and the Sonahrī—are so remarkably alike in details that one cannot but conclude that all three were built about the same time, if, indeed, they were not all designed and superintended by the same architect.

Under the platform, out in front of the mosque, are rows of vaults, as if for burial purposes, from which much of the cut-stone has been pilfered.

THE ZUMURRUD MASJID.

Between the Bukhārī Masjid and the small mosque called after Malik Ṣandal (No. 6 on the plan) is a very small mosque, perhaps the smallest in Bījāpūr. It stands upon a high platform and measures but twelve feet square. It is well constructed. Round about the *miḥrāb,* and serving as ornament to it, are some beautifully cut inscriptions, containing extracts from the Qurān, with benedictions on the Prophet and the *bismillāh* formula. It is called the Zumurrud or ' Emerald Mosque .

THE KAMRAKĪ GUMBAZ.

In the middle of the New Bāzār, about three hundred yards to the north-east of the Chhoṭa Āthār, is a small canopy covering the tomb of a female, with a ribbed, egg-shaped dome, called the Kamrakī *(Averrhoa carambola)* Gumbaz. It is an elegant little erection, with a measurement over all, of but 8 feet 4 inches each way. A great deal of its cornice has been knocked away, and only one of the little *mīnārs,* which were placed at each corner, now remains, and that without its bulbous finial ; the stumps, alone, remain of the others (Plate LXX).

THE NAU GUMBAZ.

Of, perhaps, the same date as the Mihtar Maḥall, if not earlier, is the Nau Gumbaz or ' Mosque of the Nine Domes ', situated in what, we are told, was the grounds of Khawāṣṣ Khān's palace, about two hundred yards to the north-east of Muṣṭafā Khān's Mosque (Plates LXXI and LXXIII). The peculiarity of this building is its roofing, which is carried out more on the lines of Aḥmadābād and Gujarāt work than on those of Bījāpūr. This multiple doming, so common in Gujarāt, is quite a foreign feature at Bījāpūr, and so much so that this unusual circumstance has given the mosque its present name. The body of the mosque is divided by its arching into nine bays. The four corner ones and the central one are covered by segmental domes, while the four intermediate ones have pyramidal vaults. The latter not only break the monotony of the round domes and obviate undue crowding, but also lead up to one pyramidal form for the whole group. Over each of the front corners of the roof, in the place of the usual *mīnār,* is a low domed *chhatri* ; while over the central piers rise more elongated ones, thus helping, again, towards the pyramidal aspect of the roof.

The façade, when complete, must have presented a very pleasing elevation ; but the cornice is sadly damaged, though its beautiful brackets are hardly injured. Save for the want of a little more height in the arches, this mosque is remarkably well proportioned in all respects. The arches are of the usual Bījāpūr type, and have a graceful and easy outline. The four long brackets, under the cornice, which project from the faces of the piers, between the façade arches, are particularly worthy of notice. The way in which the design of these seems to add extra rigidity and strength is interesting. This is done by the right angles of the mouldings being tilted back instead of being square with the vertical face of the wall (Plate LXXI).

The whole of the *miḥrāb*, which is but a sunk flat recess, is built of fine black, partly polished, basalt ; while, around it, and also about the small black stone niches in the side bays of the wall, are bands of inscriptions containing extracts from the Qurān. A large slab, in the back wall of the mosque, bears an inscription in eleven lines which is but the Shī'ah creed and calls forth blessings upon the twelve *imāms*. The plaster ornament in the interior has been very good, but has been choked with successive layers of whitewash.

Khawāṣṣ Khān, on whose grounds this building is said to stand, was the son of Khān Muḥammad, or Khān Khānān as he was styled, who is buried with his father in the lofty tomb near the Nau Bāgh, one of the 'Two Sisters' or Jod Gumbaz. After being *wazir* to Sikandar 'Ādil Shāh, he was eventually imprisoned at Bankapūr and put to death as a traitor.

The site of Khawāṣṣ Khān's Maḥall, or palace, is on the north side of the Nau Gumbaz. A few vaulted chambers, only, of this building were remaining a few years ago, with the entrance gateway, which stood alone, at some little distance away. Beside the *maḥall*, on the south side is a ruined well, with very clear water, all vaulted over. On its north side are openings above and below water, which look as if they communicated with chambers beyond—cool retreats, possibly, for use in the hot weather. It was in Khawāṣṣ Khān's *maḥall* that Aurangzeb took up his abode, when, for some years after his conquest of Bījāpūr, he made the city his head-quarters.[1]

THE ĀTHĀR MAḤALL.

Upon the eastern side of the citadel, across the moat, and facing the rising sun, stands the most unprepossessing-looking, yet the most sacred, building in Bījāpūr—the Āthār Maḥall

---

[1] At Mamdāpūr, about 22 miles south by west of Bījāpūr, there are two large lakes, the bigger one being probably the largest existing reservoir in the Bombay Presidency of native make, covering, when full, about 1¼ square mile. An inscription, cut in Persian on the revetment wall of this great lake, runs :—

During the career of Khawāṣṣ Khān, who was equal in rank to Āṣaf, whose family was sprung from Solomon's minister, the building of this lake, generally known as Hauz-i-Sultān, was completed on the 1st Muharram. Victory and fortune shall be in the stirrup of the king's horse as long as the sun reigns in the sky. May the just king Sultān Maḥmūd always be at the head of this prosperous country. This king of heroes ordered his minister Khawāṣṣ Khān to perform such virtuous actions as find favour with the Almighty. Bearing his precept in mind Khawāṣṣ Khān, the very fountain of benevolence, built this lake with a never failing supply of water. What an excellent lake! The sea even fails or is ashamed to equal it ; nay, more than this, it excels the seven seas of the world in beauty. Its waves are bright and pure, and its every bubble is like the moon. The fountain of immortality is as nothing compared to this lake, and, before it, appears as dishonoured as fermented liquor. This reservoir is Hauz-i-Kauthar, a well in Paradise, and its water is even far better than rose-water. The Prophet Khizer, with divine inspiration, uttered the words "Hauz-i-Sultān is rare", which gives the year in which the dam was built. The cost was 50,000 *hūns*. *Hijri* 1043. [A. D. 1633.] [*Bombay Gazetteer*, Vol. XXIII (Bījāpūr), p. 661.]

The Khawāṣṣ Khān alluded to in this inscription will be Daulat Khān, to whom Sultān Muḥammad gave that title. He served the state for eight years and was killed in A. H. 1045 (A. D. 1635). Khawāṣṣ Khān, Khān Muḥammad's son, was given the title some years after this.

or Palace of the Relic (Plates LXXIII and LXXV—LXXX). It is also known as the Āthār Mubārak and the Āthār Sharīf. Though originally intended as a Dād Maḥall or Hall of Justice, and for some short time used as such, it was eventually reserved for the safe custody of the relics of the Prophet. The building is generally ascribed to Sulṭān Muḥammad, but one account [1] says it was rebuilt by him in A. D. 1646, and it is mentioned, or, at least, the original building, as being in existence in the time of Ibrāhīm II. We read that in A. H. 1000 (A. D. 1591) a certain holy man, Shāh Ṣibghatullāh, a disciple of Ḥazrat Shāh Wajīhu-d-dīn Ḥusainī, arrived at Bījāpūr from Madīna, where he became the guest of the king. At his departure Ibrāhīm allowed him to go and see the Āthār Maḥall. The Ḥazrat, when shewn the box containing the relic, wished the attendants to open it, but was told they were not allowed to do so. Thereupon he took the box in his own hand and began to repeat a verse from the Qurān. A number of holes suddenly appeared in the sides of the box through which the hairs became visible. Then the holes closed again. The story of the relic itself—two hairs of Muḥammad—as given by Firishtah, is this: Mīr Muḥammad Ṣāliḥ Hamadāni brought some hairs of the Prophet to Bījāpūr in the time of Ibrāhīm II., who received the man with all respect. As it was the month of *Muḥarram* the king prevailed upon his guest to remain some days in the city, during which time he loaded him with presents. Mīr Muḥammad Ṣāliḥ, in consideration of the kindly treatment he had received, presented the king with two of the hairs, which Ibrāhīm placed with great care in a jewelled box, and visited it every Friday night and upon all holidays. Ultimately they were deposited in the Āthār Maḥall. It is said that Aurangzeb plundered the shrine of one of the hairs. The other is believed to be still there, but the casket is never opened.[2]

Captain Sykes says of the Āthār Maḥall :

> "It must originally have been intended for a palace, but at present it is in the hands of *religieux*, and contains a Tubrook from Mecca—a consecrated trifle shut up in a box; but as the profane are excluded from sight of it, I could not form any distinct idea respecting it. So sacred is it, however, that no woman can cross the threshold of the building; no armed man can enter; no music is permitted; and the use of flambeaus within the limits of the enclosure is interdicted." [3]

Muḥammad, in order to give the general public better access to him than they had while he held his court in the citadel, threw a bridge across the moat, from the citadel walls to the back of the *maḥall*, and established his court of justice within it. From this viaduct entrance to the building was gained through doorways off different levels into both the lower and upper floors. Right in the middle of the pathway on the viaduct, and above the citadel walls, is a water cistern, where it was probably intended to wash the feet before entering the hall. The Āthār Maḥall was thus, no doubt, connected up with the Ānaṇd Maḥall. At this time the emperor of Delhi, Shāh Jahān, was meddling with the affairs of Bījāpūr, and the 'Ādil Shāh was very apprehensive of the power of the Mughals, who had already overrun Central India and parts of the Dakhan, extorting annual tribute from its

---

[1] The *Basātīn-i-Salāṭīn*.

[2] It is recorded that the relic was first deposited in another building which was burnt down (*Journ. Bom. Br. R. A. S.*, Vol. I, p. 382). This was probably the building which Captain Little saw burning in 1790 (*Moor's Narrative*, p. 320). Captain Sydenham writes: "There is a small but neat building called the Qadam-i-Rasūl, but vulgarly and improperly so, as it is supposed to have contained a few hairs of the Prophet's beard, not an impression of his foot; Muḥammad Shāh removed them from this palace to a grand edifice which he erected close to the eastern wall of the citadel and communicating with it, and which he at first intended for his own palace. By another account it appears that they were deposited by Aurangzeb in the palace of Muḥammad which is now called Āthār Sharīf, from the holy relics, it is still believed to contain." (*Asiatic Researches*, Quarto Ed., Vol. XIII, p. 442.)

[3] *Trans. Lit. Soc. of Bombay*, Vol. III, p. 61.

states. On hearing of this new departure of Sulṭān Muḥammad, and certain other innovations, Shāh Jahān wrote demanding, under veiled threats, that he should revert to the citadel and hold his courts there as his forefathers had done before him. Being unwilling at the time to incur the displeasure of the emperor, Muḥammad shifted his court back to the citadel, leaving the *maḥall* for the use of the relic and its annual *'urs* or religious festival.

The general appearance of the building from the east suggests the idea of a great open box turned over on its side, the open lid-less side forming the front. The building is divided, longitudinally, into two parts from floor to ceiling, the forward half being a great hall supported in front by the end walls and four great wooden pillars, two others being engaged in the end walls; and the back half is divided up into halls and chambers on two floors. These are two deep from front to back, and the best room in the building is the long central one towards the back, upstairs, which is 81 feet long by 27 feet broad, and 20 feet high. A doorway leads out through the middle of the east side of this into a smaller hall or gallery, with open front, looking into the hall below, and out upon the great reservoir before it. It was here that Muḥammad sat upon his elevated *masnad*, or seat, when dispensing justice. There is a low trellis railing along the front of this, but lower in the middle than at the sides, so as not to obstruct the view. The front of this hall is supported by two wooden columns. It is known as the Gilded Hall, on account of its ceilings having been covered with gold leaf, much of which still remains.

In the room off the north side of this the relic is still supposed to be enshrined in a gold casket adorned with pearls. The room is locked and sealed, being opened only once a year at the *'urs* festival, when the box, or nest of boxes, containing the relic may be seen, but the boxes themselves are never opened, so it is said.

The two rooms on the south side of the Gilded Hall are the show rooms of the place. The three doors, leading off this hall into the great hall at the back and the rooms on the north and south, are worth notice, though they are fast being destroyed. They are, or were, the best works of art in the building, next the famous carpets. Like most Indian doors, they are folding, consisting of two leaves, with chain and staple above for fastening them. But the whole surface of each has been ribbed out with blackwood into geometric patterns, the little panels so formed being filled with ivory plates. These have, unfortunately, been subjected to rough use, and mischievous fingers have helped to make them the wrecks they are. And still the damage goes on. Between 1889 and 1903, as shewn by photographs, no less than seventy panels had disappeared. And it is difficult to stop it, for the building is entirely in the hands of the Muḥammadans, who are very jealous of any interference (Plate LXXV).

The room off the south side of the Gilded Hall is a gorgeously painted apartment, though small. The walls are covered with the interminable windings of the stems and foliage of a blue-flowered creeper *(clitorea ternatea Gokarna)*. On the backs of the niches in the walls, are painted vases and urns, containing flowers, the vases being richly lined out, somewhat in Chinese fashion, in gold (Plate LXXVII). The ceiling and its beams have also been profusely decorated in colour. A good deal of the gilding still remains upon the walls, and, like that on the ceiling of the hall outside, retains its lustre remarkably well. This is sufficient proof of the purity of the gold leaf used, else it would have tarnished long ere this.

The next room, beyond this, is also elaborately painted, but in a different style, the lower portions of the walls being covered with figures in fresco painting, but which have been so damaged that it is very difficult to trace the different forms and groups, and impossible to solve the stories of the scenes portrayed. From what can be seen they savour very strongly of western handicraft; and, indeed, in one instance regular European wine glasses are represented. These paintings are thought to have been done by European artists in the employ of Sulṭān Muḥammad, who, on their arrival in India, had little or no knowledge of eastern manners, customs, or traditions, and had, therefore, to fall back upon western ideas, and adapt them, as far as possible, to suit their eastern environment. The accompanying plates have been made from photographs, which, as such, would not have reproduced so well (Plates LXXV and LXXVI).

As these paintings are fast disappearing, and are getting less distinguishable every year, it may be as well to quote extracts from the report of an expert, Mr. John Griffiths, the late Superintendent of the Sir Jamsetji Jijibhoy School of Art, Bombay, when he examined them at the request of the Government in 1884. He says:

"The rooms which have any remains of paintings are two small ones on the right, leading off the verandah of the first floor. The first entered is decorated in the purely orthodox Mahomedan manner, with vases and flowers in niches; flowers on a gold ground in the spandrils of the arches, etc.; and painted in a free naturalistic manner is the little blue *chitorea ternata* represented creeping up from the floor to the ceiling, covering the entire wall space between the niches.

"Entering the second room it is seen at a glance that the work is totally different in character from that in the first; and on closer inspection I am of opinion that it is the work of Italian artists. The paintings are executed in fresco seeco, a kind of distemper. I am aware that they have been attributed to Portuguese artists, in the employment of the priests of Goa; but taking into consideration the facts that it was customary for the kings of Bijapur to invite to their courts, persons celebrated for their talents; that there was constant communication between Bijapur and Europe at about that period (the middle of the 17th century); and that the Portuguese did not paint in fresco, I think the weight of evidence is in favour of their having been executed by Italian artists. They are not of a very high order of merit to judge from the very fragmentary portions that now remain of them, with the exception of two compositions, and these are certainly well designed, modelled, drawn and painted. There is sufficient evidence to show that they are the work of at least two, if not more, artists who have endeavoured to comply with the wishes of their employers, in giving these figures a quasi-eastern character, by decking them up in bangles, neck-ornaments, earrings, jewelled belts and wreaths of flowers. There is not sufficient evidence to show what the subjects represented are intended to be. They may be from classic mythology.

"The subjects are painted on the lower portion of the wall of the room to the height of about four feet, the figures being a little over half life size, with a background of trees of no distinctive character, rising up nearly to the height of the ceiling, painted on a cloudy sky. The execution of this portion of the work, trees and sky, is very commonplace, and not nearly as good as some of the figure painting.

"On the wall, immediately to the left of the door entering the room, is painted a seated figure smoking a long-stemmed *chilum*, the bowl of which is supported by another figure seated on the floor. The arms are bare, while the rest of the figure is enveloped in a grey robe, adjusted in large sweeping folds, girded at the waist with a jewelled belt, and embroidered over with leaf and flower ornament, similar in character to the ornament painted on the dresses in Paul Veronese's pictures. A double plummed aigrette is worn on the head; a pendant on the forehead; a jewel in the ear; a small necklace of pearls; a bangle on each wrist, and one on the right arm immediately below the elbow. Behind this figure can be traced the head and shoulders of another; and in the background is seen the head and neck of a horse.

"The next picture is in the recess of the window, all having been destroyed between this and the last. It is composed of a group of five women and an infant, the interest of the group being centred in the child, who is nude, and is about to be wrapped up in a thin gauzy-looking material [Plate LXXVI]. It has an ornament suspended from the neck. The woman to the right is supporting the child, while the one to the left is adjusting the cloth. The others are simply engaged in watching the proceedings. The women are represented of light complexion, with long flowing hair, wearing bodices, petticoats, and embroidered scarfs passed over the head *sari*-like; and jewelled belts round the waist. All have glass and jewelled bangles, earrings, pearl necklaces and necklaces of small dark beads with jewelled fastenings; a token of marriage among Hindu and Musalman women.

"The next subject is a group of women represented with rosy cheeks, vermillion lips and of fair complexion. One behind, is drinking from a cup which is held in the right hand and a saucer in the left. Another has a wreath of white flowers worn across the body, like a sword belt, over the right shoulder and reaching as low as the left hip. The one to the left has an elaborately ornamented scarf, very thin in texture, suggesting silk or muslin, which is carried up in front from the right side over the left shoulder, round the head, and hangs loosely over the right shoulder. A portion of this picture is hidden behind a mud and stone partition which fills the archway.

"The next is composed of a male figure on the left seated, having a large wreath of flowers round the neck [Plate LXXVI[1]]; a waiting woman attending on a female figure seated on the floor at a red-covered low table, and two other female attendants standing, one in the act of drawing her *odhni* over her head, and the other represented wearing a large wreath of flowers. On the small table are four dishes which appear to contain fruit, and glasses similar in form to some old Venetian glasses, specimens of which have been found at Bijapur. The colouring of the whole is brilliant, but the work is poor in drawing. From the women wearing rings on the index finger the people represented are Musalmans, as I am informed that Hindu women never wear rings on the first finger. Another proof of their being Musalmans is from the large *basu-bands*, a broad belt-like ornament of gold and jewels, worn on the arm and tied with silk cord; and from the manner of wearing the hair, which is united and hangs loosely down the back.

"On the extreme left is a chubby fair-haired child with its mother who is reclining on a cushion. The child is nude, and the figure of the woman is depicted very delicately through thin drapery. Her limbs are gracefully and naturally folded, and very well drawn and fore-shortened. Further on to the right is a back view of a figure kneeling and bending round in the act of taking up a blue china jar, and next to this is the figure of a very dark-skinned person, with dark curly hair, carrying on his shoulders a fair-haired child. This is the only figure in all the paintings that has the face intact.

"As a piece of painting, this is decidedly one of the best. Some parts are very well drawn, the flesh tints delicately shaded without strong contrasts of light and dark.

"Another is very indistinct. At the left side is seen a portion of a figure playing on a small organ, the action of the two hands being very well rendered. Further to the right can just be traced fragments of two figures, one playing a large viola, the other a harp.

"The picture is the most important of the whole group. In the centre of the picture is a woman, nude, with a small cloth thrown loosely round the loins, reclining full length on a white cloth in an attitude not unlike one of Titian's Venuses. She is leaning on her right fore-arm, with the right leg stretched out to its full length, and the left bent, on the knee of which is resting her left hand. She has a bangle on the right arm and several on the wrists; a necklace of pearls with a large jewelled pendant, and a jewelled belt round the waist. In attendance to the left, are two Cupids, the near one, with reddish curly hair, has a quiver full of arrows attached to a red belt, worn across the left shoulder. From the neck is suspended an enamelled disc.

---

[1] The illustrations are from photographs but recently taken, and much more damaged than at the time of this description.

"On the extreme left of the picture is a back view of a figure, nude, with the exception of a thin piece of cloth thrown across the loins [Plate LXXV]. The figure is represented seated on a diapered light coloured cloth which is spread on a raised piece of ground. The left arm is bent back, and the hand appears to be resting on a winged helmet; whilst the right is extended forward towards the reclining female figure. A large wreath of white flowers is worn over the left shoulder, on both arms are large armlets tied with tasselled string; on the wrist are bangles; and round the waist is a large jewelled belt. The whole of this figure is remarkably well drawn, the modelling of the right shoulder, shewing the detoid and the muscles of the scapula, is very delicately and truthfully rendered. From the more masculine appearance of the back and arms I should say that the figure represented was that of a man, although the small feet and great width across the pelvis would incline one to the opinion that it was a female. On the right of the picture is a male figure in a sitting posture, with the two arms extended towards the female. What remains of this figure unobliterated, is sufficient to shew that the artist possessed considerable artistic power. The drawing of the left arm crossing the body, of the pelvis, of the left leg with the foreshortening of the thigh, is very well done. The figure has round the neck, a string of pearls and a large jewelled pendant suspended from a chain; a rich bangle round the left arm, and bangles on the wrist; a chain bangle round the right ankle, and a jewelled belt round the waist. To the right is a curly-haired Cupid, with wings tinged with blue, holding out a glass to the figure just described. He has a rich jewelled belt round the loins, bangles on the wrists and ankles, and pearls in the ear.

"The subject of this picture may be Aphrodite, Ares (Mars), and Adonis."

Paintings of human figures, like images, are never tolerated by strict Muḥammadans; and so, it is stated, the bigot Aurangzeb was so incensed at seeing these upon the walls of a Muḥammadan building, claiming a certain degree of sanctity, that he ordered the faces of all the figures to be destroyed.[1] In this room are kept two large chests containing a great number of coverings for the relic box, curtains and other hangings in silk and *kimkh̲āb*, which, having been carelessly kept, are falling into rags and are moth-eaten. The fine old Persian carpets, which were so badly used, especially at the *'urs* festival, when they were trodden upon by hundreds of feet, were generally kept in the room at the back of the relic room, that is, off the north end of the great hall upstairs. The best of these, however, have been rescued, other carpets having been given in exchange, and the old ones are now on view, in glass cases, in the local museum at the Gol Gumbaz (Plates LXXIX and LXXX). Beside these there are a few other articles of olden times, such as china ḥuqqah bowls (Plate XXXII), quaint copper kettles and pans, and some old glass bottles, but there is nothing among these of any great merit as works of art.

The windows on the upper floor are worth a passing notice. They are filled with geometric tracery in woodwork in which yellow and blue stained glass has been used, some of which still remains in them. An ingenious device of perforated wavy lines radiating from a centre, in the tops of some of the back windows, represent, with a strong light shining through them, the rays of the setting sun (Plate LXXVIII).

On the ground floor, at the foot of the staircase, is a closed room which was the *kitābkh̲āna* or library. Around its sides are small cupboards in which the old Āt̲h̲ār Maḥall manuscripts were once kept, the bulk of which are said to have been carted away by Aurangzeb. A few fragments of these papers were still remaining there a short time ago.[2]

---

[1] The Prophet cursed the painter or drawer of men and animals, and consequently such portraits are held to be unlawful. *Mis̲h̲kāt*, Bk. XII, Ch. I, Pt. I.

[2] Mr. Jas. Bird said, in speaking of the books and manuscripts left in the Āt̲h̲ār Mahall: "At the request of Lieut.-Col. Briggs, the late Resident at Sattara, Mir Kheirat Ali, commonly called Mushtak, the learned Persian Secretary of the Residency, made out a catalogue of the whole; but no historical works were discovered." *Journ. Bom. Br. R. A. S.*, Vol. I, p. 382.

The other rooms, on the ground floor, are all dirty lumber rooms. In the one immediately below the relic chamber, and before which hangs a curtain, is a model of the tomb of Muḥammad at Madīna. It is a poor piece of work, but rather quaint. It is carefully stowed away in a huge chest.

The general aspect of the great hall, if ever worth anything, has been ruined by the construction of two tall Gothic arches built within it, very many years ago, to strengthen the roof. The wooden panelled ceiling has been painted in light tints.

Out in front of the building is a great square tank, which is kept full, it being still fed by the Begam Talāo and Torweh conduits; and it is the addition of this, with its reflections and ripple, that, in a measure, compensates for the bare looking exterior of the palace itself.

We can well imagine Sulṭān Muḥammad spending much time in this pleasant outlook, watching, day after day, the slow and gradual rise of the walls of his own great mausoleum in the distance, and the final rounding off of the colossal dome which surmounts it. And, perhaps, he would often muse upon the shortness of life, and think of the day that was drawing nigh when his own bones would be carried away to rest beneath that vast vault.

THE JAHĀZ MAHALL.

Beside the Āthār Maḥall, on the north, and apparently forming with it part of a group of buildings connected with one another, is a ruined building, called the Jahāz Maḥall, from, it is said, its fancied resemblance to a ship (Plates LXXIV and LXXXI).[1] It is also said that, in this building, were the offices of the admiralty, hence Jahāz Maḥall or 'Admiralty Office'; and we know that Bījāpūr possessed a considerable fleet at one time, even as early as the reign of Yūsūf, when the Portuguese came into contact with it in A. D. 1498, and found it commanded by a Spanish Jew. In 'Ali's reign it is stated that there were 180 ships between the river of Gujarāt and the river of Bengal. With bare walls and hollow gaping doorways and windows, from which all its old woodwork has been torn away, it now stands a wreck indeed. It is in two storeys, the ground floor being divided, by a central wall, into an outer and an inner arcade, with a room running transversely on either side of the central gateway. At the ends of the building, on the outer sides, are, what appear to be, cookrooms, while, on the inner sides, are staircases leading to the upper storey. The upper floor was divided into suites of rooms, the walls of which are filled with pigeon-hole niches. Below, through the middle of the building, is the great gateway leading into the Āthār Maḥall, the ponderous wooden gates of which still swing in their sockets; and the huge wooden beam, which barred the door from behind, still lies upon its numerous rollers, in its long tunnel, in the wall behind the door.

On the east side of the enclosure of the Āthār Maḥall, are the ruins of a smaller building.

MUSTAFĀ KHĀN'S MOSQUE AND PALACE.

About five hundred yards east of the citadel walls are the mosque and palace of Muṣṭafā Khān (Plates LXXXI and LXXXII). The mosque is a very lofty and substantially built edifice. The façade has three tall arches, the central one being very much wider than the side ones; and, being almost devoid of ornament, the front has rather a bald appearance.

[1] There is a Jahāz Maḥall at Māṇḍū in Central India, situated between two large tanks, the two sheets of water forming, as it were, one, upon which imagination pictures the building as floating like a ship or *jahāz*. The name is not uncommon.

A deep heavy cornice overhangs the arches; and the octagonal buttresses, which were to carry minarets, flank the façade of the building. But the minarets were never built. The dome is stilted by the introduction, between it and the terrace roof, as is the Jāmi' Masjid, of a second storey, with a row of arched recesses on each face. Inside, the central bay of the ceiling is domed, the square, below, working up to a fourteen-sided figure, and this again to a smaller fourteen-sided figure which slopes off into the dome. The side bays are vaulted. The interior of the building is very plain. The *miḥrāb* niche is formed by seven sides of a ten-sided polygon.

In the façade of this mosque we find the same fault as in that of the Gagan Maḥall—the awkward combination of two narrow arches with one wide one, retaining the same height for all three. This can only be done by making the latter very squat and out of good proportion, or by making the former equally disproportioned by excessive height to width.

There is not much in this building to commend it to special notice. Behind it, across the road, are the ruins of Muṣṭafā Khān's palace, portions of which have been preserved and patched up sufficiently to give shelter to some of his descendants at the present day. Judging from the extent of the different blocks of buildings, courtyards, gateways, tanks, and gardens, it must have been an extensive residence, quite a fitting abode for the first man in the kingdom after the king. In the garden, around the large tank, may be seen lengths of shallow stone channels with serrated beds, down which the overflow from the tank was allowed to run in thousands of little ripples sparkling with lights and shadows. The bed of the reservoir nearest the palace is shallow, while that furthest away is deeper, apparently so arranged for bathing purposes.

Standing some two hundred yards to the south of the mosque and palace, upon the side of the main road leading from the citadel to the Jāmi' Masjid, is a great heavy-looking archway known as the Baṛī Kamān. It was the main entrance into Muṣṭafā Khān's grounds, though now cut off and separated from it.

Mirzā (or Mullā) Muḥammad Amīn Lāri was an officer of the state during the reign of Ibrāhīm II., who sent him with troops against the Aḥmadnagar forces. Before the king died he entrusted him with the full control of the state, and gave him injunctions to see that Sulṭān Muḥammad should succeed him. This he faithfully carried out and received from the hands of his new liege the title of Muṣṭafā Khān. He is frequently called Nawāb Muṣṭafā Khān. After serving the state faithfully for some years he died while prosecuting the siege of Chenchi in the Karnatic, and his body was brought to Bījāpūr and buried in his *sarāi* near Shāhpūr.

These buildings have also been ascribed to Muṣṭafā Khān Ardistāni, who helped to bring about the great expedition of the four kings against Rāmrāj; but this appears to be a mistake.

Muṣṭafā Khān's *Sarāi* (Caravansary), or hostel for travellers, stands near the Amīn Dargāh. When Bījāpūr was being prepared for the accommodation of the District head-quarters, this place was converted in a jail, and improved out of all semblance to its former self. A *sarāi* usually consisted of a great square open courtyard, with a well in the middle, and a surrounding arcade opening into the courtyard. Access was gained through a great gateway, with substantial doors for closing against robbers at night, in the middle of one of its sides. Merchants and others could rest in the arcade with their riding or baggage animals tethered in the court at their feet. For those who could pay a small nominal rent a few small rooms, with doors, were provided. It was always considered a very meritorious deed to build a *sarāi*, or *dharmaśālā*, as the Hindu calls it. There is an inscription over the gateway of this one which reads :

> They entered it in security. For the comfort of all people, rich and poor, this *sarāi*, called "the *sarāi* of Muḥammad is the medicine of felicity" belonging to the Pādshāh, the Asylum of Religion, Abū-l-Muzaffar, Abū-l-Manṣūr Sulṭān, the 'Ādil Shāh of the period, was built by Abd-al-Bārī Muḥammad Mustafā Khān Lārī ; and this was in the year 50 after 1000 from the prophetic exile. [A. D. 1640-41.]

Sarāis were, as a rule, built outside large cities, on the outskirts, so that travellers could arrive and depart at any hour of the night, which they could not always do inside a city after the great gates were shut.

The ruins of another large *sarāi* stand at a short distance to the north of the Amīn Dargāh. It is in two storeys, being known as the *chhoṭa*, or small, *sarāi*, and is said to have been built by a *sāhūkār* or banker.

The larger mausolea, such as the Ibrāhīm Rauza, also had ample accommodation in the way of *sarāis* attached to them, but in these cases, they were not so much for merchants and ordinary travellers as for religious mendicants travelling about the country from shrine to shrine.

AFZAL KHĀN'S CENOTAPH.

Outside the city walls, about two and a half miles west by north from the Shāhpūr gateway, and close to the village of Takki or Afzalpūr, where the tomb of Chindgī Shāh occupies the highest ground, are the cenotaph and mosque of Afzal Khān ; and three-quarters of a mile south of this, are the reputed tombs of his wives (Plates LXXXII—LXXXIV). The Afzal Khān, whose cenotaph this is said to be, was he who was *wazīr* and general under Muḥammad Shāh and 'Ali II., and who undertook the disastrous expedition against Śivājī. He, it was, who superintended the construction of the waterworks by which a fresh supply was introduced into the city from the Begam Talāo ; and his name occurs in the inscriptions upon the water tower near the Āthār Mahall. The story of Afzal Khān's last expedition and tragic end is one of the most thrilling in Dakhan history, and is told at length in the historical section of this work. As was the usual custom, he constructed his own mausoleum during his lifetime, and the double-storeyed mosque attached to it appears to have been finished in A. D. 1653, an inscription, in the *miḥrāb* of the same, giving the date A. H. 1064 and his name. The tomb appears never to have been completed, and was, no doubt, still in the hands of the architect when Afzal Khān was ordered away on that ill-fated campaign against the treacherous Śivājī. It is said that the astrologers predicted that he would never return ; and, so impressed was he by their words, that he set his house in order before starting, and put up the date of that year, A. H. 1069, in the cenotaph, and he is also said to have drowned his sixty-four wives. His death really occurred one month after the expiry of that year, *i. e.* in A. H. 1070 (A. D. 1659).[1] His body was never brought back to his own sepulchre, but was interred upon the slopes of Partabgarh, close to the spot where he was cut down by Śivājī. Consequently the central unpaved space in the floor of the cenotaph, where his grave should have been, remains undisturbed to this day ; but two

[1] In *Architecture at Beejapoor*, by Fergusson and Taylor, the latter puts the expedition in A. D. 1757, long after the 'Ādil Shāhi dynasty ceased to exist, but this is, perhaps, a printer's error.

women have been buried within the chamber, and there are several tombs and spaces in the surrounding verandah.

Close to the tomb, on the west, and separated from it by a small cistern, is the attendant mosque. This is a two-storeyed mosque, which is very unusual; that is, it has two prayer chambers, identical in plan, one above the other. It is possible that the upper floor was intended for the exclusive use of Afzal Khān's women folk, the lower prayer chamber being too small to allow of a portion being partitioned off for their use as was the custom in Gujarāt. In support of this idea we find a *mimbar* or pulpit in the lower mosque, but none in the upper, where no man would be allowed to enter to preach. There are *miḥrābs* or prayer niches in both.

There is not much calling for special remark in these buildings. The pyramidal rise of the roof from the walls of the cenotaph is rather pleasing, but the general effect of the building is spoilt by the walls and arches, below the cornice, being too squat and wanting in elevation. This gives a rather top-heavy look to the whole. These defects would have been in great measure eliminated had the building been placed upon a high basement. This is a fault that frequently occurs at Bījāpūr.

On the south side of the mosque and cenotaph are the ruins of Afzal Khān's palace; and the adjoining village, which, no doubt, was included in his *jāgīr* or fief, has been called after him. The saint who lies buried in the tomb there, Chindgī Shāh (or as it is also written Muḥammad Jangi), died in A. H. 1096 (A. D. 1684), and Afzal Khān is said to have built his tomb, that is, of course, during his life-time. On the west side of the tomb is a mosque. There is a fine large inscription stone, broken in two, near it, at the south-west corner of the platform, with Persian writing on the face and *bālbodh* on the two sides.

The reputed graves of Afzal Khān's wives, situated in a grove of trees, are on a large masonry platform, with the remains of a large tank before it, known as the 'Muḥammad Sarwar'. On the platform are eleven rows of graves, all being those of females, amounting, in all, to sixty-three, with an open empty grave which would have made the sixty-fourth. These have been so regularly placed at equal intervals, and are all so uniform in size and design, that they appear to have been made for persons who had all died at the same time. Tradition tells us that, Afzal Khān being so impressed with the prediction that he would not return to Bījāpūr, and believing he would not require his worldly goods any longer, had all his wives drowned before setting out, and that all but one, who escaped were buried here; hence the empty grave. Close by is an old well in which they are said to have met their death.

Meadows Taylor in *Tara* speaks of Afzal Khān's ladies as having accompanied him on the expedition, and mentions a Marātha chronicle in support of his statement which records that a certain 'Khundojee Kakrey', an officer of Śivājī's, was tried and beheaded for his act of treason in befriending and escorting into safety these same ladies after Afzal Khān's death. This statement is also made by Grant Duff in his *History of the Marathas.*[1]

THE GOL GUMBAZ, OR TOMB OF SULṬĀN MUḤAMMAD.

Transcending all other buildings at Bījāpūr in simple mass, and dominating the landscape for miles around, the great Gol Gumbaz, or tomb of Sulṭān Muḥammad, stands alone

[1] At Bidar, close by the tomb of 'Ali Barid, are sixty low tombs, which are said to be those of his wives, and a strange legend says they were all killed by his order in a single night. *A Guide to Bidar* by Nawab Framurz Jung Bahadur, p.11.

(Plates LXXXV—XCV). For size, few other buildings in India can be compared with it. Its noble proportions and magnificent dome are only seen to the fullest advantage from a distance. When close up to it, the dome seems to sink into the building, and to require an intermediate terrace or storey to raise it into full view. A few extra feet here would certainly have improved the general design, even when viewed from further off. The impressive grandeur of the building and its imponderable mass simply overwhelm the spectator with awe. It stands in the extreme east end of the city, its massive basement resting upon the solid rock. The vast mausoleum stands out with most striking effect when viewed, as Muḥammad himself must often have seen it, from the upper hall of the Āt͟hār Maḥall, when, backed by great storm clouds, the low western sun suddenly bursts through a rent and illumines the great building. It then flashes out into brilliant contrast against the rolling masses of angry black clouds ; the mellow tints of its walls are bathed in a golden glow, and the great dome shines like burnished brass. Under all this glory peacefully repose the mortal remains of Sulṭān Muḥammad.

Fig. 21. The Gol Gumbaz, from a distance.

King Ibrāhīm, his father, had raised the beautiful pile of the Ibrāhīm Rauza, which was the last word in decorative and luxurious magnificence. It was impossible for Muḥammad to go further upon the same lines, so he struck out in a different direction altogether, and endeavoured to dwarf it, and everything else, by stupendous mass ; and this he certainly accomplished. The Gol Gumbaz is the antithesis of the Ibrāhīm Rauza in that the strong virility of conception of the one contrasts with the delicate femininity of the other. His reign of thirty years, however, was not sufficient wherein to fully complete the building, for he seems to have died while the plastering of the walls was in progress, and it was no one else's business to complete what he left unfinished. One cannot help wondering what new departures would have been made in the further development of Bījāpūr architecture had the dynasty lived and flourished another hundred and fifty years, for they were daring builders.

A glance at the plan (Plate LXXXVIII) of the Gol Gumbaz shews what a simple building it is for all its size—just a great square hall, enclosed by four lofty walls, buttressed up by octagonal towers at the corners, and the whole surmounted by a hemispherical dome. The great size of the dome, and the neat and perfect manner in which, by means of cross-arching and pendentives, the square walls have been worked up to meet it, are the most notable features of the building. The extreme outside measurement of the mausoleum including the towers is 205 feet square; the extreme height to the apex of the dome from the base of the building is 198 feet 6 inches; the exterior diameter of the dome is 144 feet, while the interior diameter, measured 124 feet 5 inches; and the great hall, below, with no intermediate supports of any kind, inside its walls, is 135 feet 5 inches square.[1] The interior height, from the level of the floor, around the tomb platform, to the top of the dome is 178 feet. Within the base of the dome is a broad gallery, 11 feet wide, which hangs out into the interior of the building, 109 feet 6 inches above the floor. Narrow staircases wind up through the corners of the building where the towers join it, and passages lead out from them on to each of the pigeon-holed storeys of the towers. In the centre of the floor of the hall is a high platform upon which are the counterfeit tombs, the real graves being in the vault underneath, which extends over the whole length and breadth of the hall (Plate LXXXIX). It is recorded that Muḥammad, being a Shī'ah, brought earth from Karbalā, the city in 'Irāq where the martyr Ḥusain's sepulchre is situated, for use in this vault, that he might be buried in sacred dust.

The strength and stability of the building, as we have seen in other instances, really depend upon its mortar, and the fact of its foundations having been laid upon the solid rock, for its masonry is very poor, hardly better than common rubble. Most of the cut-stone masonry that is seen in these buildings is but a veneer, the blocks often standing on their thin edges, while the hearting is nothing more than the roughest rubble with a generous amount of mortar in its composition. But that the mortar used in those days was of the best, has already been seen in the case of the great flat ceiling in the Ibrāhīm Rauza

Each of the four walls of the building had been raised as three great arches, the central one being wider than the two side ones, and these have then been filled in with rubble masonry in the side ones, and cut-stone in the central one. On the north side, however, the central archway had been left open, or had been subsequently opened, as a small chapel or chamber has been built against the wall here as an annexe, communicating through the arch with the great hall within. In the central archways of the other three sides are the doors and windows; but, even here, the filling in above the windows can only be called crazy or patchwork masonry. The masonry of the great dome may be looked upon as practically concrete, it being composed of bricks in mortar, the thickness of the shell varying from ten feet at the springing to nine feet near the crown. It is thus a great rigid concrete shell without voussoirs, and, consequently, with practically no side thrusts of any kind so long as

[1] The diameter of the dome of the Pantheon at Rome is 142 feet, while the area covered, below, is but 15,833 square feet. This is reckoned the largest dome in the world.

it remains intact. It is a dead weight acting vertically downwards, partly upon the cross arching within, and partly upon the side walls—just as an inverted china basin would act upon the upper edges of a cube upon which it might rest. Being built in this way, with ring upon ring of thick brickwork, each corbelled forward until they close at the apex, it is probable that no centering or support was needed beneath it during construction, except, perhaps, for a small section near the crown, which would have been supported by that part of the dome already built. Any outward thrust that could possibly come upon the side walls would be amply neutralized by the weight of material in the pendentives which hang over inside the building. The corner buttresses take no thrust to speak of, for if we assume the point at A (see diagram) to take a certain amount of thrust from the arch L N, carried through the intermediate wall N A, then the point L would equally require a buttress to take the thrust of the other side of the same arch. But there is no provision for such, and thus it is conclusively shewn that no thrust was anticipated; and, as the building has stood over two hundred and fifty years without failing, it is clear that no active thrust exists. The arrows in the diagram show the crowns of the great arches.

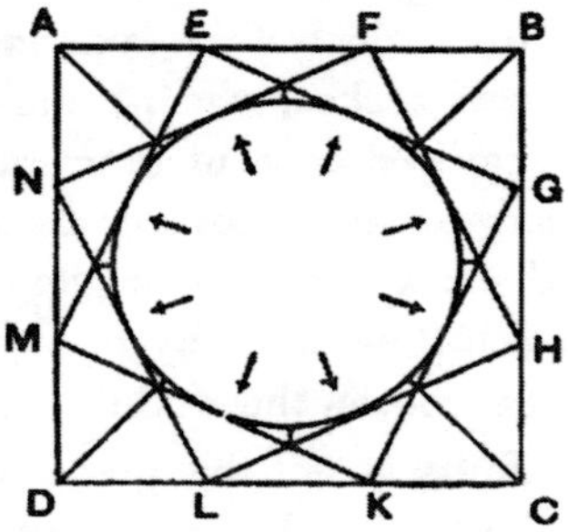

I have spoken of pendentives both here and in my account of the Jāmi' Masjid, and it may be as well, for the benefit of the uninitiated, to explain what they are. The accompanying photograph of a rough model, made by me for this purpose, will make the explanation easier (see Fig. 22). "In a spherical roof intersected with groined compartments, the term *pendentives* was applied to the surfaces included between such compartments. The same term is applied to the surfaces included in the angles formed by a groined vaulting at its spring."[1] It is in the latter sense that it is used in the buildings at Bījāpūr. The pendentives are thus a result of cross-arching or groining. In the accompanying diagram ABCD is the square room to be covered in. Points are taken in the walls at E, F, G, H, K, L, M and N so that they form the corners of an octagon. At these points piers are built up the walls to carry arches. The latter are then thrown across from one pier to an alternate pier, so that the arches, thus constructed, form, in plan, two intersecting squares EGKM and FHLN, and the crowns of all the arches fall upon a circle inscribed within these squares, and carry the dome, which may be as small, in internal diameter, as this circle.

Fig. 22. Section of the Gol Gumbaz from a plaster model.

This system of pendentives is, without doubt, the most successful and most graceful method of construction for such domes. It obviates any interference with the external

[1] *Illustrated Dictionary of Words used in Art and Archæology*, by J. W. Mollett, B.A.

contour of the dome, and adds, at the same time, a very pleasing feature to the interior—the interlacing or groining of the arches. The tendency of the dome to spread at the base, which is counteracted by the pendentives and great mass of masonry thus thrown into the interior of the building, was guarded against, in the case of the Pantheon at Rome, which possesses a dome of greater diameter, by the heaping up of masonry upon the haunches of the dome outside, thus destroying its beauty of outline.

The great hall below, which is covered by the dome, covers an area of 18,337·67 square feet, from which if we take 228·32 square feet for the projecting angles of the piers carrying the cross arches, which stand out from the walls into the floor, two on each face, we get a total covered area, uninterrupted by supports of any kind, of 18,109·35 square feet. This is the largest space covered by a single dome in the world, the next largest being that of the Pantheon at Rome, of 15,833 square feet. If we add the pendentives to the actual dome, to which they naturally belong as part of the superstructure, this then becomes the greatest domical roof in the world.

But was not this great dome, after all, but an after-thought? Compare the plan of the foundations of the mausoleum with the plan of the great unfinished tomb at 'Aināpūr. described further on (Plate XCVII), which is, so far as plan and measurements are concerned, a duplicate of the Gol Gumbaz, and it will be seen that the foundations of the 'Aināpūr tomb were laid so that the walls of the inner sepulchral chamber should carry the dome—not one half the size of the Gol Gumbaz. What was the great heavy square of inner foundations for in the lower plan of the latter? It was quite unnecessary to carry the mere thin shell of flooring above them. The plan of the 'Aināpūr tomb plainly shews what its object was. It was to have carried the walls of an inner chamber from which the dome would have risen, while the great arches in the outer walls would, no doubt, have remained open, thus forming a great verandah around the sepulchral chamber, such as is seen in the tomb of Shāh Nawāz Khān (Plate CIII). Before the walls of the Gol Gumbaz had risen many feet, it would seem that the plans were altered. The daring spirit of the architect, urged on perhaps

Fig. 23. The great cornice of the Gol Gumbaz in progress of repair.

by Sulṭān Muḥammad himself, incited him to attempt the more stupendous task of hanging a mighty dome right across the whole expanse of the outer walls; and it seems almost incredible that the man who conceived, and carried to such a successful issue, this magnificent project, should have passed into oblivion; his very name is unknown.

A very notable feature is the massive cornice which runs round the building between the tops of the arches of the walls and the parapet (Plate XCI). It is the heaviest in Bījāpūr, and is, itself, one of the most daring feats accomplished in the city. The projection is about eleven feet six inches from the face of the walls, and ninety feet above the ground. The brackets beneath the slabs are seven and a half feet in height, and consist of four courses of different heights. Each stone tails into the wall as far, in some instances, as one and a half feet. Like those already described, this cornice was in a very shattered condition; but lately, the one over the main entrance, on the south side, has been restored at very great cost and infinite labour. It was, at first, intended merely to mend the broken portions as seen from below, but when scaffolding was erected, and an examination was conducted at close quarters, it was discovered that nearly every group of brackets was cracked through in one or more places, and they were so dangerously unstable, that the slightest movement, or further disintegration of the cracked surfaces, would have brought them down in masses. There was nothing left but to restore the whole side, especially as the lives of visitors, entering or leaving the building below, were imperilled.[1]

Another remarkable feature in the building is its whispering gallery, which runs round, inside the dome, at its base. Access is gained to it from the terraced roof around the base of the dome, by eight small doorways through it. As may be seen from the section (Plate XC) and the model (Fig. 22) it hangs out into the building, being supported upon the crowns of the cross arches below; and it is about eleven feet wide, inside the low parapet wall which protects it. On entering the building a person is struck by the loud echoes which fill the place in answer to his footfall; but these sounds are intensified on entering the gallery. The footfall of a single individual is enough to wake the sounds as of a company of persons; and, in response to ordinary conversation, strange weird sounds and mocking whispers emanate from the wall around. Loud laughter is answered by a score of fiends safely ensconced behind the plaster. The slightest whisper is heard from side to side, and a conversation may be easily carried on across the diameter of the dome, in the lowest undertone, by simply talking to the wall, out of which the answering voice appears to come. A single loud clap is distinctly echoed over ten times.

Instances of multiple echoes, such as this, are the Pantheon at Rome, the tomb of Metella the wife of Crassus, which is said to have repeated a whole verse of the Æneid as many as eight times, and the whispering gallery of St. Paul's. It is not at all likely, as some suppose, that the architect of this building had the production of a wonderful echo in view when designing the dome, for the latter is no more than a duplicate, except in size, of many another in Bījāpūr. The echo is but a natural result of the size of the dome. In the smaller domes we get what is called a resonance, their diameters not being sufficiently great to allow of a distinct echo. It requires rather more than sixty-five feet between a person and the

[1] The Public Works Department deserve the greatest credit for the manner in which they carried out this work under Mr. R. M. MacFarlaine and his Assistant Mr. S. V. Rajadhyaksha. Some idea of the magnitude of the work may be gathered from the fact that the largest stones used weighed twenty-six hundredweight, and had to be raised by differential pulleys to a height of ninety feet.

reflecting surface in order that the sound of his voice may, on return, reach his ear after the cessation of the original sound, and so create the impression of a second sound or echo. If a greater distance intervenes, the echo is more distinct, as more time separates the original from the reflected sound. If the distance is less, no distinct echo results, as the original and reflecting sounds overlap and produce a confused sound or resonance. If there is but one reflecting surface there can be but one echo, for the return sound travels off into space and is dissipated; but should there be a second reflecting surface, opposite the first, as in the case of the two sides of the dome, the return sound or echo is intercepted and reflected back again to the first surface. Thus the sound is bandied backwards and forwards, producing a series of echoes, each time losing some of its intensity until it becomes too feeble to catch the ear.

Upon the great raised platform in the centre of the mausoleum, under the dome, are the counterfeit tombs of the grandson of Sulṭān Muḥammad (son of 'Ali II.); Muḥammad's younger wife, 'Arūs Bībī; the Sulṭān himself; his favourite mistress Rambhā; his daughter; and his older wife, in this order from east to west.[1] Over Muḥammad's grave is a very shabby-looking wooden canopy (Plate XCV). The real graves, where the bodies lie, are, of course, in the crypt or vault immediately below, the entrance to which is by a staircase under the western doorway. The tombs in the vault do not correspond exactly with the position of those above, as Muḥammad has three instead of two to the east of him, and two instead of three to the west. The central four are in the central vault, while the outermost one on each side is in the side vaults.

Over the south, or main doorway, inside, there is a large boldly-cut inscription in three compartments (Fig. 24). Each of these three sections is a complete sentence in itself, and each, on computing the values of the Persian letters, gives the date of Muḥammad's death as A. H. 1067 (A. D. 1656). These sentences read:

The end of Muḥammad has become laudable.
Muḥammad Sulṭān whose abode is in Paradise.
The abode of peace became Muḥammad Shāh.

Fig. 24. The inscription in the Gol Gumbaz.

Captain Sydenham, who saw this building a hundred years ago, says:

"Over a lofty doorway through which you enter on the southern side, are some Arabic inscriptions in Togra letters which are sculptured in alto-relievo. The characters are gilded, and the ground is painted with a liquid preparation of *lājaward* or lapis lazuli which gives the whole an appearance of a beautiful distribution of gold and enamel."[2]

[1] Meadows Taylor puts his mother, Tāj Sultāna, in the place of his older wife, but Tāj Sultāna was buried in the Ibrāhīm Rauza. The most eastern grave has also been said to be that of his youngest unmarried daughter, but this cannot be since the tomb has a ridge on the top, indicating a male occupant. Captain Sydenham, about 1811, says "On the right of the Sulṭān's tomb, as you enter, are the tombs of his son and daughter-in-law."

[2] *Asiatic Researches*, Quarto Ed., Vol. XIII, p. 437.

The portion added to the back, on the north side of the building, is said to have been intended as a last resting place for Jahān Begam, wife of Muḥammad Shāh. This could hardly have been since it was customary to place the wife beside her husband; but it may have been intended for his spiritual preceptor. Whatever it was built for, it was never finished, and never occupied. An inspection of the masonry shows that it was added after the main building was erected. Below it is a vault of the same dimensions.

Projecting from the top of the dome, some eight feet or so, is the rod which carried the great metal finial. It is said that this crescent finial was carried away during the time of the Rājās of Sātāra to Gulburgah to adorn the tomb of Pīr Khwājah Banda Nawāz.

Hanging from under the cornice by a chain, above the main entrance on the south side, is a meteorite *(bijlī-patthar)* which is said to have fallen in the vicinity during Muḥammad's reign.

On the south side of the Gol Gumbaz, and standing a short distance from it, is the great outer gateway, the upper storey of which was used as the *naqqār-khāna* or drum room, where music was played at stated times (Plate LXXXVII). Like the tomb it appears never to have been finished. Projecting from the edge of the roof, all along the sky-line, are brackets, which were intended to carry a cornice, above which would have risen a low parapet wall, with *mīnārs* at the corners. The upper hall has, of late, been converted into a museum for a local collection of objects of interest. When the citadel walls were being demolished, years ago, and the various buildings were being converted to modern use, many objects were found during the excavations and clearances; but the best of these subsequently disappeared, and the rest, after lying in a heap in an outhouse behind the Ānand Maḥall, and thereafter being moved about from place to place, were more or less broken up and lost. The collection is therefore, at present, rather poor. The most important objects are the much worn carpets from the Āthār Maḥall, which belonged to the old dynasty, and are most excellent specimens of old Persian carpet weaving. To convert the *naqqār-khāna* into a museum it was necessary to insert windows into the open arches of the upper floor, and these were designed after the pattern of those in the west wall of the Āthār Maḥall. Out in front of this building has been arranged, as a gun trophy, many of the old cannon collected from various parts of the city fortifications. Guns connected with their bastions by inscriptions or special historical associations have been left on them.

Standing in the middle of the gun trophy is a great granite column upon whose shaft is a long old Kanarese inscription, but which has no connection with Bījāpūr. The column was brought from Mahākūṭeśvara, some three miles to the east of Bādāmī, for its better safe keeping.

Standing on a low plinth, out before the Gol Gumbaz, and between it and the *naqqār-khāna*, is the mutilated small stone image of an elephant, which is, perhaps, one of a pair which originally stood here, one on either side, facing inwards.

To the west of the great mausoleum, and standing upon the western side of the terrace, is the mosque which is attached to the tomb, and which was, for many years, used as a travellers' bungalow (Plates LXXXVI, LXXXIX and XCII). It is a well-proportioned and elegant building, with slender minarets and rich deep cornice, the latter, however, being much damaged. Owing to its use as a travellers' bungalow, with people coming and going, a great deal of the cornice was dismantled, and the rest was supported with wooden framing as a temporary measure. The whole, though appearing intact, and in good condition from a distance, was, like that of the mausoleum itself, in a very rickety and unsafe condition. The minarets here, as in all Bījāpūr mosques, being but purely ornamental features, contain no staircases as they do at Aḥmadābād, access to the roof terrace being gained by stairways through the thickness of the end walls. The general style, proportions, and finish of this mosque shew that it was not due to the want of skilled labour that the Gol Gumbaz was built so plainly, and was covered with plaster instead of richly chiselled stonework.

JAHĀN BEGAM'S TOMB AT 'AINĀPŪR.

Away to the east of the city, beyond 'Ain-ul-Mulk's tomb already described, are the foundations and piers of a great mausoleum whose plan and measurements are identical with those of the great Gol Gumbaz, even to the corner towers (Plates LXXXVI, XCVI and XCVII). But in this case, the four façades of the building were to be open, with three great arches in each face, between the corner towers. This seems to be clearly indicated by the presence of niches on the inside of the arch piers, which would have been blocked up had walls been introduced to close up the arches. But the principal points in which this, had it been carried out, would have differed from the Gol Gumbaz, were the construction and size of the dome. Here an inner sepulchral chamber, 76 feet square, has its walls built up to very near the springing lines of the dome, which was to rise above this, and not upon the outer walls as in the case of the Gol Gumbaz. It would, therefore, have been, perhaps, not more than seventy feet in external diameter or just half the diameter of the other. In order to show off so small a dome to advantage, these inner walls would, in all probability, have been carried up a considerable distance above the outer walls, resulting in a building much on the lines of the tomb of S͟hāh Nawāz K͟hān (Plate CIII), or of S͟hāh Karīm's tomb near the Jāmi' Masjid (Plate CVI), with the addition of the corner towers. The dome would, perhaps, have been less bulbous, and more after the shape of that over 'Ain-un-Mulk's tomb. It will be seen from the plan that the inner piers were to carry the dome, from the projecting mouldings which would have been carried up round the intersecting arch rings. The inner chamber, too, has three great open arches in each of its four sides.

Within the sepulchral chamber, upon a double platform—one upon another—is a row of five graves. Occupying the centre is a small tombstone, apparently of a male child. Upon the east side of this is a very large tombstone whose flat top shows that it is of a woman. It does not seem to be known whose these are. To the west of these are three very small plaster graves. It is said that they are the graves of 'Abd-al-Raḥmān, father of the mother of Sulṭāna Jahān Begam; Jahān Begam, herself, Muḥammad's wife, and 'Abd-al-Raḥmān's children. Meadows Taylor says the mausoleum was begun for Muḥammad's mother, Tāj Sulṭāna, but he also says she is buried in the Gol Gumbaz beside him. But this is quite wrong, for she is buried in the Ibrāhīm Rauza. Hājī Fāṭimah Sulṭāna, Muḥammad's mother, died and was buried at Makka, whither she went on pilgrimage, so we are also told.

MUBĀRAK K͟HĀN'S MAḤALL.

Situated in the south-east quarter of the city and near the walls, are a couple of small buildings, side by side, known as Mubārak K͟hān's Maḥall. The one towards the west is a little pavilion, while the other in front of it, is a combination of fountain and pavilion, which stood in the middle of a large cistern, now filled up. Another such group, described fully later on, stands upon the margin of the lake at Kumatgī, about ten miles east of Bījāpūr. In both cases they were, evidently, pleasure or garden houses belonging to the nobility, where they could retire at any time from the press of public business, and there enjoy the quiet surroundings of extensive gardens, and listen to the soothing sound of plashing water. In the sultry noontide of the hot weather days they could bathe in the cool element in the many little ornamental cisterns within these pavilions.

The three-storeyed structure, which stood in the middle of the great cistern, just as the *jalamaṇdir* does in front of the Sāt Manzil, is full of pipes laid about through the masonry. Two pipes run round the top of the plinth of the basement, outside, from which short pipes led through the peacock brackets and out at their mouths, there being nine of these brackets on each face exclusive of the corner ones, or forty all round (Plate XCIX). Similarly, some of the brackets, above, had pipes through them for water to pass through. There is a cistern in the floor of the first storey, and traces of another in the uppermost one.

The only Mubārak Khān that we know of in Bījāpūr history was a slave belonging to a noble named Chānd Khān, towards the close of the reign of king Ibrāhīm II., who was raised to power and affluence; but who, in the reign of Muḥammad, together with Khawāṣṣ Khān, a fellow slave who had also risen to power, met with a violent death. Both were beheaded, their heads being taken to Randaulah Khān in a basket.

GREEN-STONE SARCOPHAGUS.

Fifty yards to the south of the tomb of 'Ali 'Ādil Shāh I. is a beautifully cut and moulded tombstone, in a dark greenish-black basalt, standing upon a high and extensive ornamental basement (Plate XCVIII). It has been so carefully wrought and finely finished, that one is led to believe it must be the resting place of some one of note, yet both tradition and history are silent regarding it. Those peculiar corner feet of the basement are such as might be found as supports to a low stand in chased metal. They are seen at the foot of the *mīnārs* of some of the mosques of the time of Ibrāhīm II., and at the corners of the grave platforms of the great unfinished tomb at 'Aināpūr (Plate XCVI). It must be to about the close of Ibrāhīm's reign or the beginning of that of Muḥammad that we must place this work. Beneath the platform is a vault wherein the body was deposited.

TOMB OF 'ALI 'ĀDIL SHĀH II.

The last royal mausoleum, which was begun but never finished, is that of 'Ali 'Ādil Shāh II., which lies at a short distance to the north of the citadel and the Gagan Maḥal (Plates XCVIII and C). The great elevated basement, upon which the building stands, is 215 feet square. The basement of the Gol Gumbaz is 158 feet square. The former, with the projecting corner buttresses, has a total width of face of 225 feet, while the latter, with its towers, measures but 205 feet over all. This, then, covers the greatest area of any building in Bījāpūr.[1] But this tomb of 'Ali was not to rise to any great height, nor was it to be surmounted by a dome covering the whole of this great area. Like that of the great tomb

[1] About 11,000 square feet more than the Jāmi' Masjid, without its side corridors.

at 'Aināpūr, the dome was to cover only the sepulchral chamber, 79 feet square, in much the same way as the dome covers that of the Ibrāhīm Rauza. This is plainly shewn by the plan of the piers of the inner chamber where the necessary offsets are worked upon the inner sides, from which the cross arching of the pendentives was to spring in the usual way. The interior diameter of the dome would not have exceeded 60 feet, or 70 feet across the exterior. If the plan is compared with that of the Jāmi' Masjid, it will be seen that they are almost identical, so far as the great central space under the dome, and the inner corridor around it, are concerned, the scale of the 'Ali Rauza being a trifle larger. We may assume, therefore, that the roofing and dome would have been carried out, in the latter building, on much the same lines as in that of the earlier one. Plate C shows the building as it would probably have looked when completed. The very lofty basement would have added considerable dignity to the finished building. Its object, however, was to provide the necessary vaults for the actual graves beneath the mausoleum, the arched entrances to which are on the east, north and west sides, but now closed up.

Another similarity to the Jāmi' Masjid would have been in the finish of the wall surfaces, which, judging by the unfinished and rough surfaces of the present masonry, were to have been plastered. There is no indication that any elaborate surface carving was going to be indulged in, such as we find on the Ibrāhīm Rauza. In each of the great corner piers of the mausoleum is a square-planned winding staircase.

The most characteristic feature in this building is its arches. These are purely Gothic in outline, having been struck from two centres, the curves being carried up to the crowns. The form of arch, otherwise universal in Bījāpūr, is that where the curves, struck from two centres, and rising from their springings, meet, at a certain point, tangents to the curve, which continue the arch rings to the crown. This departure from the usual type gives the building rather the appearance of an old Gothic ruin, and these arch rings, which remain to this day, have regular voussoirs and key-stones. The centering for them was formed by rubble walling built up between the piers, with the top smoothed and plastered off to the curve for the soffit of the arch. The death of 'Ali, after a short reign of sixteen years, stopped the work and dispersed the workmen, and it was no one's business to complete it for him. Until lately, in fact, the chips and débris from the work remained piled up around the basement, and the temporary ramp to ascend to the tomb platform, in the absence of the steps, not begun, still serves that purpose. 'Ali's successor, Sikandar, had a shorter reign; and the anxiety and worry caused by the threatening attitude of the Mughals during his time, together with constant internal dissension, all working towards the disintegration of the kingdom, prevented this young king from even beginning a mausoleum for himself.

The south side of the inner chamber has had four or five feet of walling, with the bottom of a doorway, inserted between the piers. The central bay on the east side is still open, and so is that on the south. The west side is closed up by a temporary mosque. The corner bays, between the piers, are all closed in with walling. It is certain, therefore, that the sepulchral chamber, like that of the Ibrāhīm Rauza, was to be enclosed.

Although left unfinished, 'Ali was interred within the building, his grave being represented by the great tombstone upon the central platform; while, in the south-west corner, on a small platform, is the tombstone of a female, with the *bismillāh* formula inscribed around it, which is said to be the tomb of Khurshe Khānam, the wife of 'Ali 'Ādil Shāh and mother of Sikandar.[1] Beside these two graves there are fourteen others, twelve of them being the graves of females.

Very roughly built, within the mausoleum, is a small temporary mosque, put in, apparently, after 'Ali's death, to which the members of his household could resort for prayer for the dead. It is doubtful whether the general design for 'Ali's tomb ever included a mosque; if it did, the building would have been erected upon a separate platform, to the west of the great tomb platform. Such a mosque was never begun, or, at least, no evidence of such now remains.

The tombstone, itself, is very plain and severe in design. Around the top of the platform there are holes, about 10 inches square, for the posts of a railing or canopy of some sort which it was intended to put up.

THE 'ARSH AND PĀNĪ MAHALLS.

A building of which we know nothing, is that known as the 'Arsh Maḥall, which has been converted from a ruin into a residence for the local Civil Surgeon (Plates CI and CII). It, however, has no further interest for us since it is, as it stands, an almost entirely new construction. Reference has already been made to it in the section on the "Description of the City," where it has been identified with the Sikka ("Sicca") Maḥall of Captain Sydenham's account. But, out in front of it, upon one of the bastions of the old citadel wall, are the ruined walls of a little pavilion known as the Pānī Maḥall. This was, no doubt, originally, a little garden house or pleasure resort, occupying an elevated position overlooking the moat and plain beyond it. It is said that the king used to sit here and watch the parades of troops and elephant fights which took place upon the esplanade before it, which was called the Ālat-kā-Maidān. We are told in the *Basātīn-i-Salāṭīn* that Dilāwar Khān, on one occasion, invited king Ibrāhīm II. to sit upon a bastion of the *ḥiṣār* (citadel) in order to review the new troops which he had raised. The shifting of the parade ground, upon which also the elephant tournaments took place, from the inside to the outside of the citadel, was one of the things the emperor Shāh Jahān took umbrage at when he advised Sulṭān Muḥammad, under threats, to remove his court from the Āthār Maḥall back again to the citadel. But, from the inscriptions upon the walls of this little pavilion, it appears to have been erected by 'Ali II. If Muḥammad really used this particular bastion as tradition says he did, he probably sat beneath some temporary canopy on those occasions. It has probably been called the Pānī Maḥall as it overhung the surrounding water of the moat.

The front of the little building, of which a few small walls only remain, judging from the grooves in the masonry for the insertion of woodwork, was hung with curtains or screens of some kind; while, behind, are traces of brickwork where a cookroom appears to have been; and where, let into the middle of the floor, is a stone with a cup-shaped hollow in the middle of it, as if intended for husking rice or pounding curry stuff. The walls are covered with clean-cut surface ornament, in which is represented in low relief, plates with melons and other fruits and Persian wine bottles. There are a number of inscriptions, so disposed as to add to the surface decoration, one of which tells us that "on this bastion is built the

[1] It is also said to be that of 'Ali's nurse.

mansion of pleasure ". Another gives the name of 'Ali II. as Abūl Muzaffar Pādshāh 'Ali 'Ādilī. A third gives the date A. H. 1080 (A. D. 1669). A fourth says: "The writing was written by the slave of the palace, Taqī Al-Ḥusainī, in A. H. 1081." A fifth has the Shī'ah declaration of faith. A sixth tells us the verses (or it may be read houses) were composed (or built) by his majesty 'Ali 'Ādil Shāh Ghāzi. The masonry of these walls is particularly well-finished, and bears a striking resemblance to that of the little Makka Masjid, about three hundred yards to the south.

THE MAKKA MASJID.

One of the most perfect buildings, though very small, is the little Makka Masjid, shut in by very high walls in the south-eastern quarter of the citadel. These same high walls have always been a puzzle to visitors. They enclose, on three sides—north, south, and west, a large rectangular enclosure. They are very lofty and very solidly built. The eastern end was never completed, the ends of the north and south walls at this side remaining unfinished. Built within this end of the enclosure is the Makka Masjid, itself being enclosed, with its courtyard, within its own surrounding corridors. Embedded within the eastern end of these corridors are two old *mīnārs,* with spiral staircases ascending them; rotten remnants of wooden bracketting project from where the first gallery encircled them. These *mīnārs* have already been mentioned in describing the early buildings of Bījāpūr. They were, no doubt, part of an old mosque, which, falling into decay, or having been destroyed by the Hindus, was rebuilt at a much later period as the present Makka Masjid. It is possible that, while the original mosque was a ruin the great walls, behind it, were built, the intention being to remove the ruins of the old mosque and absorb the site within the projected enclosure. One can imagine the outcry, at such a juncture, of some fanatics, at the impiety of laying sacrilegious hands upon the ruin, for it is contrary to strict Musalman tenets to divert to any other use either the material or site of a once-built mosque. In spite, therefore, of the fact that the canons of Islām were being openly and freely violated in other directions in the city, the voice of religion prevailed in this case, and the building of the great walls at this end was discontinued, and a new mosque was subsequently built. But what were these high walls for? It is certain that they were not intended as a defence of any kind, for the four great arched openings in the south face have never been provided with doors, nor has any arrangement been provided in the masonry jambs for their insertion. On examining the end and north walls, inside, we find great square holes in the masonry, in a line, at a good height above the ground, which were apparently intended to receive the ends of beams that supported a lean-to roof or shed of some kind. The most plausible solution of the puzzle, then, is that here were the elephant stables, the high walls being intended to shut off all noise and smells from the palaces to the north and west of them. The arched entrances, on the side away from the palaces, are high enough to allow elephants, with their *mahāuts* upon them, to pass in and out freely. This idea receives some confirmation from the fact that, just outside the enclosure, on the south, and almost touching the wall, is a tower,[1] which on close inspection, turns out to have been a storehouse for grain.

[1] Called by some writers the 'Bijjanhalli' or 'Bickkanhalli' tower, as it had hitherto been supposed to be the old watch-tower of the village of Bijjanhalli, Bajkanhalli, or Bachaknalli, which village existed somewhere in this neighbourhood before Bījāpūr became a city.

It was roofed over, as may be seen from inside, where the slots in the top of the wall shew where the timbers were let in, and it was covered with eight or ten inches of concrete. Outside are the plastered channels or drains down the sides to carry off the rain water from the roof, such as exist down the west face of the Sāt Manzil. A doorway was made on the north side, near the high wall. Steps lead up the outside to the top, up which, as in the old granaries near the Jāmi' Masjid, the grain was carried and poured down through an opening in the roof into the chamber, being drawn off as required from the small doorway below.

But to revert to the Makka Masjid, which is so called because it is said to be on the same plan as the mosque at Makka (Plates CI and CII). It consists of the mosque chamber, which stands at the west end of a courtyard completely surrounded by a colonnade, the east end of which is deeper than the other three sides. There are two entrances—one on the north and one on the east. The style of masonry, the surface decoration, the finish, and the material used, agree more closely with the little Pānī Maḥall than with any other building in Bījāpūr; in fact, one cannot help thinking the same workmen were employed upon both. The edges of the masonry and the carving are almost as sharp today as when they left the hands of the masons; and this is due, in most part, to the protection of the high walls around. There is some very neat and crisp surface carving round the central *miḥrāb,* representing tombs, niches, hanging lamps or censers. It is worth while examining the masonry of the sides and back of the mosque, where it will be seen how indifferent masons were then with regard to laying their courses level and parallel. The blocks of stone, as they obtained them, were dressed to the nearest straight-lined figure, thus producing a regular patchwork. The absence in the mosque of a *mimbar* or pulpit, and the manner in which it is so thoroughly enclosed, point to it having been built for the use of women.

TOMB OF SHĀH NAWĀZ KHĀN.

By the roadside, on the way out to the Amīn Dargāh, and rather more than a mile from the Shāhpūr gate, is the tomb of Shāh Nawāz Khān, *wazīr*, who died in A. H. 1058 (A. D. 1647), or nine years before Muḥammad Shāh (Plates CIII and CIV). He was one of Bījāpūr's nobles, but his name does not figure very prominently in Bījāpūr history. This tomb, though of little architectural merit, is interesting as giving a general idea, on a small scale, of what Jahān Begam's tomb at 'Ainăpūr was probably intended to be like. The building, or rather group, is fairly complete. On the west of the tomb is the mosque, with a tank between them. The very stilted look of the upper walls of the central chamber, and the dome above, is not altogether pleasant, and there is a lack of good proportion between the different parts of the general design. Taken altogether it shows signs of a general decadence in monumental building, which set in in Bījāpūr with the interference of the Mughal emperors in the affairs of the state; and the drain on the state revenues, caused by excessive tribute exacted by Delhi, probably had also some effect upon the downward trend of architectural activity.

YĀQŪT DĀBULĪ'S MOSQUE AND TOMB.

Yāqut Dābuli, the Abyssinian slave, who was entrusted by Muḥammad Shāh with the elaborate colour decoration of the great *miḥrāb* in the Jāmi' Masjid, lies buried just outside the citadel to the north-east. His remains repose within a very small mausoleum, close beside which is the mosque, in this case a larger and more important building than the other (Plates CIII and CIV). The tomb is a compact little square structure with stone lattice work filling each of the three sides, the doorway being on the south side. Inside is a single tombstone over the grave of a male. Above the doorway is an inscription which reads, according to the late Mr. Rehatsek's translation :

> One atom of divine grace
> Is better than to be chief of 1,000 villages.

Between the two compartments of the inscription :

> Malik Yāqūt Chīnī.

The surname 'Chīnī' has, however, been challenged by a local Musalman gentleman, with considerable knowledge of Bījāpūr and its history, who maintained that the name should be Malik Yāqūt Jannatī. It is sometimes difficult to read these inscriptions correctly, when, as so often happens, the correct transcription in stone is made subservient to the decorative effect of the design formed by the interlacing of the letters. If there is not room for the necessary diacritical marks which distinguish letters whose forms are otherwise identical, they are left out, and often additional unnecessary and misleading ones are inserted to fill up vacant spaces. Here, for instance, the 'J' and 'Ch' are represented by the same shaped letter but with a different arrangement of dots, and without the dots either letter might well be read. Probably 'Jannati' is the correct reading. In the inscription in the *miḥrāb* of the Jāmi' Masjid, which gives his name, only the first two are given. Is it possible that this Malik Yāqūt could have been the architect of the Gol Gumbaz ?

The mosque, as it stands, does not seem to be the original edifice, which is encased within subsequent additions. A glance at the plan (Plate CIV) will shew that the central thick-walled portion is the original mosque, and that the side rooms and forward hall were added afterwards. The side additions are two-storeyed, the upper floors having no staircases to them ; there may have been a wooden one originally. The masonry of these additions is much superior to that of the original mosque. The additions account for the number of minarets upon the roof, the old mosque having its own, and the newer part having others.

The ceiling of the forward hall is worth notice. It is a wagon-vaulted one, divided into nine spaces, the central one being flat, as in the tomb of Pīr Sayyid Ḥamīd Qādirī and the Ibrāhīm Rauza.

On the roadside, under a *pīpal* tree, near the Kālī Masjid, is set up an inscribed slab which is said to have been brought from Yāqūt Dābulī's mosque. Of it the late Mr. Rehatsek wrote : "The inscription being rather barbarous, and, although intended for a mosque, not commencing with the usual *Bismillah,* had probably been rejected for these reasons, and never occupied the position intended for it. After the praises of the Prophet, those of Muḥammad Shāh Ghāzi are sounded in this inscription ; it contains, however, no date, and the words 'this mosque' occur in the last line. Probably the inscription was never completed."

Across the road from the mosque and tomb is the Travellers' Bungalow, constructed out of the ruins of Yāqūt Dābulī's Maḥall. The whitewashed grave in the enclosure is said to be that of Hazrat Hājī Rūmī, who came from Makka in A. H. 808, and died in 875 (A. D. 1368). If this be correct, it is the oldest known grave in the city.

THE TOMBS OF KHĀN MUHAMMAD AND 'ABDUL RAZZĀQ QĀDIRĪ.

These two tombs, the domes of which are very conspicuous objects, are known to European residents as the 'Two Sisters', and to natives as the Joḍ Gumbaz, or 'Twin Domes,' on account of their close proximity and likeness, in size and shape, to one another (Plates XCVI and CV). The octagonal building, on the south, is the resting place of the traitor Khān Muḥammad, or Khān Khānān as his sovereign called him, and of his son Khawāṣṣ Khān, *wazīr* to Sikandar. Khān Muḥammad, who was in command of the troops in the field, was bought over by the commander of the imperial forces of Dehli, and remained inactive at the critical juncture, when he had the enemy entirely in his hands. Afzal Khān, who was in the field with him, thoroughly disgusted, withdrew and returned to Bījāpūr, and reported to the king how matters stood. Khān Muḥammad was recalled, and, as he came into the city through the Makka gate, he was assassinated. Subsequently, Aurangzeb gave instructions that the tax for one year, which Bījāpūr was now annually obliged to remit to Dehli, should be used for the building of a tomb over Khān Muḥammad. Khawāṣṣ Khān, his son, *wazīr* to Sikandar, was infected with the same treasonable impulses which possessed his father, and he, too, after being imprisoned at Bankapūr, fell under the executioner's sword. His body was brought to Bījāpūr, and buried in the tomb of his father, which is thus generally called after him.

The larger square tomb is that of 'Abdul Razzāq Qādirī, Khawāṣṣ Khān's religious tutor or domestic chaplain, and was, no doubt, built at the same time as the other.

The floors of both tombs are at a very considerable elevation above the surrounding ground level, which is due to the vaults, containing the graves, being built upon the ground rather than beneath its surface, as is the case in most tombs. The tomb of 'Abdul Razzāq Qādirī is exceedingly plain, the square wall rising almost unbroken from the ground to the dome.

To the west of these two tombs is a third, which is said to be that of Sīdī Raiḥān. Sīdī Raiḥān Sholāpūri was an officer of note who distinguished himself during the reign of Sulṭān Muḥammad. It is alleged that he was purchased as a boy of seven years old, with his mother, by Ibrāhīm II. from a merchant at Nauraspūr, and was sent to the palace to be the playmate of young prince Muḥammad who was of the same age.

Within Khawāṣṣ Khān's tomb is one of the finest halls in Bījāpūr, unoccupied even by the usual counterfeit tombstones. This is unusual, and the absence of these has been taken to indicate that the hall was used as a dwelling. This was hardly so. As the tombs were built by Aurangzeb, it is very likely he had ordered marble tombstones from northern India or elsewhere, such as are usual in Gujarāt and Hindustān, but for some reason or other, they never reached Bījāpūr. He did precisely the same thing for his wife's tomb in the Nau Bāgh, and some of the marble slabs still lie in the lower rooms of the Āthār Maḥall.

This building was used, with the mosque attached, as an Executive Engineer's office and dwelling, but, owing to the great reverence with which the Muḥammadans hold the memory of the saint 'Abdul Razzāq, his tomb was not converted into a dwelling. These two tombs are the only other buildings, besides the Gol Gumbaz, that have galleries within the domes, but, owing to the small diameter of the latter, they have no distinct echo.

On the south side of the road, and close to the Joḍ Gumbaz, on the east, were two great baobab *(Andansonia digitata)* trees, known in the vernacular as Gorak Imlīs. Only one of these now survives, the greater one, of over fifty feet girth, having fallen a few years ago. Tradition points to these as the original execution trees of the 'Ādil Shāhi régime.

Fig. 25. One of the baobab or execution trees.

It is said that beneath them all executions took place, when the grim executioner, sword in hand, made his last salam to his victim. For the greater part of the year these trees look forbidding enough, with their gaunt and gnarled branches, bare of all foliage, and their bloated trunks. They might well be associated with the last terrible penalty of the law and the dread work of the executioner. Yet, in their season, they produce a fruit from which the Muḥammadans make a refreshing sherbet, which is much appreciated in the hot weather. Another tree, even more connected with the dead than this, is the custard apple, which thrives in old graveyards. These baobabs, with others in the suburbs, are supposed to have been introduced from Africa by Abyssinians who settled in Bījāpūr. They are often found on the sites of old Muḥammadan towns in western and central India—Nālchā, below Māṇḍū, in the Dhār State, for instance, is full of them ; and it is doubtful which are the more numerous, the baobabs or the ruined tombs and mosques scattered about among them. Fig. 25 shews one of the Bījāpūr execution trees.

THE TOMBS OF HAZRAT SAYYID KARĪM MUḤAMMAD ṢĀḤIB AND HAZRAT SAYYID 'ABDUL RAḤMĀN.

Close to the south-east corner of the Jāmi' Masjid is the small tomb of Hazrat Sayyid Karīm Muḥammad Ṣāḥīb, a local saint and son of Muḥammad Mudris, who died in A. H. 1105 (A. D. 1693). The mausoleum, however, does not seem to have been erected over his remains until 1731, if the chronogram in the inscription over the doorway is correctly deciphered. The inscription tells us that this wonderful *dargāh* had become a delightful place of pilgrimage for disciples, and the chronogram is in the words "The world is in the shadow of this cupola of Shāh Karīm". (Plate CVI.)

The general design of the building is similar to that of Shāh Nawāz Khān's tomb, except that the exterior arches are walled in and filled with doors and windows. The proportions of the building are better, the inner chamber being larger in proportion to the outside walls, with the result that the second storey, rising above the first roof, is larger, and, with the dome, forms a better and more pleasing pyramidal form of outline than the other.

The interior of the dome and the pendentives have a silvery sheen, due, it is said, to the use of powdered mother-of-pearl used in the whitewash that has been applied. Around the windows on the west, inside, is some very good surface decoration in stone, while upon the doors are decorative iron bosses like those at the Mihtar Maḥall, but simpler in design (Plate LXVII). Within the tomb, under the dome, are four graves—three male and one female—and in the west verandah is one male tomb. The eastern grave, beneath the dome is that of Shāh Karīm, that in the west verandah is that of Hazrat Pādshāh. The building is under the care of the Jāgīrdār of Fatḥpūr. At this tomb is kept the old Bāra Imān *panja* or *'alam* (standard), which is carried at the time of the Muḥarram procession. It is said to be composed of five metals. It is a beautiful bit of work (Fig. 26).

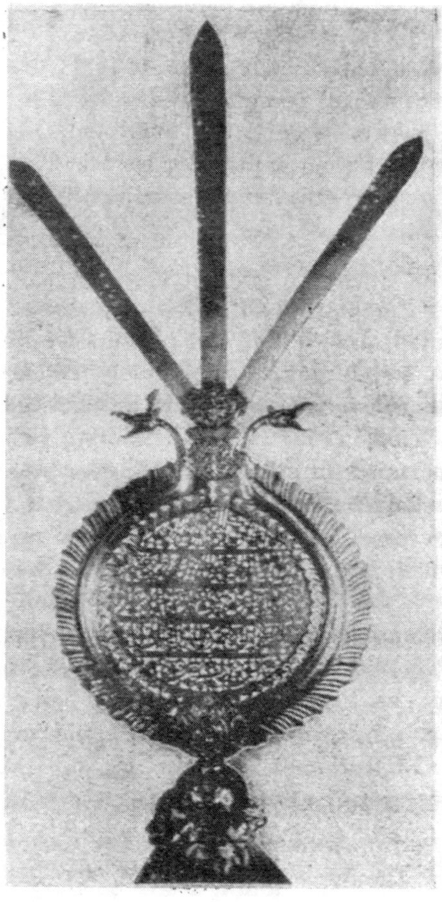

Fig. 26. Metal *panja* or standard.

Opposite the last, on the east, is a very similar tomb, said to be that of Hazrat Sayyid 'Abdul Raḥmān, another son of Muḥammad Mudris, whose death is put in A. H. 1120 (A. D. 1710). The inside of this building has the same silvery lustre, but here the decoration is in raised plaster work, which is picked out with red (Plate CVII). This building is in the charge of the Jāgīrdār of Nandihāl.

ALLĀH BĀBŪ'S MOSQUE AND TOMB.

A group of small buildings, which goes by the name of Allāh Bābū's mosque and tomb, not far to the south-west of the Gol Gumbaz, shews how debased the style had become towards the end of the 'Ādil Shāhi period (Plates CV and CVI). Placed upon a very high basement, under which is a series of burial vaults, these little buildings are more conspicuous than interesting from any historical associations; for who Allāh Bābū was no one knows. They are badly built of rubble and plaster, and consist of a small square tomb pavilion and a mosque. What is most noticeable is the very stilted, narrow-necked domes. The dome has, practically, parted company with the ceiling and roof; it no longer even pretends to fulfil the function of a domical ceiling to either the tomb or mosque. It is a mere ornamental excrescence upon the roof, the little square, upon which it is raised from the roof, having become a second storey, but with no means of access to it. In this group may be plainly seen the transition to the style of work carried out in later years at Hyderābād and elsewhere.

As the tomb pavilion stands in front of the addition to the north end of the mosque, which is, in fact, an older and very much more roughly-built mosque, it is possible that the grave was, at first, without shelter, in the open, beside which this old mosque was built. Subsequently the pavilion was built over it, together with the newer mosque to match, the older one just being allowed to remain. Judging from the size of the vaulted chambers, there must have been many interments here; and, if the pavilion covers the remains of a saint, it would be but natural for his followers to wish to be buried beside him. But in the local list of Bījāpūr's saints the name of Allāh Bābū does not occur.

THE CHINCH DIDDĪ MASJID.

Perched upon a lofty bastion of the citadels walls, on its eastern side near the Āthār Maḥall, and, in this conspicuous position, overlooking the city to the east, north, and south, is a small mosque, commonly called the Chinch Diddī mosque, after the *diddī* or postern gate below it (Plate CVIII). It is a very plain building with little about it of interest, save the remains of some wall painting within, which is very poor and weak, and has more the appearance of cheap common wall paper. It is said that the proper name of the building is Chindaṛi Masjid, *chindaṛi,* referring to the chintz-like pattern on the walls, which is similar to patterns of clothes commonly worn by women. The building known as Mubārak Khān's Maḥall, in the south-east quarter of the city, was decorated in the same way; but, in neither case is the work anything like the more solid wall painting at Kumatgī, described further on. Muḥammadans are fond of elevated spots for their evening prayers, and the terraces on the roofs of houses were favourite places. It is not unlikely that it was built by Muḥammad Shāh when he erected the Āthār Maḥall; and it would have been a pleasant spot for his evening's devotions, where he could have passed away an hour at sunset watching the busy hive of workmen and the gigantic network of scaffolding enveloping the rising walls of his own great mausoleum.

It is, without doubt, a late building. To make the old bastion stouter and stronger to carry the mosque, it was further encased within an extra thickness of arched masonry; while a firm foundation was obtained upon the top by laying great heavy cross beams of wood under the foundations of the building.

THE MULLĀ MASJID.

The Mullā Masjid, also called Malik Raiḥān's Masjid, is situated within the suburb of of Shāhpūr or Khudanpūr, without the Shāhpūr gate. It is a very neat little building, in a good state of preservation, having its cornice and parapet almost intact. The front minarets are very graceful and well-proportioned, and the little *minārs* over the central piers enhance the general effect. The façade is, perhaps, just a trifle spoilt, as that of Malikah Jahān Begam's is also, by the arches being a little too low for the best proportions. The dome is of the high stilted type, drawn in at the neck where the band of leaves encircles it; and, as was the tendency in later buildings, it has become but a ball ornament. The mosque has been used, of late, to house a Hindustānī school.

The only Malik, or Sīdī Raiḥān, of note was he whose tomb is close beside that of Khawāṣṣ Khān, and who has already been briefly noticed in the account of the tomb. It is doubtful if there is any connection between the two.

In the garden, on the north side of this mosque, is a very neat little square tomb, said to be the resting place of Shamsah Māī Ṣāḥiba, a local saint, and grand-daughter of Sayyid Muḥammad Ḥusainī. Her father was Avval Chishtī. Another saint buried here was Hazrat Shāh Abū-l-Ḥusain Faqrābādi, grandson of Khwājah Banda Nawāz, who came to Bījāpūr during the lifetime of Ibrāhīm II. and died in the reign of Muḥammad Shāh.

A little way beyond this, again, is a curious long arcade, open along the south side, containing a row of tombs which give it the appearance of a family burying place, more especially as the tombs are those of both males and females. There are about sixteen, the majority being those of the latter. The arcade is divided by its pillars and cross beams into bays; and it would seem that each bay had been set apart for one man and his near relations, who are buried on either side of him. Thus, in some, the central space, reserved for the head of the family, has not been occupied, the space for the grave being left unpaved, while other graves are on either side of it. In the sixth bay from the east end is a tomb more ornate than the rest, being partitioned off from them by cross walls. All the tombs up to this, on the east, are of cut-stone, set upon high plinths, while those that continue on the west are meanly built of brick and mortar, and are set flat upon the floor without plinths. This may, perhaps, be the result of a sudden fall of the family from opulence to poverty, and thus exhibits, in its silent way, the uncertainty of life and fortune in those days. The only inscription to be found in this arcade is upon one of the cut-stone tombs, which is nothing but the simple name 'Alif Khān', and which leaves us no wiser than before. The family appears to have gone on using this place for their interments, for, after filling this arcade, two further bays have been added, though not joined to it, of inferior construction. In this are two tombs.

THE DHĀĪWĀDĪ MASJID.

Two hundred and fifty yards west of the Allāhpūr gate, on the south side of the road, is a mosque known as the Dhāīwādī Masjid, which is said to have been built for the husbands of the *dhāī* women, or wet-nurses, who lived in this *wādī* or hamlet. Its minarets, only one of which now rises above the roof, are of a different pattern to any others in the city. In plan, their outline might be called an octofoil, that is, it is bounded by eight convex curves, so that, in elevation, they have something of the appearance of clustered columns, tied round with narrow fillets at intervals. The pendentives, within, are rather well designed, those in the central bay being prettily ornamented. On the façade are some good plaster medallions containing interwoven Persian or Arabic letters, and other ornament decorates the crowns of the arches. The cornice is fair, but the slabs are damaged.

THE AMĪN DARGĀH AND HĀSHIM PĪR'S TOMB.

This first tomb, one of the two most sacred in Bījāpūr, the other being that of Hazrat Hāshim Pīr, near the Gol Gumbaz, is that of Ḥazrat Khwājah Amīn-ud-dīn, a saint and son of Shāh Burhān-ud-dīn, who died in A. H. 1075 (A. D. 1664). The building is said to have been erected by Afzal Khan, *wazīr,* whose cenotaph lies about a mile to the west by south of it. There is nothing particularly interesting about it architecturally. It is a very conspicuous landmark for miles around owing to its elevated position and its whitewash, which has been liberally applied to it.

Hāshim Pīr was Ḥazrat Hāshim Ḥusaini, nephew of Wajīhu-d-dīn Gujarāti,[1] who died in A. H. 1056 (A. D. 1646).

THE DAULAT KOṬHĪ AND 'AINĀPŪR MAḤALL.

There are very few remains of the palaces of the nobles left in Bījāpūr. Besides that of Muṣtafā Khān and the pavilion of Mubārak Khān, already noticed, there are the remains of the Fatḥ Mahall (No. 8 on plan), said to have belonged to a Fatḥ Khān, *wazīr.* It was, a short time ago, a picturesque ruin, consisting of a large square tank surrounded by a high wall, with remains of buildings on the south side. Its material will probably now have been carted away to make room for modern progress and requirements.

Two standing examples of the lesser palaces, or dwellings of well-to-do folk, are the palace at 'Aināpūr and the Daulat Koṭhī in the town, not more than about three or four hundred yards north of the Jāmi' Masjid. The latter is a large solid-looking building, composed of fairly good masonry, and in a fair state of preservation. It faces north. The general plan of the rooms may be seen on Plate CIX, a large open hall on both the north and south sides being separated from one another by a central line of rooms, and flanked by suites of rooms which lay at right angles to the direction of the middle ones. The great halls open outwards, and each has two columns in front to support the roof. In the larger buildings of this class there was an upper storey over the central block and wings and the height of the hall was the full height of these two storeys, so that the windows of the upper rooms looked down into the hall. Ornamental niches for oil lamps, and other decorations adorn the walls. This building is said to have been erected during the time of Sulṭān Muḥammad.

The 'Aināpūr *maḥall* is in the fields at a short distance to the west of 'Aināpūr village. It is a very complete structure, and is in very good repair (Plates CVIII and CIX). It is built on the same general plan as other *maḥalls,* and has the same vaulted roof over the outer hall. Above the entrance doorway is inserted a slab bearing an inscription, which is rather illegible, but seems to contain neither date nor name of any person.

[1] This saint's tomb is in Aḥmadābād.

For the size of the building, and the general appearance from outside, the interior accommodation is very limited indeed. There are but three rooms that could be closed, and the forward hall which is open in front. The two side ones, which measure 33 feet by 15 feet 6 inches, were each, perhaps, divided into two apartments by *pardahs* or curtains hung across under the central arch. The men of the household would spend most of their time in the large open hall or the ample verandah in front of it. From the section it will be seen that there are two fine terraces on the roof, which could be used for sleeping out upon during the hot sultry nights of the hot weather, the lower one quite sheltered by high walls for the women folk. The lighting of these interiors was very poor, as bad almost as the ventilation, but light and air were not essentials in designing them. Then again, what windows were provided, were generally closed by grills and lattices, for the sake of privacy for the women.

AMBĀR KHĀNĀS.

A large city like Bījāpūr could not hold out long in a siege without having ample stores of grain laid up for such an emergency, and for this purpose extensive storehouses were necessary. Two of these, called *ambār khānās,* still exist, and stand by the road side some three or four hundred yards to the east of the Jāmi' Masjid. Each range is divided into rooms, and each room is provided with a circular hole, about eighteen inches in diameter, in the roof. There is a doorway, with shutters fitting in grooves, and air vents in the roof for ventilation. There are ten doorways in the front of the longer range, and three in that of the other. A staircase ascends to the roof, up which the grain was carried and shot through the apertures above into the rooms. This staircase does not extend right down to the ground, but stops short at about seven feet from it. No doubt, portable wooden ones fitted the gap, which were removed when not required, so preventing unauthorized persons or animals from getting on to the roof. As required, the grain was drawn off at the doorways below, the shutters being manœuvred accordingly. Brackets run along the front face, with a little circular notch in the top of each, as if for the purpose of supporting a temporary lean-to roof, perhaps, to cover the clerks and servants engaged in doling out the grain. On the face of the longer block of store rooms (No. 173 on plan) is an inscription which reads:

> When Muḥammad Shāh Ghāzī constructed that maḥall
> He raised the middle of the citadel like a ball.
> This edifice, how strong it appears! He built with joy in the year 1053
> which had elapsed since the Hijrah.
>
> [A. D. 1643-44.]

The small ruin, marked No. 190, in the south-east quarter of the town, appears, also, to have been a granary or *ambār khānah.*

THE GRAVE OF SIKANDAR 'ĀDIL SHĀH.

Sikandar, the last of the Bījāpūr dynasty, does not appear to have attempted to build a mausoleum for himself. He was but five years of age when he ascended the throne and not more than twenty when he was dispossessed. He had, therefore, hardly time to think about the matter, more especially as the state was rapidly falling to pieces. He was buried in a simple grave, in the open air, situated in the *bāzār,* almost midway between the Dakhanī 'Īdgāh and the unfinished mausoleum of 'Ali 'Ādil Shāh II.

THE WATER-WORKS OF THE CITY.

NOT only was the storage of grain in sufficient quantities of vital necessity to Bījāpūr but an adequate supply of water was also most essential. We find that provision for this was not neglected ; and the plentiful distribution of tanks or reservoirs, wells and water towers, together with a great ramification of water pipes and aqueducts, shows how keenly alive the 'Ādil Shāhis were to the due provision for these needs. The immense population, crowded into Bījāpūr during the reigns of Ibrāhīm II., Muḥammad and 'Ālī II., required a great deal of water, perhaps, twice as much as a modern city of the same size, with its restrictions as to waste and unnecessary consumption. Not only did the Hindu love to wallow in it, and require a great deal for his many ceremonial ablutions, but the well-to-do Muḥammadan was, in those days, more lavish of it still. The latter had great partiality for the presence of water, and he knew full well, and appreciated the cooling effects of tanks and cisterns of cold water within and around his dwelling. When he could afford it, he loved to have it gurgling down his garden in ornamental channels, splashing in and out of cisterns on its way. To give a prettier effect to the running water, the floors of these channels were often cut into zigzag ridges, or were strewn with little fishes in relief, against which the water plashed and spirtled in myriads of sparkling ripples. These channel beds were, in many instances, of very complicated patterns. Some of the larger were divided into compartments, each of which was channelled into a maze of windings. The water, entering at one end, and travelling round and round through all these tiny channels, in and out, redoubled upon itself a dozen times, and finally slipped out at the opposite end into another, only to go through its tortuous meanderings, again and again, down the length of the garden. The effect, though bewildering, must have been very pleasing, for the divisions between the channels are very narrow, being just enough to separate the various streams racing in opposite directions (Plate CXIII).

These, together with cool chunam or marble pavements, covered in with thick masonry walls and roofs, afforded luxurious retreats from the glare and scorching heat of a summer sun. In their palaces, even in cool subterranean vaults, they had their chunam-lined baths and fountains. In the Sāt Manzil, as already noticed, they had, at least, one masonry basin or bath upon each floor, with octagonal, square, or fluted sides; and, away upon the highest storey now remaining, are traces of a bath. Their palaces usually had a large square tank within the walled enclosure. It may be seen in the ruined palaces of Fatḥ Khān and Muṣṭafā Khān. *Ḥammāms,* or public baths, were also much in vogue and some of them, judging by the remnants that remain, were often very complex and luxurious apartments. Truly the waste of water must have far exceeded its use!

Fortunately Bījāpūr has water near the surface, and wells were sunk everywhere. These may have sufficed for the ordinary needs of the people. The only way to get water in larger quantities was to bring it in from great reservoirs located upon higher ground without the city. Some of these exist to the present day, though their connections are either completely ruined or are sadly out of repair. Nevertheless some of the pipes are still working. One of these large reservoirs was the Begam Talāo to the south of the town, from which water was brought in through earthen pipes. These were in short lengths, made with a flange at one end and embedded firmly in concrete. In some cases the pipes have a narrow neck at one end to fit into the next. At intervals along the lengths of piping were built lofty square water towers, intended as traps to intercept silt and prevent the pipes being choked, as well as to relieve the pressure in the pipes. The inlet pipe enters the tower at a comparatively low level, whereas the take-off pipe leaves it at a much higher level, carrying off the clearer water from which the silt has subsided. The towers, no doubt, were periodically cleaned out. Some of the larger towers in the town are distributing centres; and from one of these alone, that on the north side of the Makka Masjid, upwards of seventy pipes lead away in different directions amongst the buildings in the citadel.

From the Surang Bāurī, near Torweh, water was brought towards the city by a great subterranean tunnel. At the *bāurī,* near the Khān Sarvar at Afzal Khān's wives' tombs, it may be seen, low down in the north side of the well, as a masonry tunnel with an arched top, curving rapidly round to the eastward. It then makes a bee-line for the Motī Dargāh, where it deflects more to the east, and passes beneath the gardens of the Ibrāhīm Rauza enclosure. To this point its direction is easily traced by the manholes, or air shafts, placed at frequent intervals along its course; beyond this it is lost, and only extensive excavations would settle its further course. For the greater part of its length, it is roughly cut through the *murum,* or disintegrated rock, the water being in some parts over sixty feet below the surface. A curious thing, at first sight, about this tunnel, is that it is built up with masonry upon one side only. The reason for this is that the strata of rock and *murum,* through which it passes, dip from south to north, so that water percolating down through the strata is intercepted and falls into the tunnel where it is diverted towards the city, the opposite side of the tunnel being concreted to prevent its escape. It is thus a catchment tunnel, for the small well—the Surang Bāurī from which it starts—could not, of course, supply any quantity of water. As far as can at present be gathered, the tunnel appears to have entered the city by the Makka gate, and then to have branched off in different directions, one branch steering westward through the old palace of Khawāṣṣ Khān, thence under the road in front of the Tāj Bāurī, being probably connected with it by pipes,[1] on to the garden at Khawāṣṣ Khān's tomb (the Joḍ Gumbaz), and thence along the road, on the south side

[1] In the north-east corner of the *bāurī* nearest the tunnel, is a perennial flow of water into the tank which probably comes from the tunnel.

of the tomb towards a spot on the south side of the road near the citadel gateway. Another branch seems to have started off in a north-easterly direction, possibly supplying water to the water towers between the unfinished tomb of 'Āli II. and Fatḥ Khān's palace.

Three of these water towers have inscriptions upon them. Upon that numbered 67, a little to the north of the tomb of 'Ali I., is a slab bearing the following effusion:

> Let it be manifest to the intellects of those that belong to the noble profession of constructors of wonderful works and rare edifices in the picture gallery of the world that—by the command of the glorious and powerful Pādshāh, whose court is prosperous like that of Solomon, and the zenith of eminence, the Sulṭān Muḥammad Ghāzi—the Khān, twin brother of prosperity, commander-in-chief of the period, foremost of the nobles in the country of the Dakhan, recipient of the lights of divine grace, Afzal Khān Muḥammad Shāhi—if he should aspire to the highest sphere he would be the excellent among the excellent, and the most excellent of the excellent, his praises resounding from every region when Afzal, Afzal [most excellent, most excellent] is mentioned—has with full care made this excavation of the tank—which is called after Muḥammad, a name of the greatest comfort to the people of God—that the thirsty-lipped people of the world may drink to their heart's content of this water, and that having become contented, they may always keep their tongues moistened with prayers for the ever-enduring Sultanate of the Pādshāh, who is the asylum of the universe, year 1062.
>
> [A. D. 1651-52.]

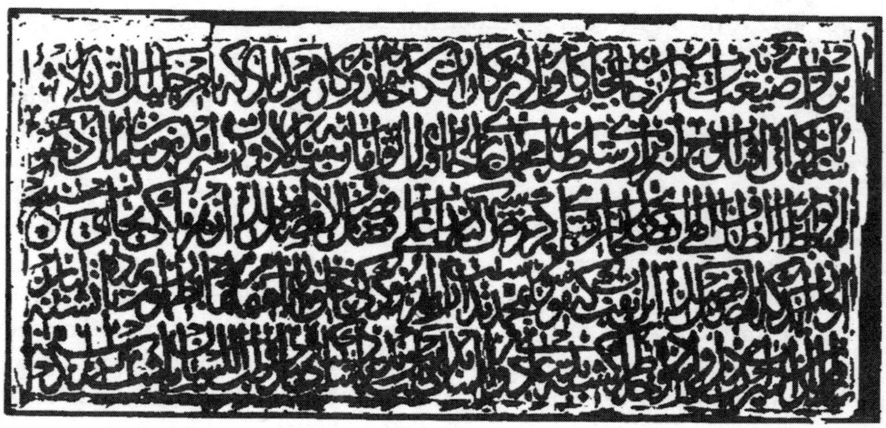

Fig. 27. The inscription on water tower No. 67.

Upon the water tower near the Anḍā Masjid, No. 91, are three inscriptions, the first reading:

> If the sagacious son, endowed with the sign of prosperity, the commander-in-chief of the period, were to aspire to the highest sphere [it would be] excellent, excellent, and the excellence of Afzal. In every land his praises are sung when Afzal, Afzal [most excellent, most excellent] the quintessence of well-wishers, the conqueror of the region is mentioned. Afzal Khān Muḥammad Shāhi has made the excavation of the tank, etc. [The rest is entirely as in the preceding.]

The second is much in the same strain, while the third is the same as that on water tower No. 67, only that the date of the year at the end is omitted. Three more inscribed slabs are found upon the tower, No. 115, near the Āthār Mahall. Of these, two are duplicates of two on tower No. 91, while the third is the same as that on tower No. 67.

The principal tanks and wells in the town are, the great Tāj Bāurī, the largest and most important; the Chānd Bāurī, near the Shāhpūr gate; the Barī and Mubārak Khān's Bāurīs in the south-east; the Māsā and Nīm Bāurīs in the north-east quarter of the city; the Hilāl and Nagar Bāurīs; and the Jāmi' Masjid Bāurī. There were many other large ones, the ruin of which may still be seen, but they have fallen into disrepair and now hold no water.

THE TĀJ BĀURĪ.

The great Tāj Bāurī is situated in the west end of the city, near to the Makka gate. It is square in plan—223 feet each way—and is enclosed within high walls on the east, south, and west, and a range of apartments along its north side (Plates CX and CXIV).

Fig. 28. Broken arch at the end of the east wing of the Tāj Bāurī.

The entrance is through the middle of this, by a broad flight of steps over which is thrown a lofty arch, 35 feet in span, flanked by octagonal towers. The apartments on the east and west of this entrance were intended for the temporary accommodation of travellers.

Descending the broad flight of steps between the towers, and passing under the great arch, we come upon a broad terrace or landing which juts out into the water of the tank, from which flights of steps on both sides lead down to the water's edge. Around the inner side of the high wall that encloses it, runs a narrow gallery or terrace, with a low parapet wall on the inner side. This communicates with sets of rooms in the middle of each of the three sides which overlook the tank, those on the south side being appropriated and converted into a Hindu shrine dedicated to Baladeva. Above the sides of the tank are arrangements for raising water, those on the south being still used to irrigate the gardens behind.

Part of the western wing of the rooms on the north side is used as municipal offices while the eastern wing has been used by a Kanarese school, and is partly in ruins. In connection with the description of the flat ceilings in the Ibrāhīm Rauza and the Mihtar Maḥall already described, it may be well to notice the construction of a large, but rather flat dome, partly fallen, at the end of the east wing here (Fig. 28), and observe how the stone slabs form a lining to a concrete roof, and are not really self-supported; they are held in their places simply by the adhesiveness of the mortar used.

There are different stories current accounting for the construction of this work. One says it was built by Malik Ṣandal, the architect of the Ibrāhīm Rauza, in honour of Tāj Sulṭāna, the queen of Ibrāhīm II., in the year A. D. 1620. Another affirms that Sulṭān Muḥammad, having done Malik Ṣandal a great injustice, and wishing to make reparation for the same, asked him to name anything he liked and he would grant it him. Having no children through whom to hand down his name to posterity, he asked that he might be allowed to construct some substantial piece of work by which his name might be perpetuated. This was granted, and the king, himself, supplied him with the necessary funds for constructing this tank which was to be his memorial.

THE C̲H̲ĀṆD BĀURĪ.

Another tank of the same class, but very much smaller, is the C̲h̲āṇd Bāurī near the S̲h̲āhpūr gate. It is also called the C̲h̲aṇda Bāurī. This was the model upon which the Tāj Bāurī was designed; and, in general arrangement, it is like that one, though not so fine. The arch spanning the entrance, which is on the east, and the terrace around the inside, with rooms in the south, are copied, with improvements, in the Tāj Bāurī. Its construction is attributed to the famous C̲h̲āṇd Bībī, Meadows Taylor's *Noble Queen.*

THE PAVILIONS AT KUMATGĪ.

AT the small village of Kumatgī, ten miles east of Bījāpūr, on the Hippargi road, are some old buildings which are interesting enough to be described with those of the city itself. It was, at one time, a place frequented by the nobles and, perhaps, the court of Bījāpūr, as a pleasure resort. There is at this place a large lake—except in times of drought when it dries up—on one side of which are the remains of several buildings, walls and gateways. Chief among these, are some little pavilions with tanks and cisterns about them. Upon the walls of one of these are some very remarkable and interesting frescoes, which must be well over two hundred years old (Plates CX—CXIII).

Over one archway is a spirited representation of the game of polo, where not only the men but the horses, too, seem to enjoy the sport (Plate CXIII). Two horsemen, in the centre, have the ball between their sticks, which are of the usual shape as used at present, and each is trying to get possession of it by hooking it away from the other. Two other horsemen, also equipped with polo sticks, are standing by waiting for the release of the ball. Over an opposite arch is a hunting scene, where the mounted hunters are chasing tigers, leopards, and deer. Around the lower parts of these two arches is some very pretty bird ornament. There are also representations of persons who, from their peculiar dress and light complexions, appear to be Europeans of note: they are possibly portraits of envoys or ambassadors who visited the Bījāpūr Court (Plate CXI). On another wall is the full length figure of a musician who plays upon a guitar whilst a queen and her maid sit listening. It is evident the musician, who, from his head-dress and flowing robes, might be a Persian, is trying to make an impression upon the ladies, for he holds his head on one side in a very lackadaisical manner as he plays. It reminds one strongly of a scene from 'Lalla Rookh', but for the absence of the grumpy old chamberlain. But, although he is not here to interrupt the pleasure of this little entertainment, we have him on another part of the walls, or a portrait that might well be his. Another scene, rather indistinct in parts, depicts a wrestling match that is going on before a seated and several standing figures. On another wall are two seated figures, clad in tiger-skin garments, with tiger-face visors thrown up on the forehead. They are armed and have their horses beside them. They appear to have met on the road, and are sitting under a tree that has some most curiously shaped birds in its branches. Strapped on the arms of the two figures are guards, which are, no doubt, intended to take the place of shields in hand-to-hand combats (Plate CXIII).

The surface of the walls, and, consequently the paintings, have suffered very great damage from having been scribbled over, scratched and smoked. Kumatgī was very likely resorted to by the nobles of Bījāpūr for hunting; and the great artificial lake, upon the border of which several of these little chateaux stand, must have made it a favourite and pleasant spot. Its wild-fowl attract the sportsmen at the present day, and a trip to Kumatgī for a day's shooting, in the season, is one of the pleasures the Bījāpūr folk still enjoy.

There are here extensive ruins of a small town or *bāzār,* which appears to have been walled in, and there is a long broad road, down each side of which is a fine row of stabling arcade for horses of masters and followers. From this a broad road led down, through a great gateway, along the margin of the lake and past the different pavilions.

Not the least of their enjoyments were the cool refreshing fountains and cisterns. In fact, the elaborate waterworks in, and around, these buildings, is the chief characteristic of them. Out in front of the painted pavilion, and rising out of the large square tank, is a two-storeyed building, through the masonry of which, pipes are carried up to scores of jets on both storeys. These all open outward, and when the water was turned on, and spouted forth from every possible point, splashing into the tank below, it must have been a very refreshing sight. The water was raised by manual and bullock labour to a cistern on the top of a high tower, and from this was distributed through pipes to the various points below.

Not content with this grand display before the pavilion they must needs have more of it within. From a large chunam-lined tank on the roof, water was allowed to descend through a great perforated rose sprinkler in the centre of the ceiling, forming a splendid shower bath, with a cistern below it to wallow in. What thorough enjoyment this must have been in the hot, dry weather! Surely those proud old warriors, who made the welkin ring with the clash of steel when occasion demanded it, knew, too, how to make the best of life in their idle moments!

THE COINAGE OF BĪJĀPŪR.

It is very probable that for some time after Yūsuf's secession from Bīdar that the Bījāpūr state continued to use the Bahmanī coinage. When the 'Ādil Shāhis began to coin their own money is not known, and, until recently, nothing was definitely known of any distinctive Bījāpūr currency. During my last two or three visits to that city, I made special enquiries for 'Ādil Shāhi coins with the result that I was able to collect between two and three hundred copper coins, which, from the little I was able to glean from their superscriptions, I concluded were mostly, if not all, of that dynasty. I passed these on to the Reverend Dr. George Taylor of Aḥmedābād, an expert upon Muḥammadan coins, who examined them very carefully and eventually wrote a paper upon them to the *Numismatic Supplement* to the Journal of the Asiatic Society of Bengal.[1] This article is accompanied by a plate of reconstructed representations of the inscriptions upon the coins, that is, of the dies used. No single coin was found to contain more than a portion of the legends, but by copying a bit from one and a bit from another it was possible to build up superscriptions of all except for a small area on Nos. 6 and 7 in the plate. Nothing on them, however, shews that they definitely belong to Bījāpūr. The names of regnant kings, without the fathers' names, alone are given. But, as pointed out by Dr. Taylor, that apart from the fact of their having been found at Bījāpūr, the names of the five kings found upon them—'Ali, Ibrāhīm, Muḥammad, a second 'Ali and Sikandar—and their order, where dates are given, agree with the names and order of five of the Bījāpūr kings as known from history, and this fully warrants us in assuming, without any reasonable doubt, that they are Bījāpūr coins. Moreover, the inscriptions upon one of the types bears the title of 'Ādil Shāh, a distinctive title of the Bījāpūr dynasty. Dr. Taylor says :

"So far as I am aware, no coins of this dynasty have hitherto been published, and a Bījāpūr currency, prior to Aurangzeb's annexation of the kingdom, has not been registered in any book on Numismatics. But, having regard to the pomp and splendour of the 'Adil Shāhs, a glory attested by the noble monuments and graceful memorials that still remain in the city of Bījāpūr, 'the Palmyra of the Dakhan', it is well nigh incredible that these proud monarchs, during the two centuries of their independence, should have been content to use an alien currency. More than once, indeed, had the conjecture been hazarded that they did strike coins of their own, and today some of these coins of theirs we hold in our hand."

---

[1] No. XV, arts. 90 and 91, p. 678.

The only reference he had found to any actual Bījāpūr currency is that in Beale's *Oriental Biographical Dictionary*, where that writer states, with reference to Muḥammad 'Ādil Shāh, " He was the last king of Bījāpūr who struck coins in his own name ". There is a reference to Bījāpūr coinage in the *Basātīn-i-Salāṭīn*, where it is said that Ibrāhīm II. struck copper coins, stamped with the name *nauras* in honour of the foundation of the new city of Nauraspūr, and the royal coin, whatever value that was, was designated the 'Ibrāhīm Nauras'. In another place it is stated that the coins in existence in the time of Sulṭān Muḥammad were the *muhur, hūn, dharan,* and *partāb,* the *partāb* being a quarter of a *hūn,* and the *dharan* a half *hūn.* These were, no doubt, gold coins. 'Ālamgīr introduced rupees.

Plate CXV shews specimens of these coins side by side with the complete dies, and represents nine different types. There is a tenth which has not been reconstructed. No. 1 is of 'Ali I.; Nos. 2, 3, and 4 are of Ibrāhīm II.; Nos. 5, 6 and 7 are of Muḥammad; No. 8 is of 'Ali II.; and No. 9 of Sikandar.

Silver or gold coins of the ordinary shape are not known, but silver currency of quite a different type was in use along the Bījāpūr sea coast, superscribed with an 'Ādil Shāhi legend. These are constructed of silver wire, about an eighth of an inch thick, in lengths of about three to four inches, bent double like a hair-pin or cotter-pin. The two arms seem to have been flattened against one another in a vice between dies, which at the same time left the inscription in relief upon these arms. They are known as *lārins,* and have been found at different places along the western coast from the Persian Gulf to Ceylon; and, being supposed to have originated in the district of Lār at the head of the Gulf, they have received the name they go by. They were probably coined by other states beside Bījāpūr, and their uncommon shape may be due to some peculiar manner of carrying them. They have been noted by European travellers as far back as about 1620 (Plate CXV).

Gold coins have been found at Bījāpūr, one of which was a fine specimen of a Chālukyan coin. Vijayanagar coins have also been found there. But on one occasion fifteen small dumpy gold coins were unearthed, in shape very like a small medicinal tabloid, weighing fifty grains each. Most of these have a very small mark on one side—a dot, a circle, or group of three or four dots—and a small mark very like a Persian letter on the other side. These could hardly be 'Ādil Shāhi pieces: but Firishtah distinctly says that no gold coins were struck by the several kings of the Dakhan after the dissolution of the Bahmanī dynasty, except by the Quṭb Shāhi kings.[1]

Since writing the above, I have had a communication from Dr. Taylor telling me of the discovery of two small gold coins of the 'Ādil Shāhi currency. Casts were sent to him by Mr. J. Allan of the British Museum. They are undated, but bear the name of Muḥammad Shah, and are identical with the same king's copper coins. They weigh 51·7 and 51·8 grains respectively, and measure between ·35 and ·4 of an inch in diameter. They belong to Colonel Biddulph, who has presented a third specimen to the British Museum. Firishtah closed his account of the 'Ādil Shāhis before Muḥammad came to the throne, and it is possible, though hardly probable, that there were no gold coins struck in the State before that. And yet Firishtah, who held various offices for some years at Bījāpūr, could surely not make a mistake about the coinage which he himself had been handling for so long.

[1] Briggs' *Ferishtah*, Vol. II, p. 300.

OLD BĪJĀPŪR SANADS.

AMONG miscellaneous relics appertaining to the Bījāpūr of olden times, some of the most curious, and often interesting, are old *sanads,* or deeds, petitions and letters. There are few of these to be had there now, although some fifty years ago, before the sound of the engine whistle was heard in those valleys, or tourists went out of their way to visit the old forgotten city, many of these still existed. They were possessed by a few of the old families, who, through the pinch of poverty, have since been glad enough to part with them to generous visitors, and they have thus been nearly all dissipated. The demand for old *sanads,* indeed, was so brisk that unscrupulous persons manufactured them, and many an unsuspecting collector of rarities burdened himself with these worthless documents. But not alone for this innocent deception were they fabricated; there was one case, at least, where one was forged to support a claim to some land, which, when accidentally held up against the light in court, displayed a European watermark with a recent date. It is needless to say the claimant lost his case, and, for a time, his freedom.

During my visits to Bījāpūr, I collected a few of these old *sanads,* which I can only say, I believe are genuine. Two illustrations are given on Plate CXVI. That with the diagonal lines, flowers and crescents, which are emblazoned in gold on the original, is a fragment of a letter, which seems to have been a reply from one of the Bījāpūr kings to a communication from the reigning Emperor of Delhi, conveying some special news. The fragment reads as follows:

"...... the Royal Throne, the Abode of Khilāfat, of the Protector of the World, the Conqueror of Kingdoms, sitting in the highest place of honour; a Soloman in dignity. The Viceregent of God, the Lord of Felicity—may the life of the world be sacrificed to him! Hearing the heart-cherishing news of the blooming state of the garden of the kingdom, this humble self was so much delighted, that it is beyond human power and control to express this in words. If I sacrifice my life to this happy tidings it is admissible, because the happy news has been the cause of our welfare. Meetings of festivity and joy were at once convened, the lamps were lighted and the drums and trumpets were sounded. The bāzārs were decorated, and the citizens were feeling so much delight and pleasure that more than that can never be expected. This state continued for many days, and we thanked God for giving us such a blessed gift. We all pray that the foot of that precious Pearl of the Imperial Treasury be welcome to all the well-wishers of the state. It was in these days of festivity and joy that the envoy of the happy news brought the Grand Mandate, with a pair of bracelets, a state robe, a jewelled sword, a chair, and three horses, one of which named Jaswant can well be described in the words of the following verses:

"'(1) Oh excellent! The horse, like a moon in beauty, he treads the heaven like the imagination of an astronomer.

"'(2) His hooves are soft, his tail is thick, and his haunches are heavy.

"'(3) He is beloved, and his hairs are intertwined with the thread of life; he is a new bride, and his hands (*sic*) are coloured red with the blood of enemies.

"'(4) He is the deer of Khutan; his locks are waving about; and over his haunches is a saddle-cloth of Turkish velvet.

"'(5) He is of Persian birth, and wanders about in the jungles like Majnūn; his tail excels the locks of Laila.'

"The above gifts, which had been sent to exalt this humble self, I have received from Malik Sandar. He gave me also a robe of honour, which has conferred upon me all the more dignity. Hearing the glad tidings that so many presents were coming for me, I went at once to receive them. Eagerness has made me so swift, that I travelled three stages in one. After fulfilling the ceremonies of respect and deference I received the Imperial Mandate and the presents and held them above my head. By receiving the present and by putting on the state robe I was so much exalted . . . . . ."

The other document on the plate appears to be a *sanad,* issued by Sulṭān Muḥammad. It bears the royal seal, which, however, owing to imperfect stamping and subsequent wear, is not very distinct. It consists of a circle, within which is the sun, whose rays are plainly seen; and within this is certain obliterated writing. Whether merely a coincidence or not, it is interesting to note the sun's rays used for the lights of the top of some of the windows in the Āthār Maḥall, already described, which building was erected by Muḥammad. The document reads:

"In the name of God the merciful and compassionate.

"The mandate obeyed by the whole world is issued, and informs the exalted officer, the most distinguished of the nobility, the most illustrious of great men, the exalted Khān of high dignity [possibly Khān Muḥammad who lies buried in the Joḍ Gumbaz] . . . . . . and all the present and future revenue and agricultural officers of Muḥammadpūr [Bījāpūr], that in A. H. 1046 [A. D. 1636] a petition was submitted in the Imperial Court by . . . . . . to this effect: that Jannat Makānī assigned some land and gardens as a subsistence to the servants in charge of the shrine of Quṭb-ul-Aqṭāb, the king of saints—may the most high God hallow his grave. The daily allowance of the refuge of saintly people—Shaikh Muḥyu-d-dīn, son of Shaikh Aḥmad—as well as the expenses of the mosque and *langarkhānah* [bedehouse] were also defrayed out of the income of the above land. But after the death of Jannat Makānī the above lands and gardens were taken away from their possession, and consequently they are all in a sad plight, and the mosque and *langarkhānah* have fallen into decay. The Imperial court now pitying their miserable state gives them back the above land and gardens, and expects that they, living on the income of this estate, will pray for the long life of the king."

One *sanad* is in reply to a petition, restoring land that had been alienated, and is of the reign of Muḥammad Farrukh-Siyar and bears the seal of his *wazīr* of the year A. D. 1716. Another, of Aurangzeb, with his seal, issued in the 40th year of his reign, grants certain land to two individuals, tax free. Another is issued by 'Ali 'Ādil Shāh II. in the year A. D. 167., as an order for the apprehension of certain evildoers. In it, as well as in several others, Bījāpūr is called Muḥammadpūr. One other, a royal mandate, as most of these Bījāpūr *sanads* are called, grants leave of absence to a certain Qāzī, at an outlying station, to visit his family at Bījāpūr ; gives orders for his daily allowance to be paid from the local treasury, and instructs him to return to his duties punctually. One is a petition by a certain Arab, together with fifty others, for a royal grant-in-aid on account of their large families and other dependants in Bījāpūr and Arabia, and the dearness of provisions. They ask all who are interested in them to append their signatures and seals. Of the latter there are no less than twenty-five impressed upon the document. One more is a letter from a certain person to another, offering his daughter in betrothal to his son. Others are more or less of the same nature as these.

The Nawāb Ṣāḥib, the descendant of Muṣṭafā K͟hān Lari, who lives in the ruined palace of the latter, possesses a number of these old documents, some of them being of considerable interest. One of these is worth transcribing on account of its very characteristic and extravagant language. It is a letter from Aurangzeb, when he was stationed at Aurangābād during the reign of his father S͟hāh Jahān. It runs thus :

"This may be known unto the asylum of state and grandeur, the officer of the court of justice and felicity, the most illustrious of the house of honour and eminence, the support of glory and greatness, the centre of the circle of magnificence and splendour, the circumference of justice and honour, the gem of the mirror of purity and cleanliness, the most distinguished of the nobility, the most illustrious of the pious people, the possessor of dignity and greatness, the holder of honour and grandeur, the receiver of royal favours, the recipient of the Emperor's clemency, the light of the eye of fortune, the splendour of the garden of grandeur, the most illustrious of the exalted K͟hāns, the most distinguished of the well-wishers of the state, under the special favour of God, the seer of His attributes, enjoying his particular kindness and clemency, and nourished by his chosen gifts, 'Adil K͟hān, exalted by royal favours and kingly gifts; that his petition containing congratulations on the auspicious weight of His Imperial Highness [Aurangzeb] sent with the worthy officer Muḥammad Razā, to the exalted and grand Court, has been perused by His Imperial Highness at the noble city of Aurangābād, which is the resting place of state and fortune. The present which he sent, as a token of his pure loyalty and true obedience, has been accepted by those who have influence in the Imperial Court. As he has enumerated the favours of the Emperor, so according to the verse, 'If you will thank us, we shall shower more blessings upon you', His Imperial Highness has become more kind and attentive to that distinguished and illustrious chief. God be thanked and praised, that the true obedience, and the pure loyalty of that sun of the sky of justice and equity is fully impressed upon the most high mind of His Imperial Highness, and His Imperial Highness is anxious to make this fact known to the bright mind of that shining luminary also. The royal favours will always increase the rank and dignity of that full moon of the sky of grandeur and splendour. He should send a report regularly, about the state of affairs in that province, to the Imperial Court, and he should regard the angelic mind of His Imperial Highness as most interested in the solution of the difficult problems of that province. In these auspicious days, the weighing of His Imperial Highness' body has caused universal joy. The scales, on account of having the honour of weighing the most blessed body, have become the envy of the highest heaven. On the occasion of this grand jubilee His Imperial Highness has honoured all loyal and obedient officers by conferring upon them high titles and kingly gifts. As that planet of the constellation of splendour and light is under the special favour of His Imperial Highness, so the diamond aigrette, which he had sent as the nucleus of his present to the Imperial court, and had desired through his trustworthy representative Ḥakīm Muḥammad Huṣain, that His Imperial Highness using it once, should return it to him, so according to his wishes His Imperial Highness has used it once, and it is now being returned with Jalāl, who is the most reliable and trustworthy servant of His Imperial Highness; and as that just and benign noble had expressed through his confidential servant, that he is very fond of hawking, so His Imperial Highness has sent to that sun of the sky of state three sparrow hawks, two hawks and two falcons. In addition to this, His Imperial

Highness, being very kind and benevolent to him, instructs him, that he should, trusting in the kindness of His Imperial Highness, write to the Imperial court for anything which may be pleasing to him. As His Imperial Highness is very much pleased with that crown of dignity and grandeur, so his wishes will be immediately fulfilled. That sun of the sky of justice and equity should consider the angelic mind of His Imperial Highness as particularly attentive to him.

Regnant year 12 of Shāh Jahān."

Another is a letter from Shāh Jahān's Court in reply to a petition, saying that, as it was not forwarded through the proper official channel, it should be so sent, when it will be attended to.

These are sufficient to give some idea of the style of official correspondence and government resolutions in those days. From the *sanad* given in full above, it will be seen how, although nominally independent, the king of Bījāpūr was looked upon as a vassal of the Emperor of Delhi. He is styled "Khān" merely, *i. e.* a noble, and is not accorded the title of "Shāh".

PLATE II

THE GAGAN MAHALL, STATION CHURCH, AND SAT MANZIL.

THE WALLS OF THE CITADEL.

PLATE III

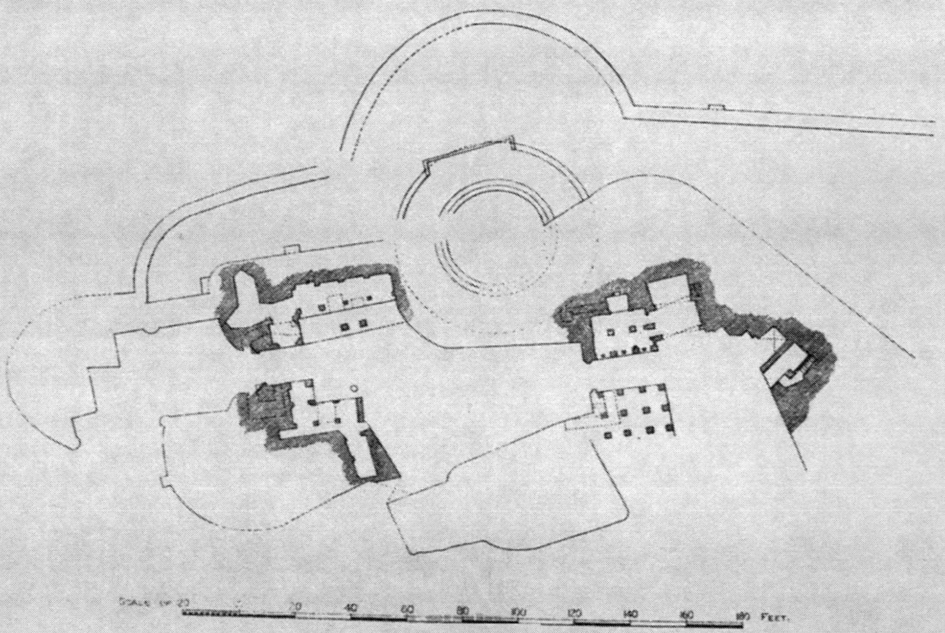

PLAN OF THE CITADEL GATEWAY.

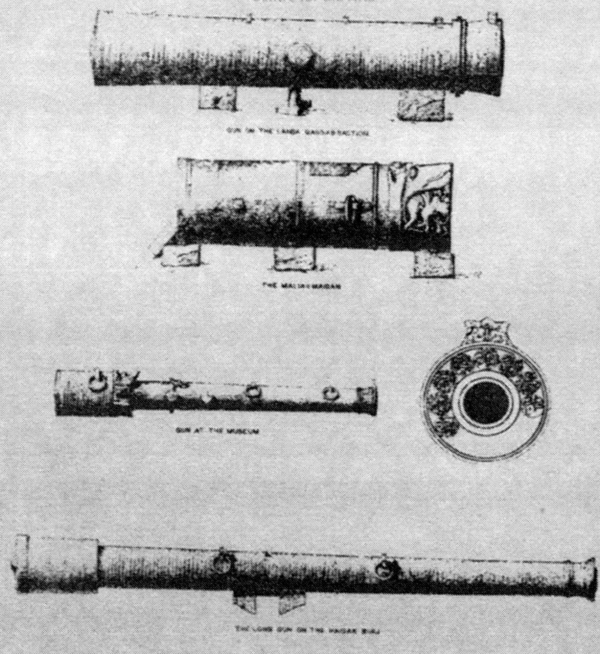

THE GUNS OF BIJAPUR.

THE MALIK-I-MAIDAN GUN

THE LANDA QASSAB GUN.

THE LAMCHARRI GUN.

PLATE V

THE ALLAHPUR GATEWAY

PLATE VI.

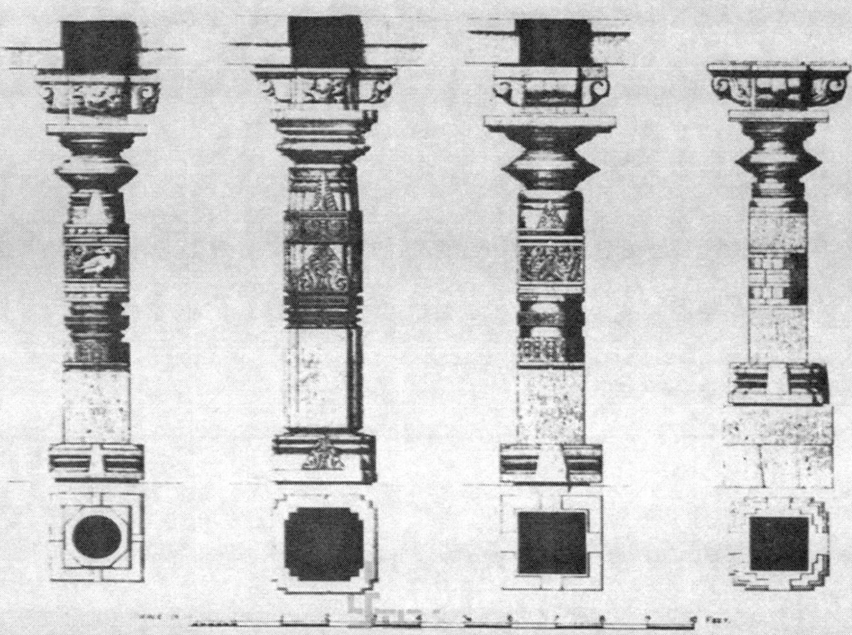

HINDU PILLARS IN THE GATEWAY OF THE CITADEL.

HINDU PILLARS LYING AT BIJAPUR.

KARIM-UD-DIN'S MOSQUE.

KHWAJAH JAHAN'S MOSQUE

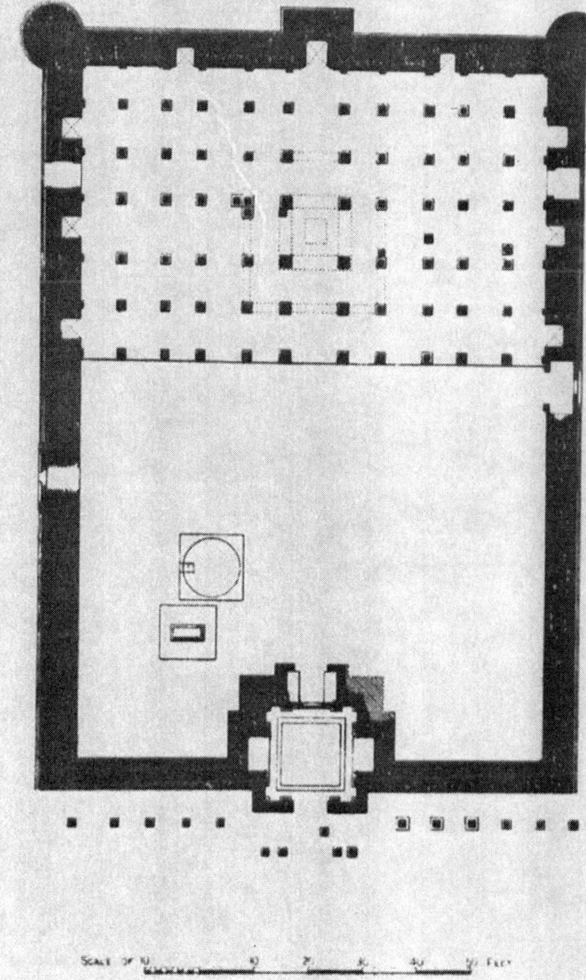

PLAN OF KARIMU'D-DIN'S MASJID.

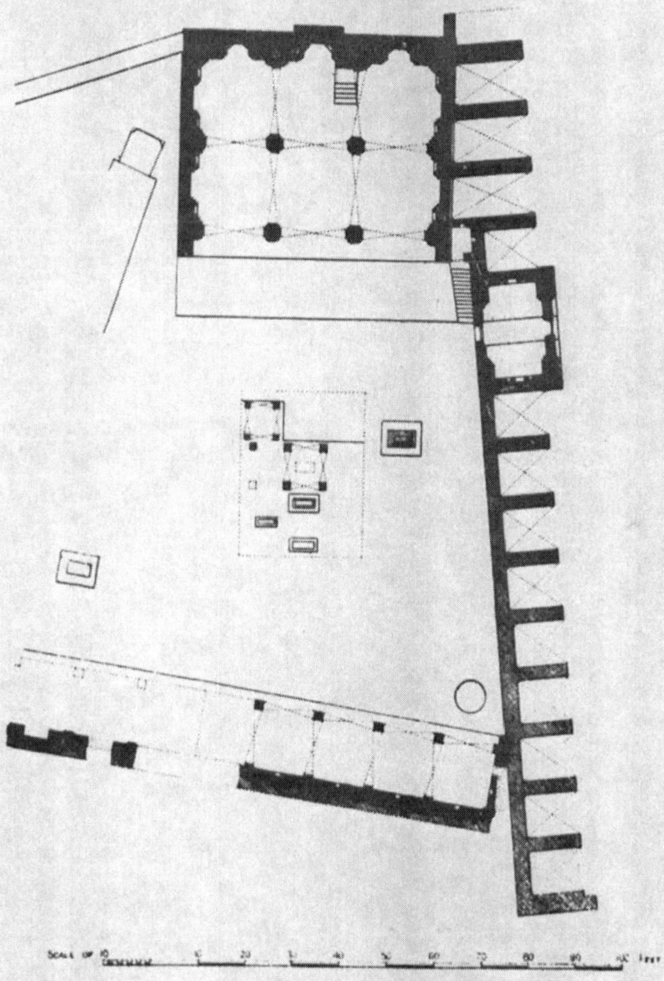

PLAN OF IBRAHIM'S OLD JAMI MASJID.

IBRAHIM'S OLD JAMI MASJID.

IKHLAS KHAN'S MOSQUE.

PLATE X

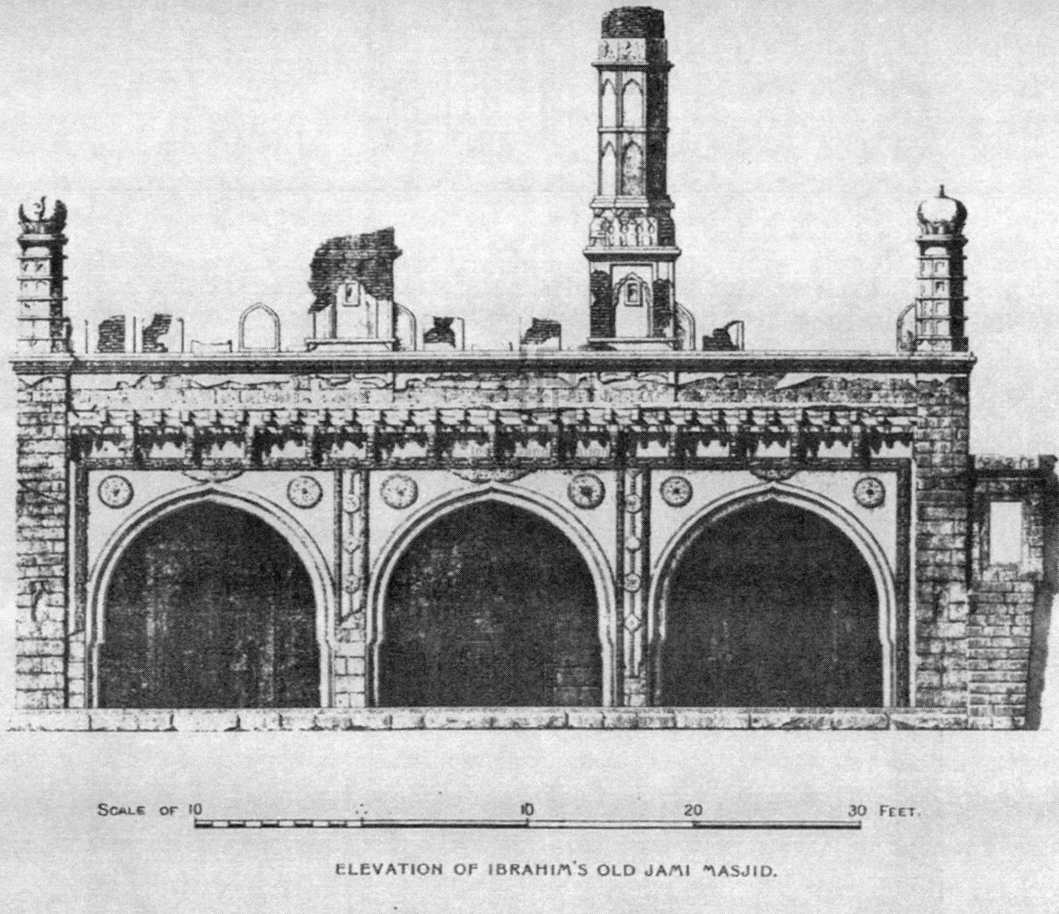

ELEVATION OF IBRAHIM'S OLD JAMI MASJID.

ELEVATION AND PLAN OF IKHLAS KHAN'S MOSQUE.

CROSS SECTION OF IKHLAS KHAN'S MOSQUE.

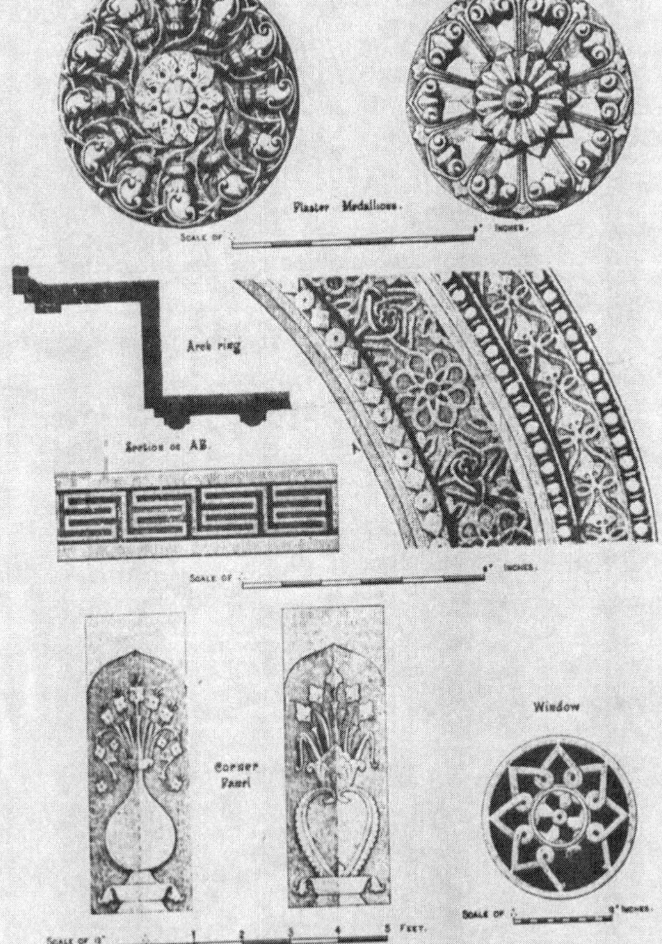

DETAILS OF ORNAMENT FROM VARIOUS BUILDINGS.

THE RANGIN MASJID.

AIN-UL-MULK'S MOSQUE AT AINAPUR

AIN-UL-MULK'S TOMB AND MOSQUE.

TOMB OF ALI I.

PLATE XV

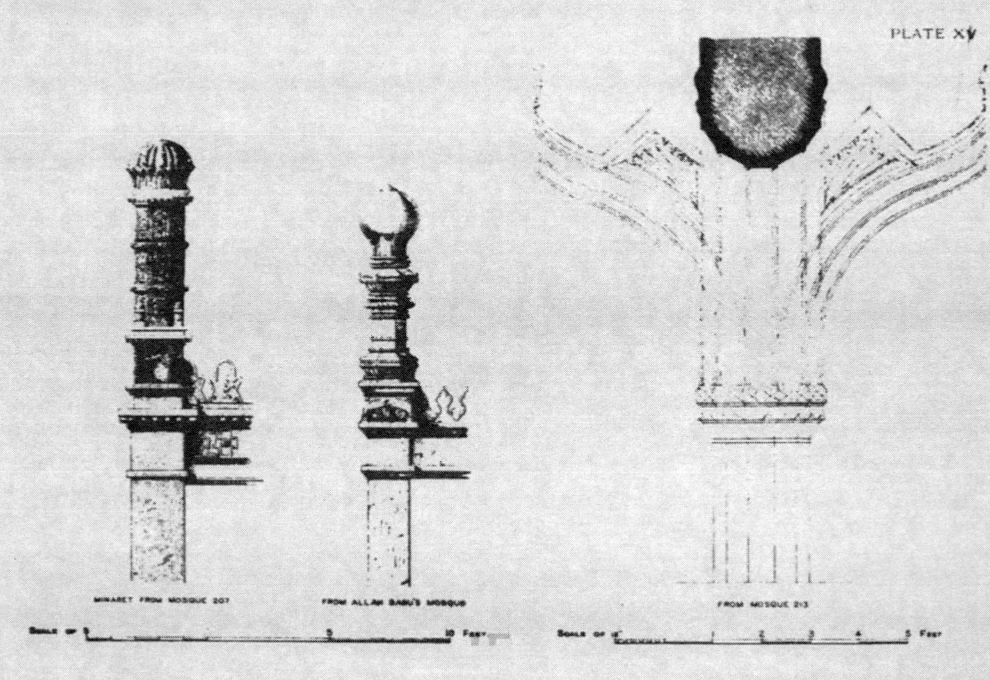

DETAILS FROM ALLAH BABU'S MOSQUE AND MOSQUES NOS. 213 AND 207.

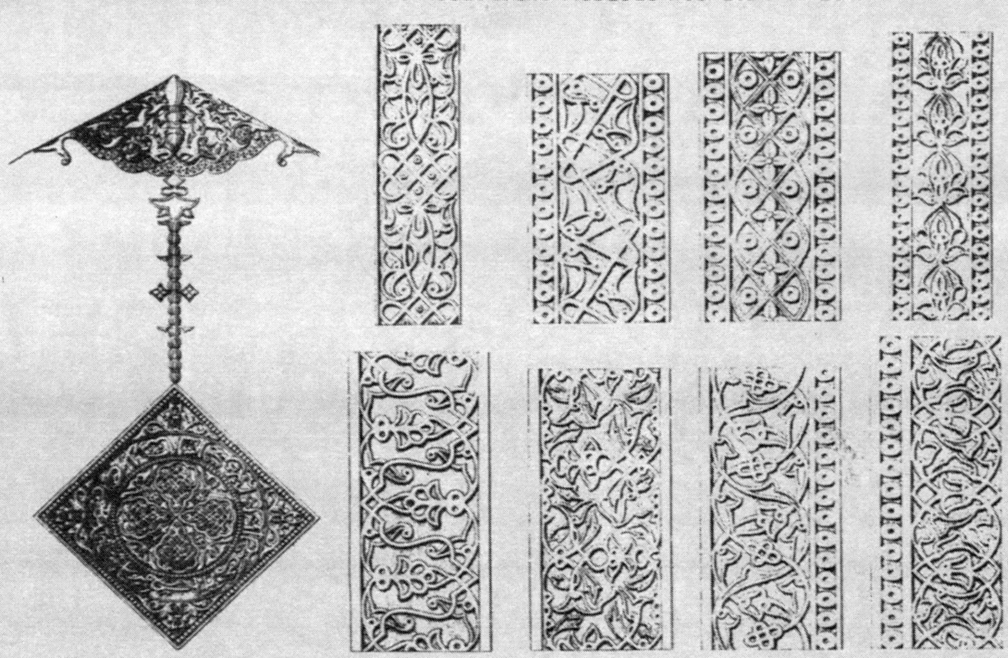

STUCCO ORNAMENT FROM AIN-UL-MULK'S TOMB.

THE IBRAHIMPUR MOSQUE.

THE GAGAN MAHALL

PLATE XVII

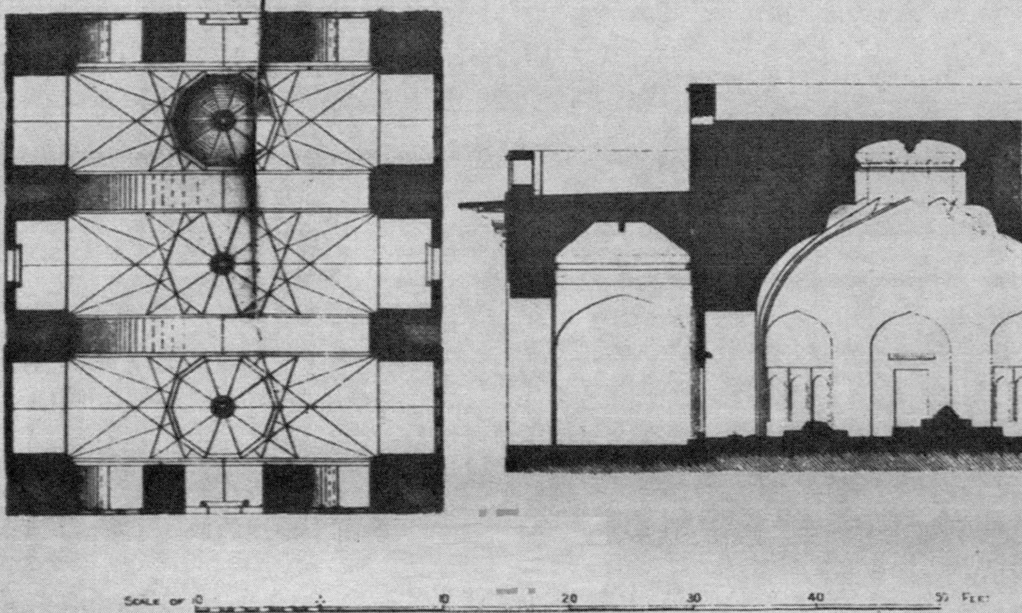

PLAN AND SECTION OF THE TOMB OF ALI I.

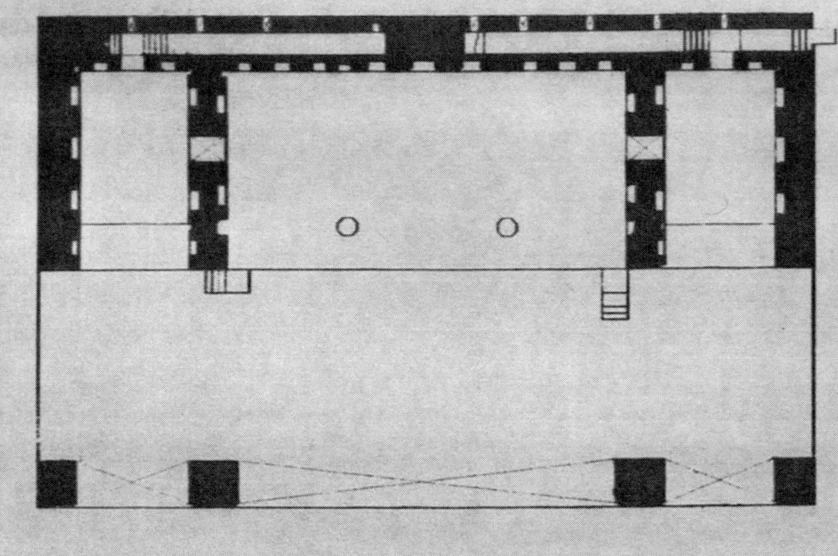

PLAN OF THE GAGAN MAHALL.

PLATE XVIII

OLD CARVED WOOD WINDOW FRAMES.

THE GAGAN MAHALL AND MOAT.

THE SAT MANZIL AND MOAT 60 YEARS AGO.

THE JAMI MASJID. FROM THE SOUTH-WEST.

THE FACADE OF THE JAMI MASJID.

PLATE XXI

THE INTERIOR OF THE JAMI MASJID.

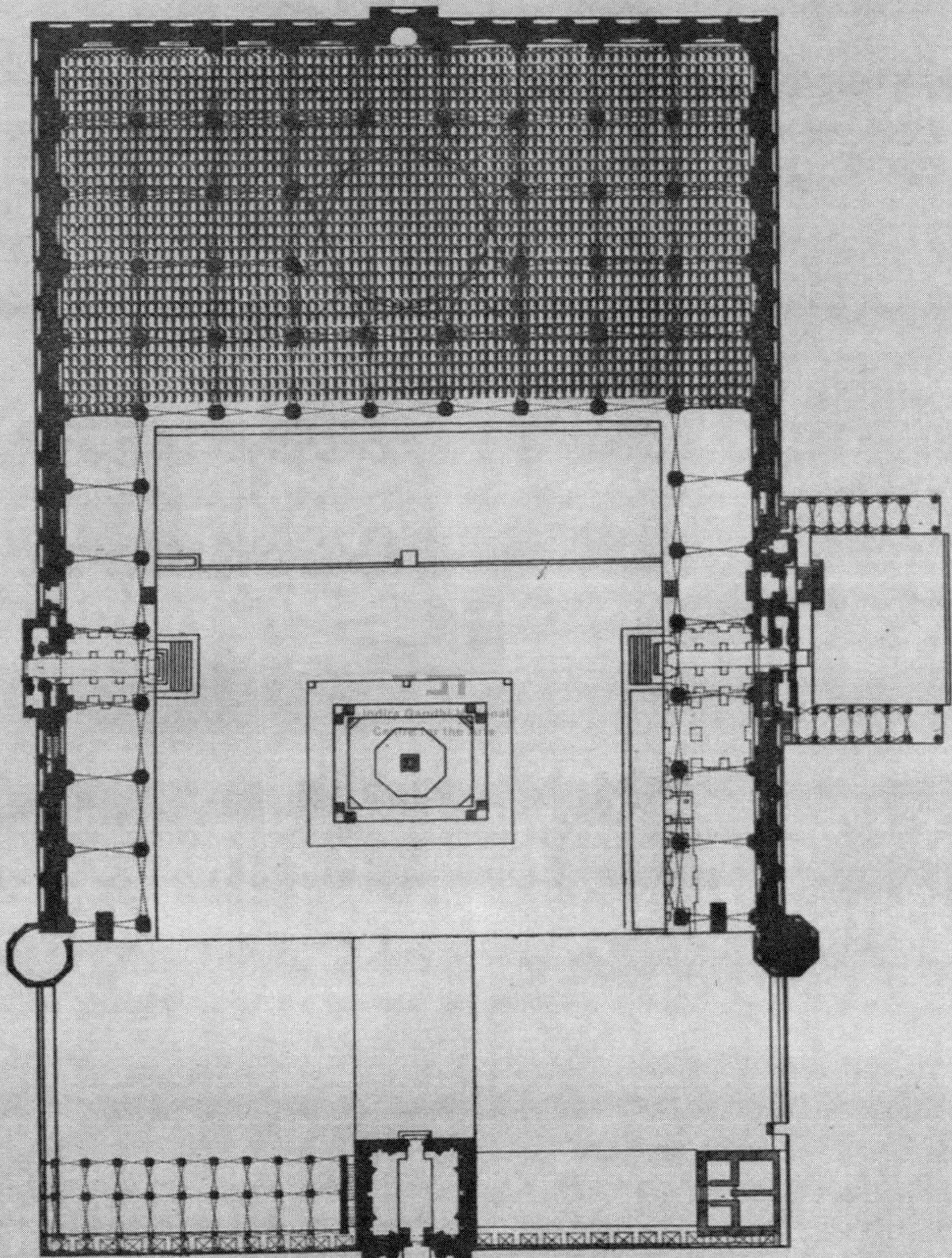

PLAN OF THE JAMI MASJID.

PLATE XXIII

PERFORATED WINDOWS FROM THE JAMI MASJID.

PLATE XXIV

PORTION OF A CARVED WOOD CEILING PANEL.

PATTERNS OF PRAYER CARPETS FROM THE JAMI MASJID.

ALI SHAHID PIR'S MOSQUE

ARCH IN THE FACADE OF ALI SHAHID PIR'S MOSQUE.

THE SAT-MANZIL AND JALAMANDIR.

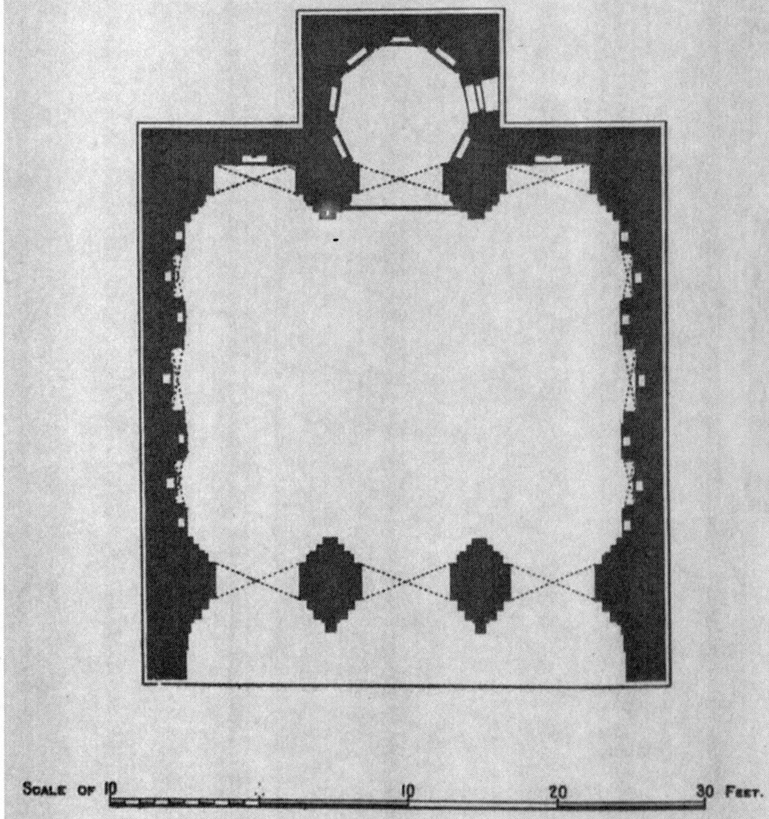

PLAN OF ALI SHAHID PIR'S MASJID.

LONGITUDINAL SECTION OF ALI SHAHID PIR'S MASJID.

PLATE XXVIII

SCALE OF 10 — 10 — 20 FEET.

FRONT ELEVATION OF ALI SHAHID PIR'S MASJID.

CROSS SECTION OF ALI SHAHID PIR'S MASJID.

DETAILS FROM ALI SHAHID PIR'S MASJID.

PLATE XXX

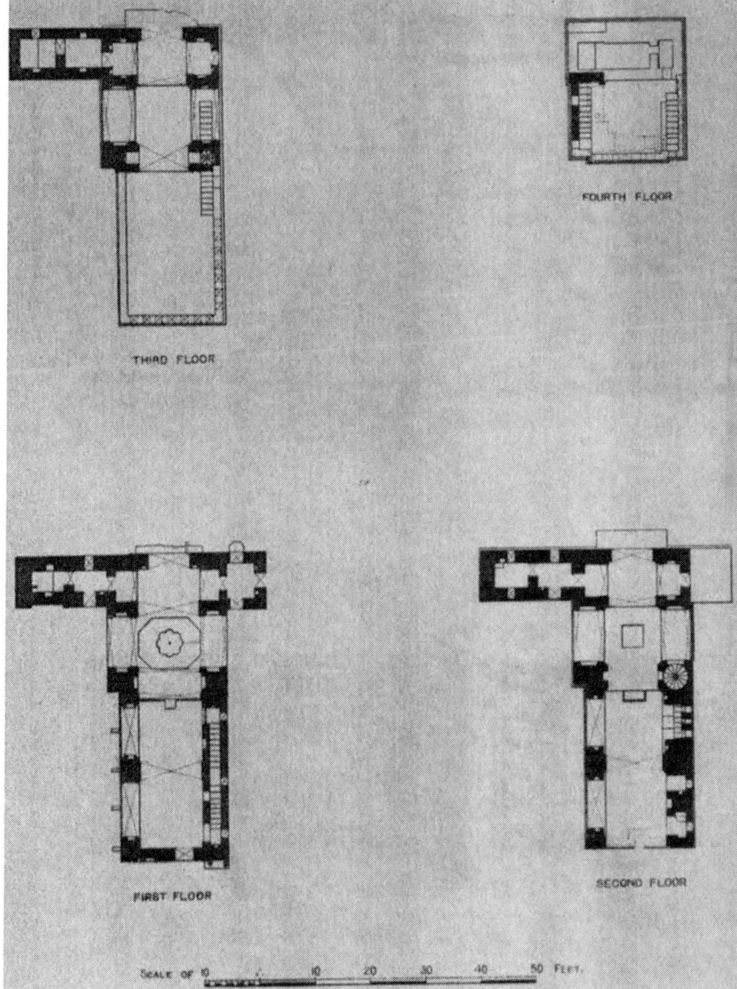

PLANS OF THE FLOORS OF THE SAT MANZIL.

STUCCO ORNAMENT ON WALLS OF RUIN ON EAST OF SAT MANZIL.

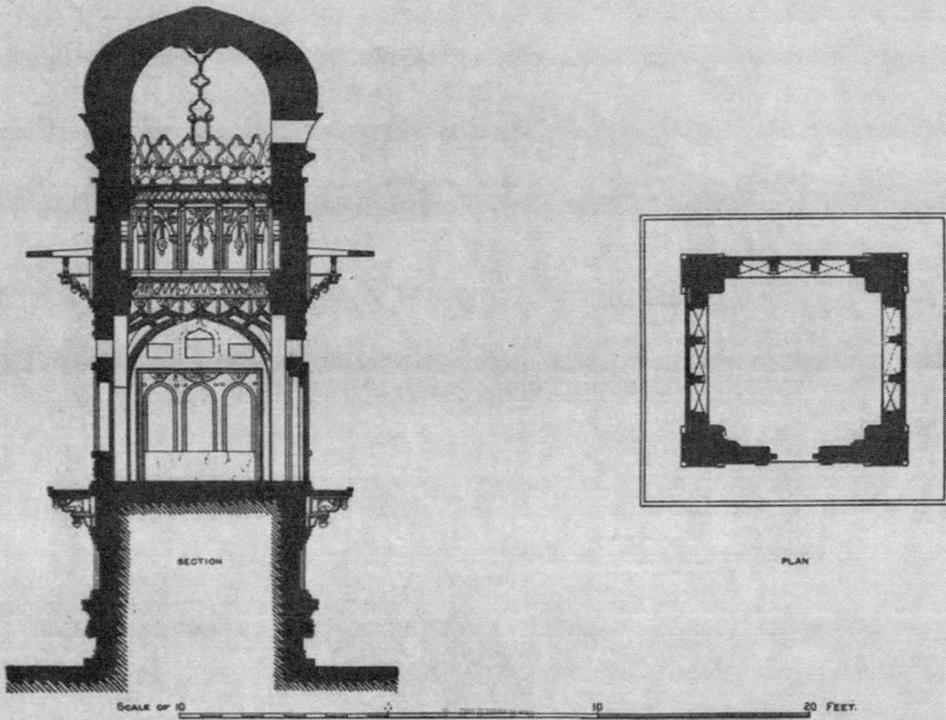

PLAN AND SECTION OF JALAMANDIR.

ELEVATION OF JALAMANDIR, AND SAMPLE OF WALL MASONRY.

PLATE XXXII

BIJAPUR OLD CHINA.

PLATE XXXIII

DECORATED CEILINGS IN STUCCO IN RUIN ON EAST OF SAT MANZIL.

DECORATED CEILINGS IN STUCCO IN RUIN ON EAST OF SAT MANZIL.

PLATE XXXV

DECORATED CEILING IN STUCCO IN RUIN ON EAST OF SAT MANZIL.

DECORATED ARCH FROM THE CHHOTA ASAR.

FLATE XXXVI

STUCCO CEILING FROM THE CHHOTA ASAR.

HALF EVEVATION OF THE BACK WALL OF THE CHHOTA ASAR.

PLATE XXXVII

MALIKA JAHAN BEGAM'S MOSQUE

PORTION OF FACADE OF MALIKA JAHAN BEGAM'S MOSQUE.

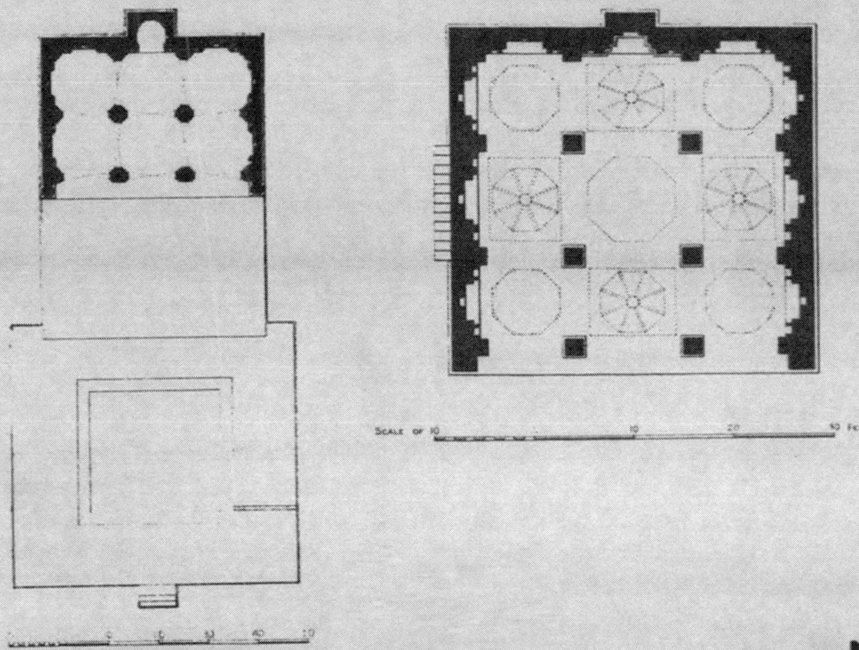

PLANS OF THE NAU GUMBAZ AND MALIKA JAHAN BEGAM'S MOSQUE.

CORNICE FROM MALIKA JAHAN BEGAM'S MOSQUE.

PLATE XXXIX

MINARETS FROM VARIOUS BUILDINGS AT BIJAPUR.

PLATE XL

ELEVATION OF PART OF THE FACADE OF MALIKA JAHAN BEGAM'S MOSQUE.

THE KALI MASJID AT LAKSHMESWAR.

THE OUTER GATEWAY OF THE KALI MASJID AT LAKSHMESWAR.

THE BUKHARI MASJID.

GENERAL VIEW OF THE IBRAHIM RAUZA.

THE MOSQUE OF THE IBRAHIM RAUZA.

THE TOMB OF THE IBRAHIM RAUZA.

PORTION OF THE FACADE OF THE IBRAHIM RAUZA.

THE WALLS OF THE TOMB OF THE IBRAHIM RAUZA.

PLATE XLVI

PERFORATED WINDOW IN THE TOMB OF THE IBRAHIM RAUZA.

PLATE XLVII

WEST DOOR IN THE TOMB OF THE IBRAHIM RAUZA.

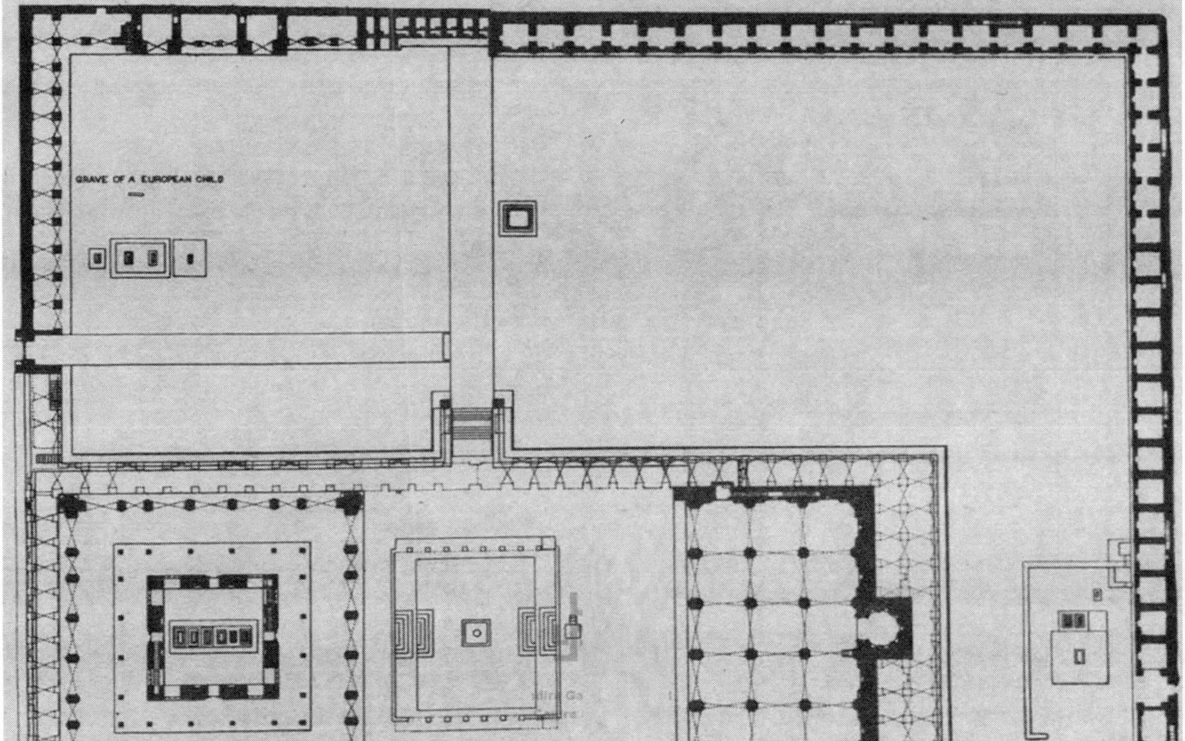

PLAN OF THE IBRAHIM RAUZA.

ELEVATION OF THE IBRAHIM RAUZA MOSQUE.

PLATE L

ELEVATION OF PORTION OF THE WALLS OF THE TOMB OF THE IBRAHIM RAUZA.

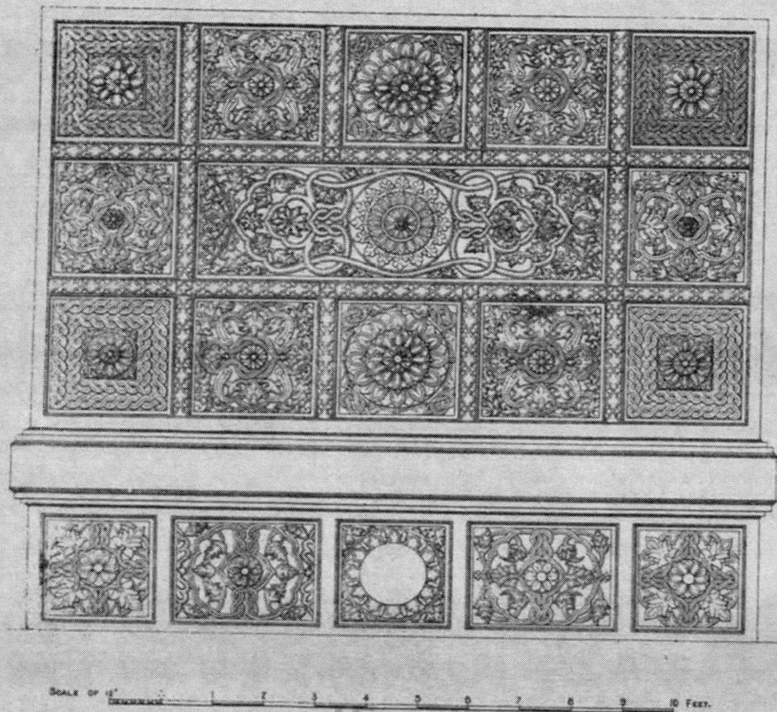

CEILING PANEL FROM THE TOMB OF THE IBRAHIM RAUZA.

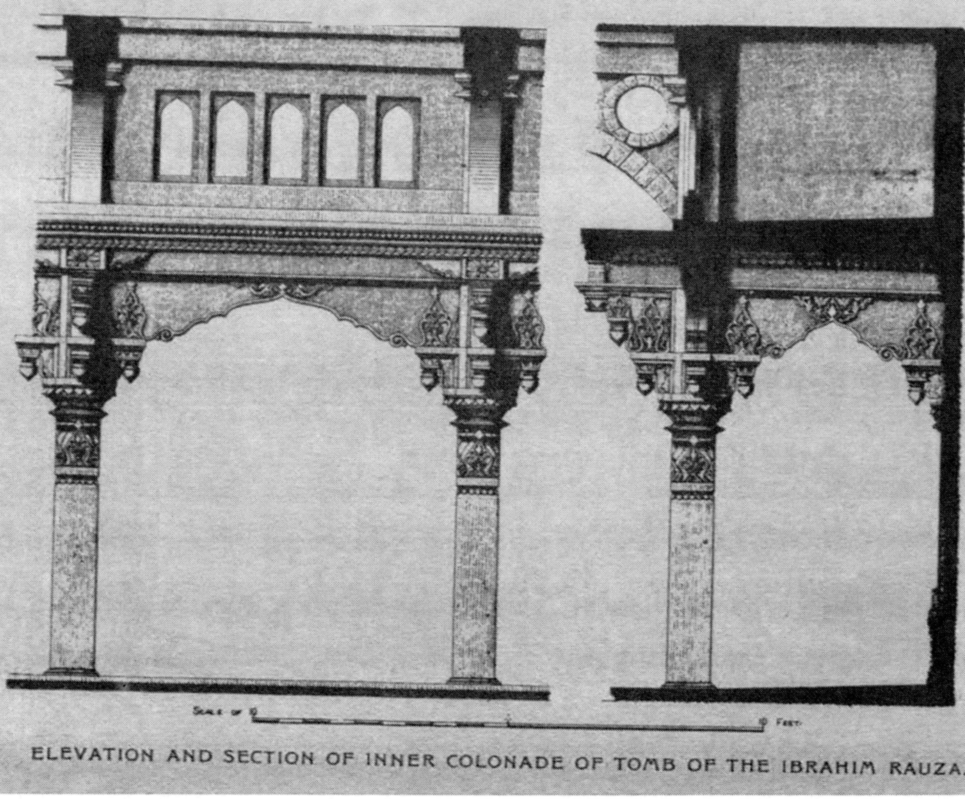

ELEVATION AND SECTION OF INNER COLONADE OF TOMB OF THE IBRAHIM RAUZA.

PLATE LII

SECTION OF THE TOMB OF THE IBRAHIM RAUZA.

REPRODUCED FROM "ARCHITECTURAL ILLUSTRATIONS OF THE PRINCIPAL BUILDINGS AT BEEJAPOOR."

PLATE LIII

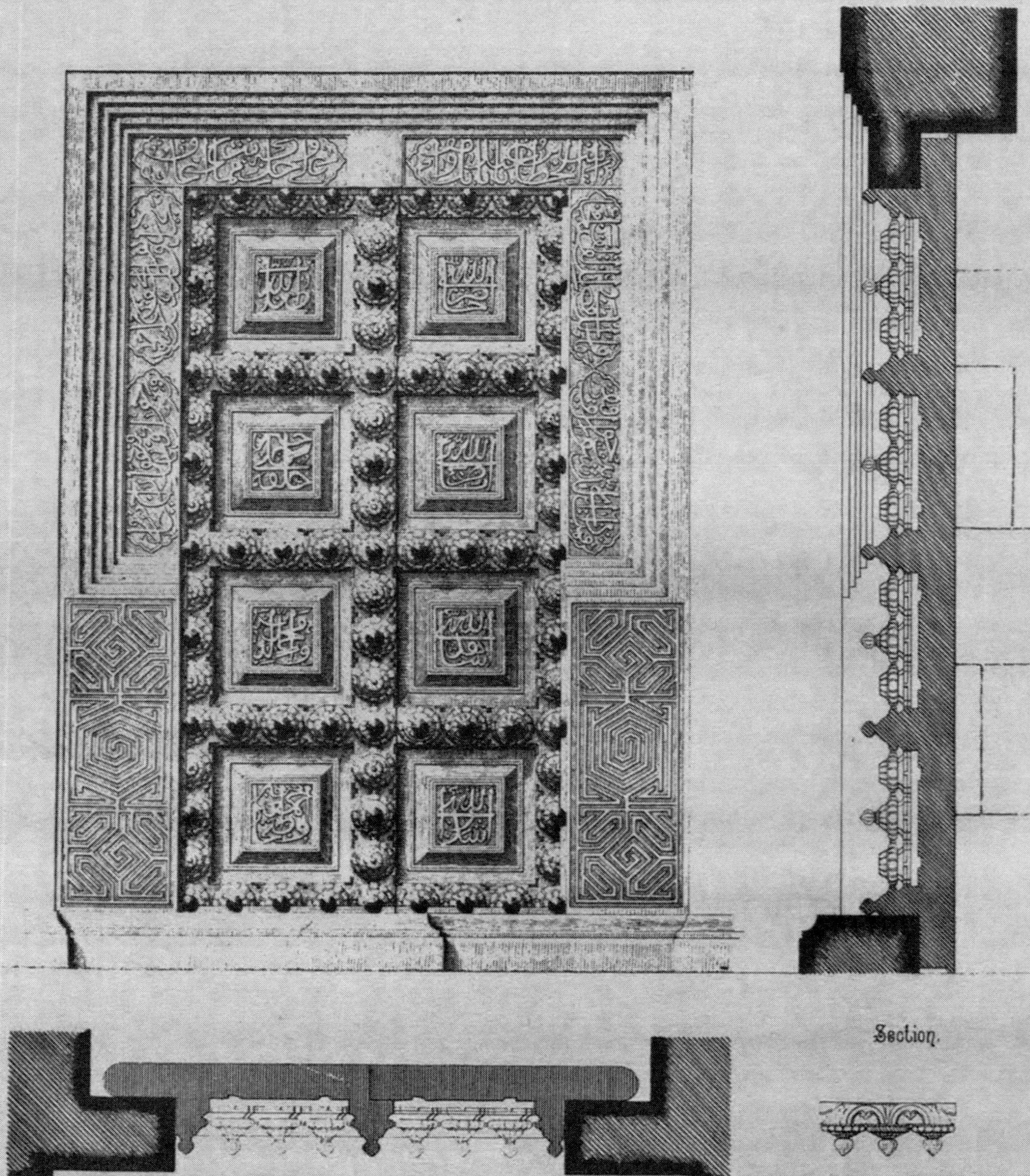

ELEVATION OF A DOOR OF THE TOMB OF THE IBRAHIM RAUZA.

PERFORATED WINDOW FROM THE TOMB OF THE IBRAHIM RAUZA.

PLATE LV

THE ANAND MAHALL, BEFORE CONVERSION.

THE ANAND MAHALL, AFTER CONVERSION.

THE ANDA MASJID.

PLATE LVII

PLAN AND ELEVATION OF THE ANDA MASJID.

PLAN AND SECTION OF CEILING IN MOSQUE NO. 231.

PLATE LVIII

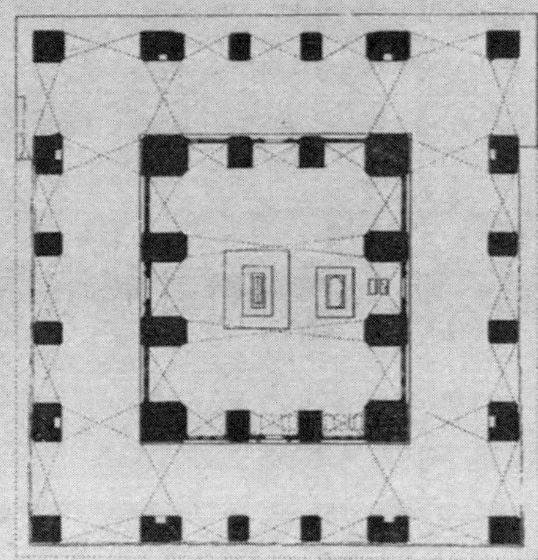

Scale of 10 10 20 Feet. Scale of 10 10 20 30 40 50 Feet.

SECTION OF THE ANDA MASJID, AND PLAN OF TOMB OF ALI I.

SECTION OF CORNICE

ELEVATION OF CORNICE

PLAN OF CEILING LOOKING UP

Scale of 10 10 Feet.

PLAN OF CEILING AND DETAILS OF CORNICE IN BATULA KHAN'S MOSQUE.

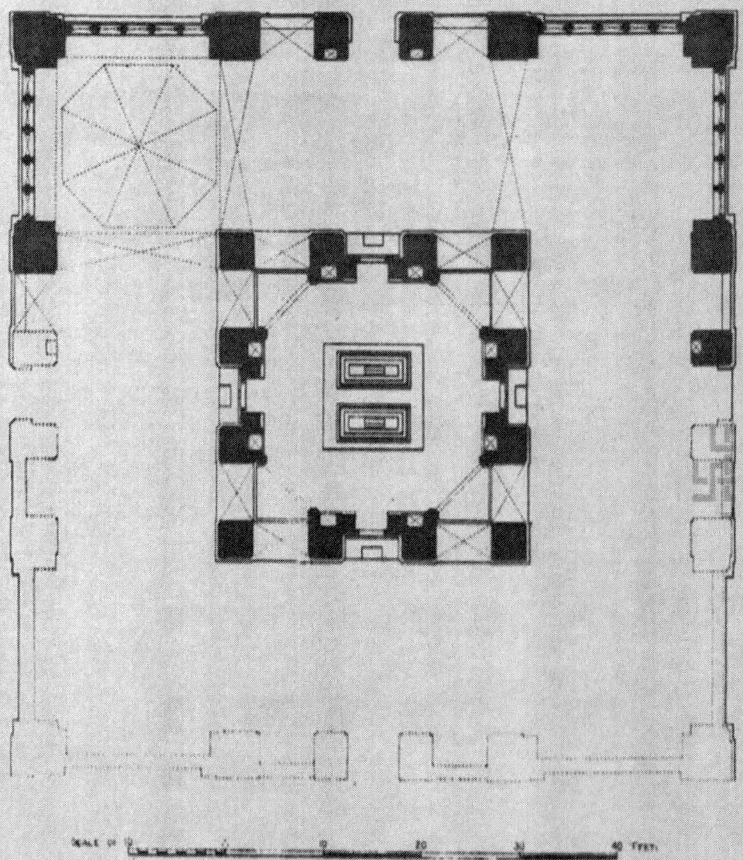

PLAN OF MAUSOLEUM OF SHAIKH HAMID QADIR.

SECTION OF MAUSOLEUM OF SHAIKH HAMID QADIR.

PLATE LX

PATTERNS OF KANGURAS (PARAPETS) FROM VARIOUS BUILDINGS.

PATTERNS OF KANGURAS (PARAPETS) FROM VARIOUS BUILDINGS.

PLATE LXII

THE SANGAT MAHALL AT NAURASPUR

THE MIHTAR-I MAHALL MOSQUE.

THE SANGAT MAHALL AT NAURASPUR, SHEWING CONCRETE ROOFING

BRACKETS AT THE INNER DOOR OF THE MIHTAR-I-MAHALL.

PLATE LXIV

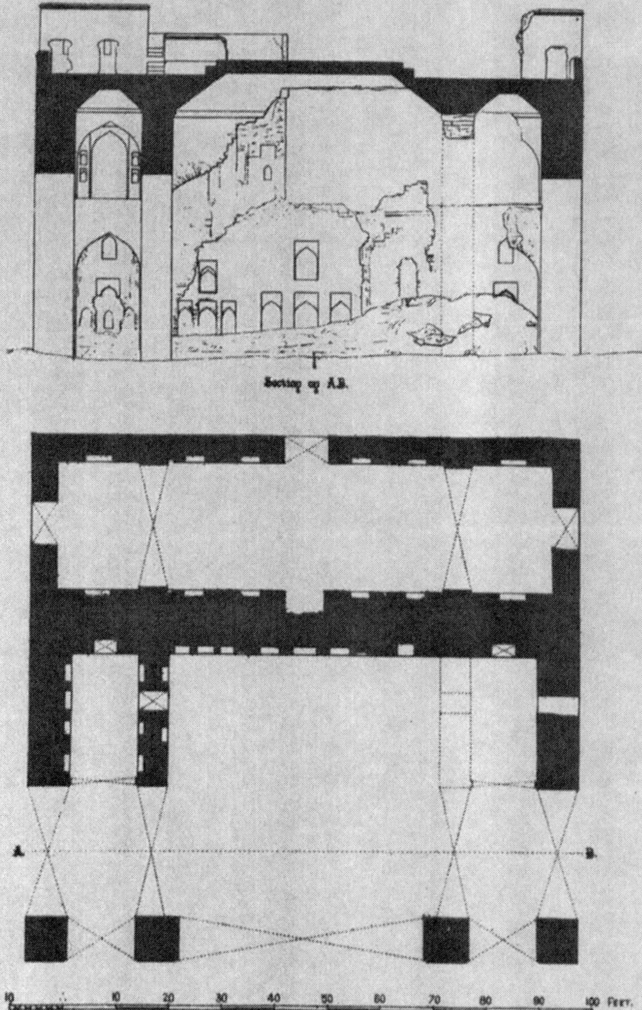

PLAN AND INNER ELEVATION OF THE SANGAT MAHALL.

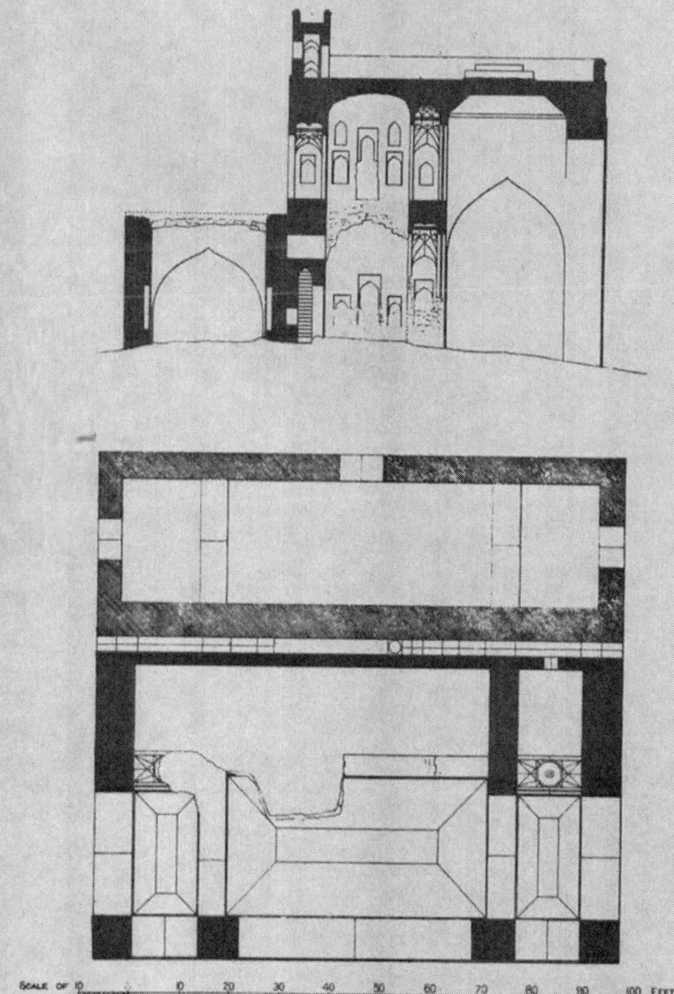

PLAN OF CEILING AND CROSS SECTION OF THE SANGAT MAHALL.

THE MIHTAR-I-MAHALL.

LOWER PART OF THE FACADE OF THE MIHTAR-I-MAHALL

MOSQUE IN THE SHAHPUR SUBURB

PLATE LXVII

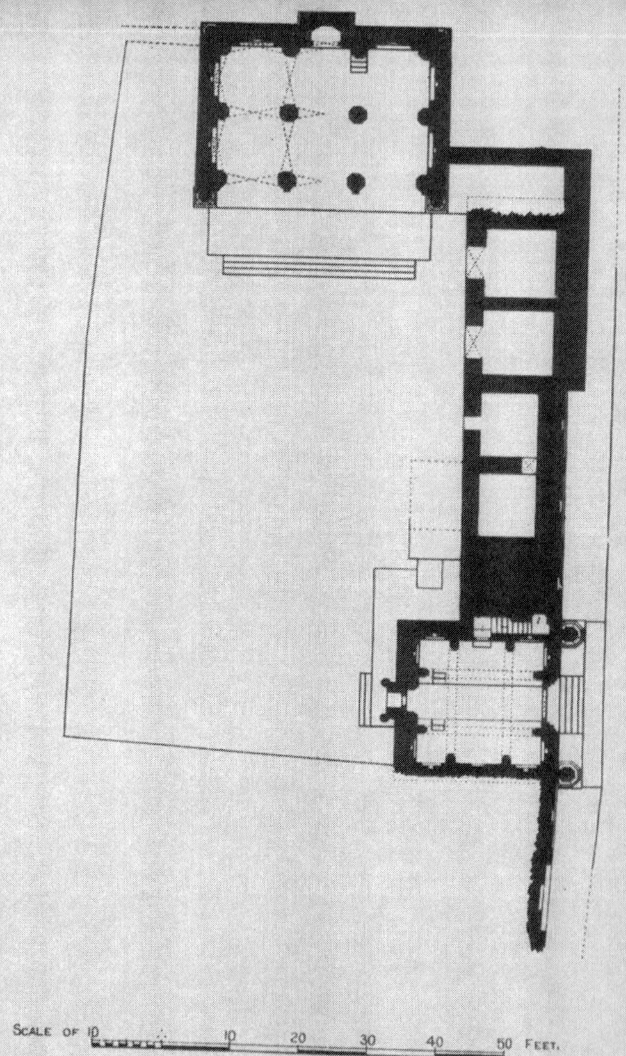

PLAN OF THE MIHTAR-I-MAHALL AND MOSQUE.

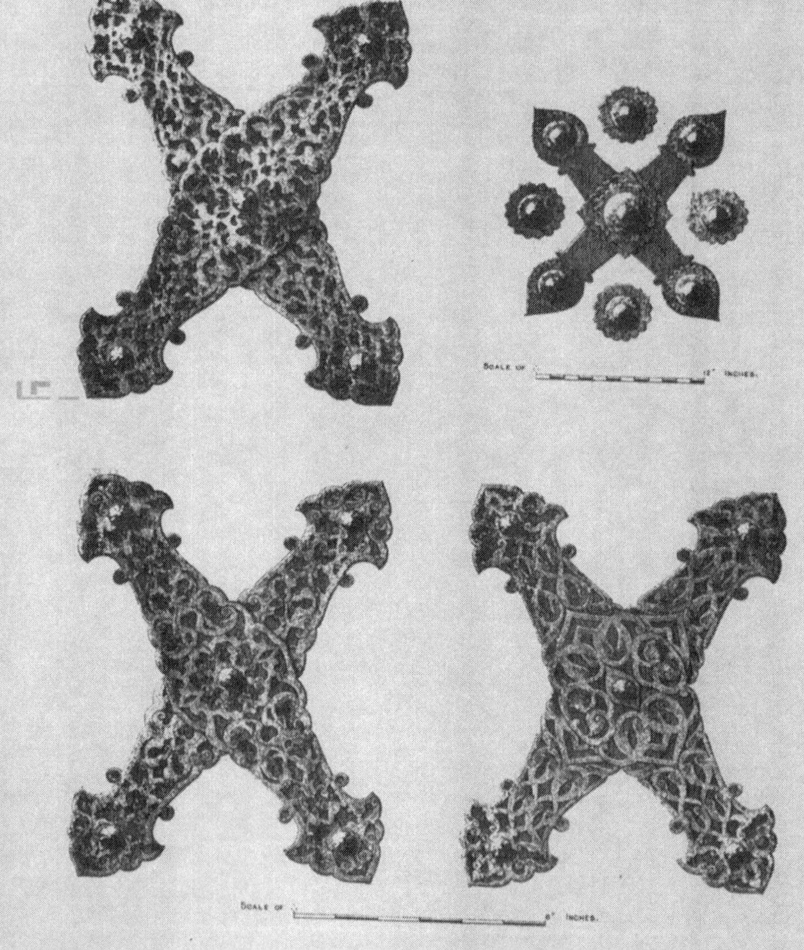

IRON BOSSES FROM DOORS OF THE MIHTAR-I-MAHALL AND SHAH KARIM'S TOMB.

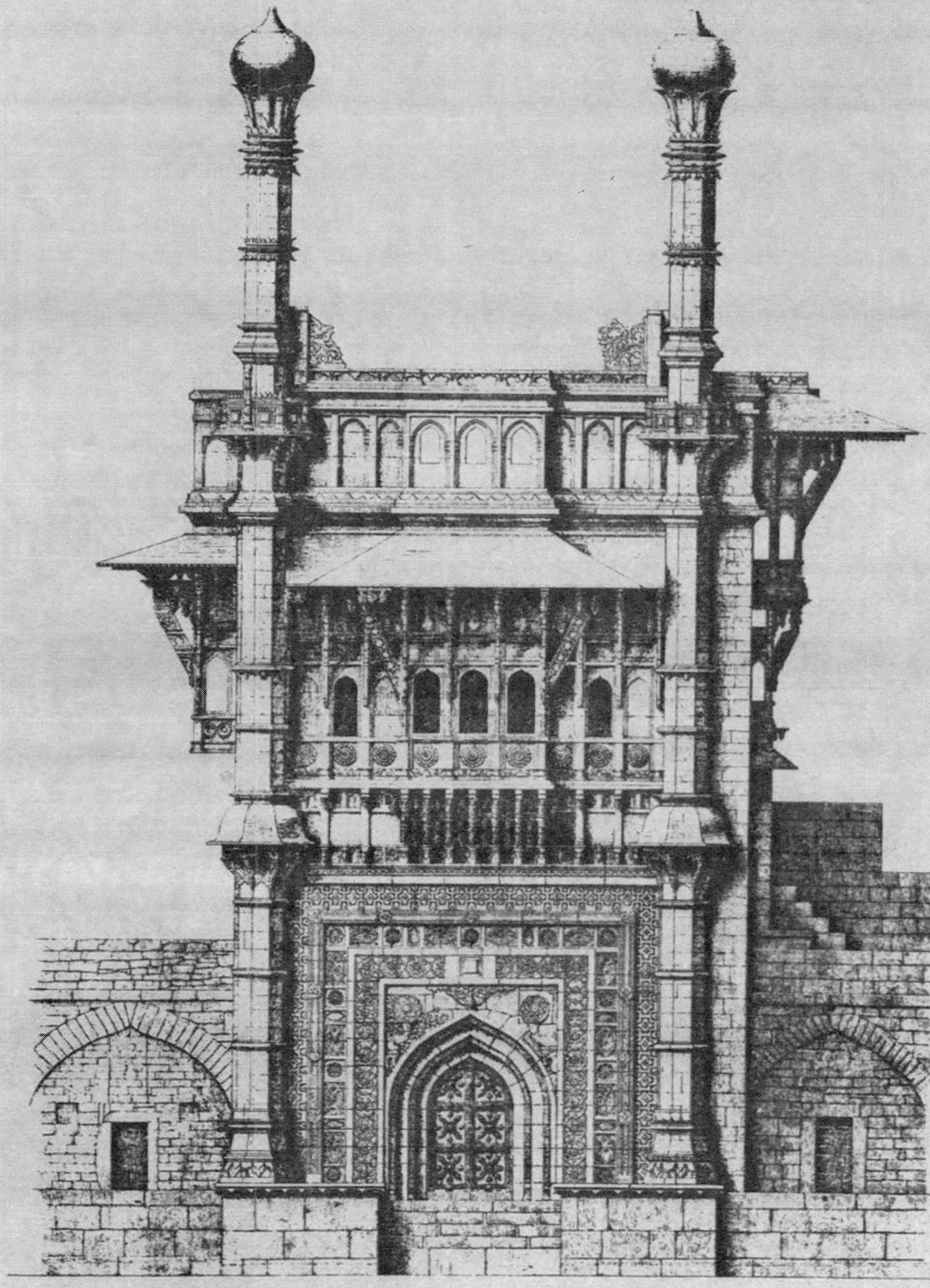

ELEVATION OF THE MIHTAR-I-MAHALL.

ELEVATION OF FACADE OF THE MOSQUE OF THE MIHTAR-I-MAHALL.

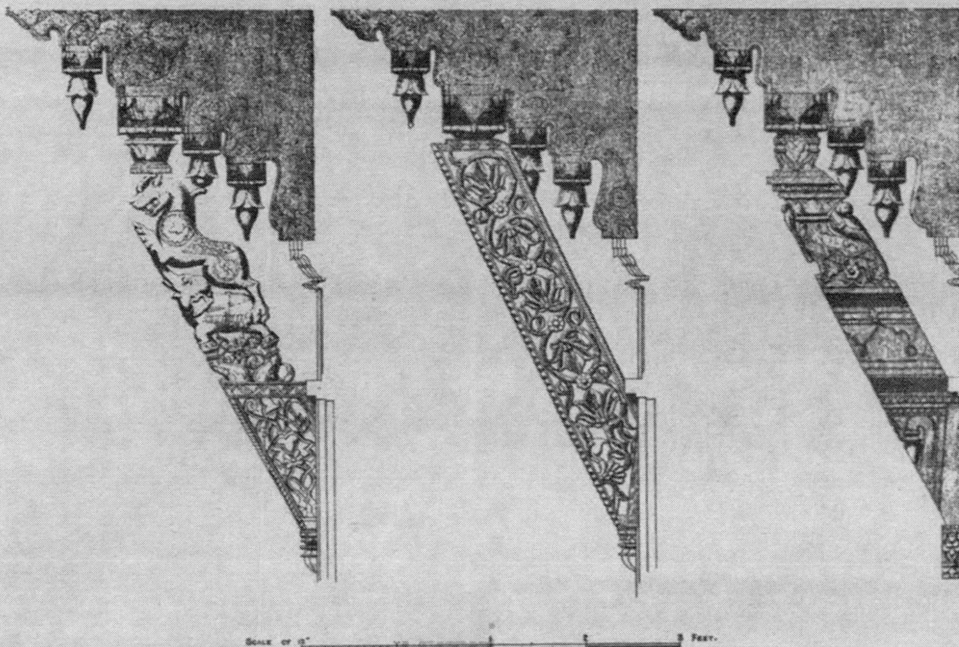

ORNAMENTAL BRACKETS FROM THE MIHTAR-I-MAHALL.

PLAN, ELEVATION AND SECTION OF THE KAMRAKI GUMBAZ.

'HALF INNER, AND HALF OUTER DOORWAYS OF THE MIHTAR-I-MAHALL.

CORNICE BRACKETS FROM THE NAU GUMBAZ AND KHUMBAR'S MOSQU

MOSQUE No. 329. IN THE SHAHPUR SUBURB.

MOSQUE No. 311. IN THE SHAHPUR SUBURB.

PLATE LXXIII

THE NAU GUMBAZ.

THE ASHAR MAHALL.

PLATE LXXIV

GREAT ARCH OVER MOAT BEHIND THE ASHAR MAHALL.

THE JAHAZ MAHALL.

PLATE LXXV

PANELLED DOOR FROM ASHAR MAHALL

PAINTING ON WALL OF ASHAR MAHALL.

PAINTING FROM WALL OF ASHAR MAHALL.

PAINTING FROM WALL OF ASHAR MAHALL.

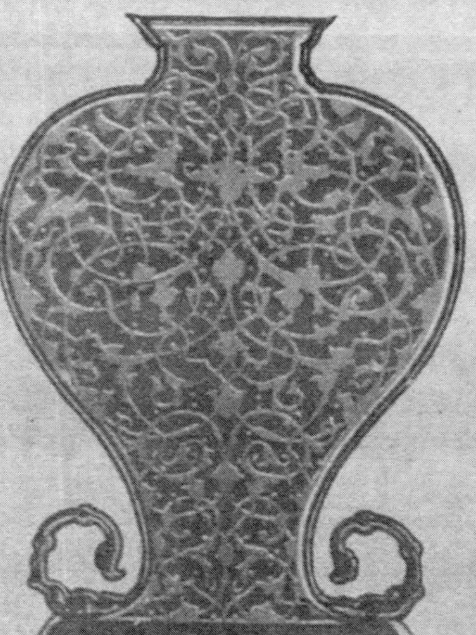

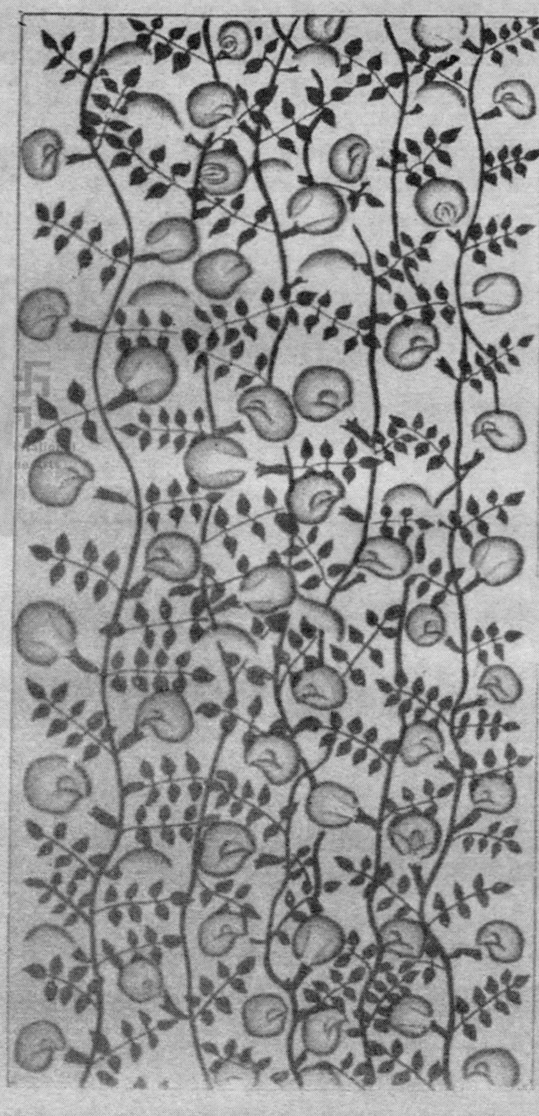

SCALE OF 12" 2 FEET

TRELLIS WINDOWS FROM THE ASHAR MAHALL.

OUTLINE DRAWINGS OF THREE OLD CARPETS FROM THE ASHAR MAHALL.

PANELLED CEILING IN THE ASHAR MAHALL.

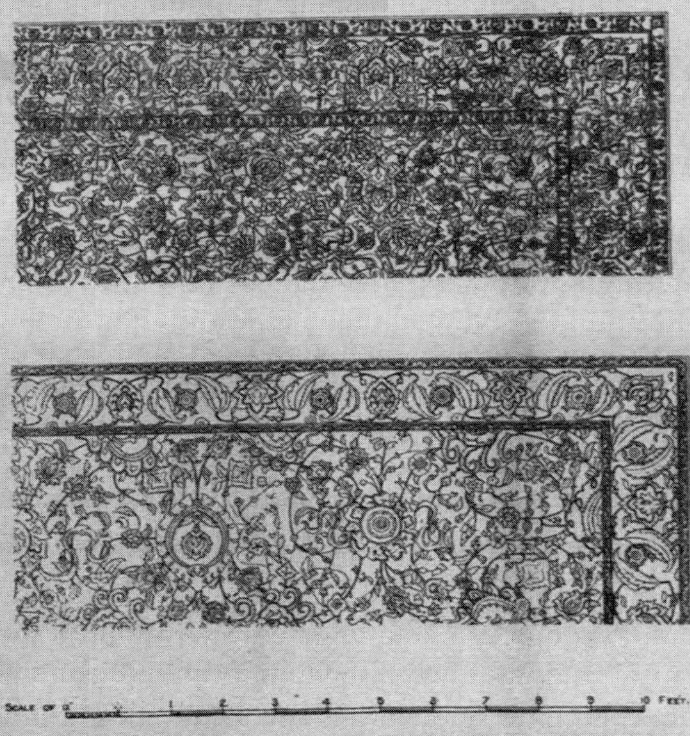

OUTLINE DRAWINGS OF TWO OLD CARPETS FROM THE ASHAR MAHALL.

PLATE LXXXI

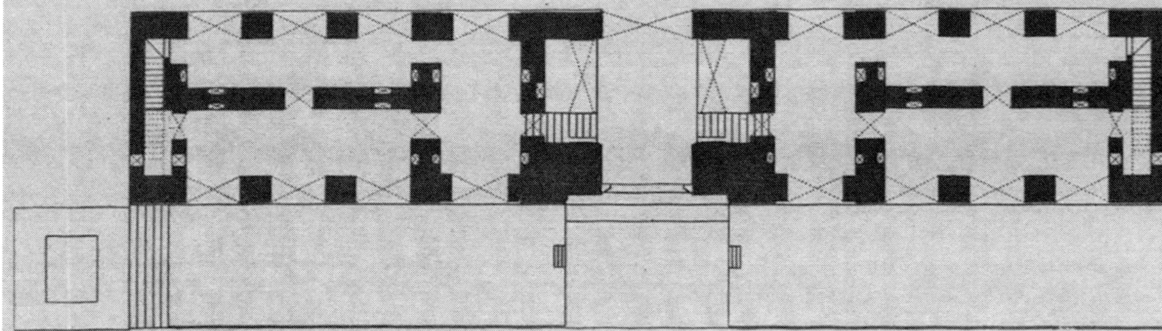

SCALE OF 10 10 20 30 40 50 60 70 80 90 100 FEET.

PLAN OF THE JAHAZ MAHALL.

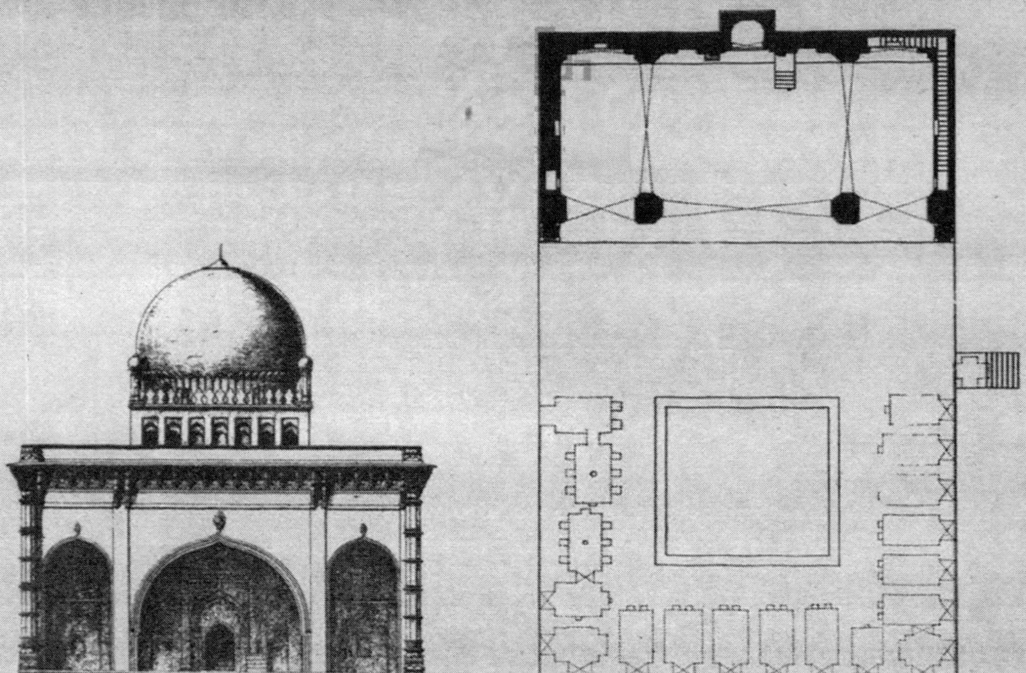

SCALE OF 10 10 20 30 40 50 60 70 80 90 100 FEET.

PLAN AND ELEVATION OF MUSTAFA KHAN'S MOSQUE.

MUSTAFA KHAN'S MOSQUE.

AFZAL KHAN'S CENOTAPH AND MOSQUE.

PLATE LXXXII

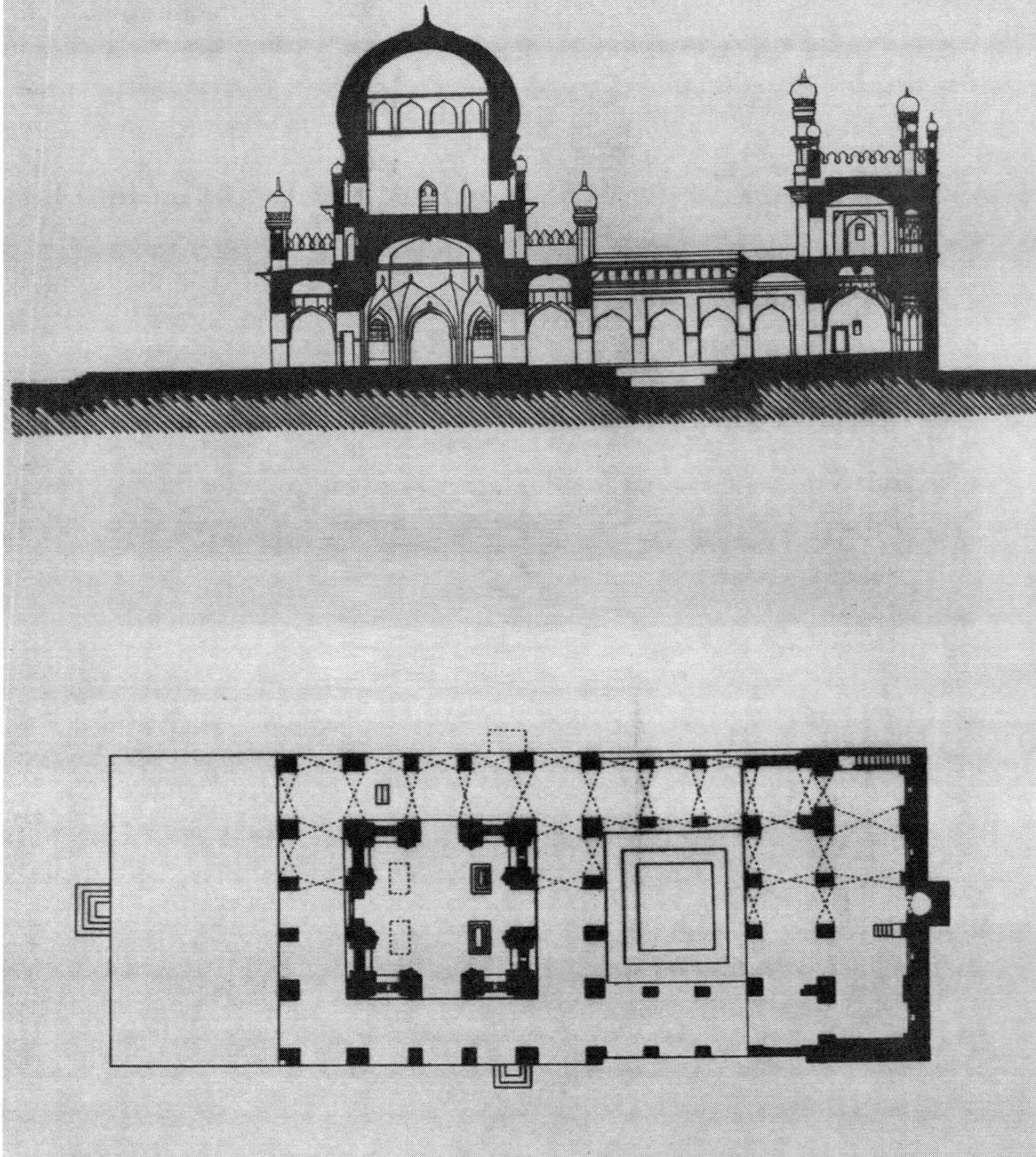

PLAN AND SECTION OF AFZAL KHAN'S CENOTAPH AND MOSQUE.

PLATE LXXXIV

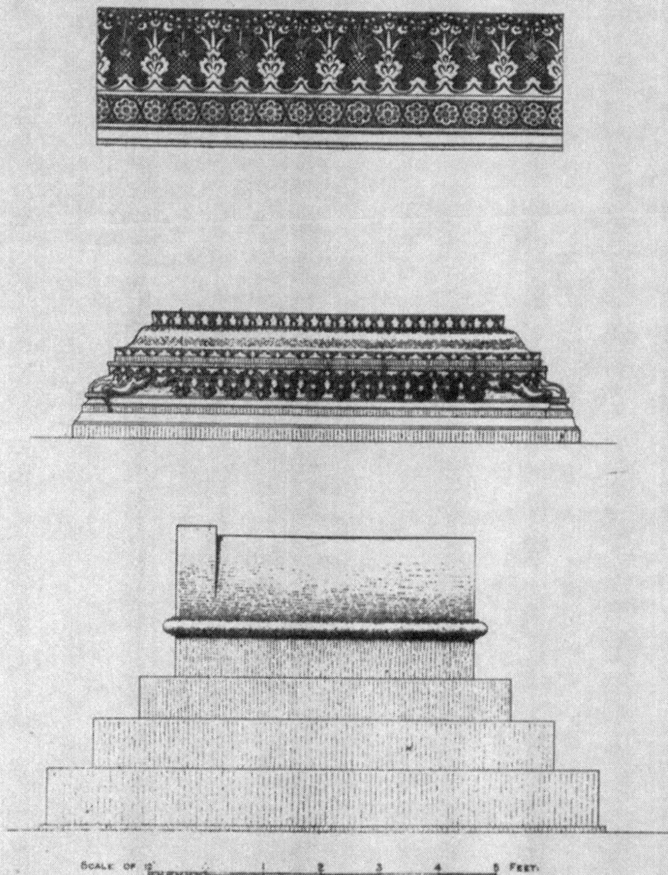

BAND OF STUCCO ORNAMENT AND ELEVATION OF TWO TOMBS.

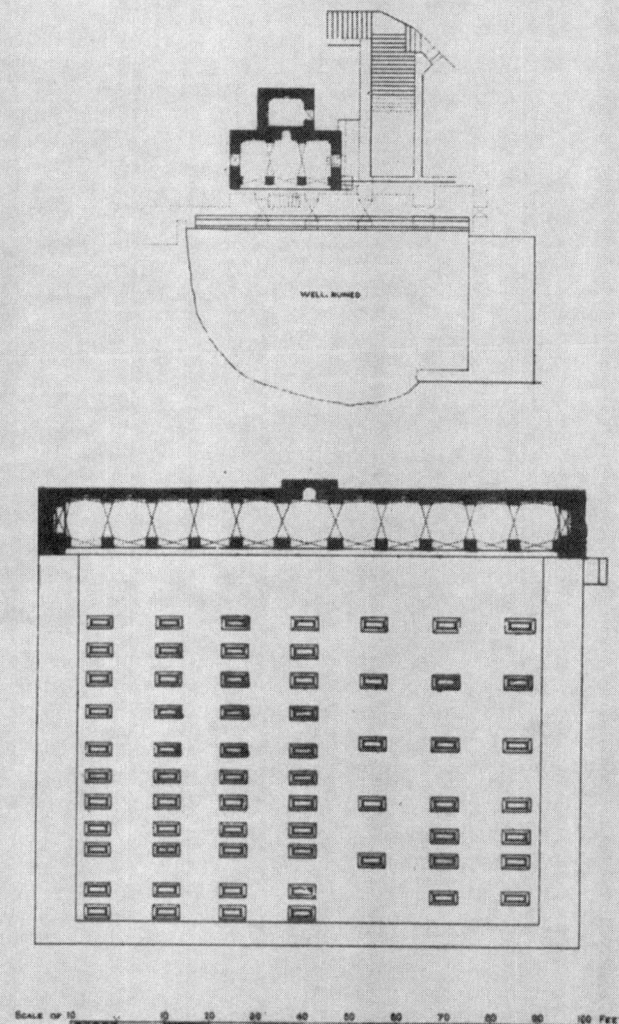

PLAN OF AFZAL KHAN'S WIVES' TOMBS.

THE GOL GUMBAZ FROM THE SOUTH-EAST.

THE MOSQUE OF THE GOL GUMBAZ.

JAHAN BEGAM'S TOMB AT AINAPUR.

THE NAQAR-KHANA OF THE GOL GUMBAZ BEFORE CONVERSION

THE NAQAR-KHANA OF THE GOL GUMBAZ AFTER CONVERSION.

PLATE LXXXVIII

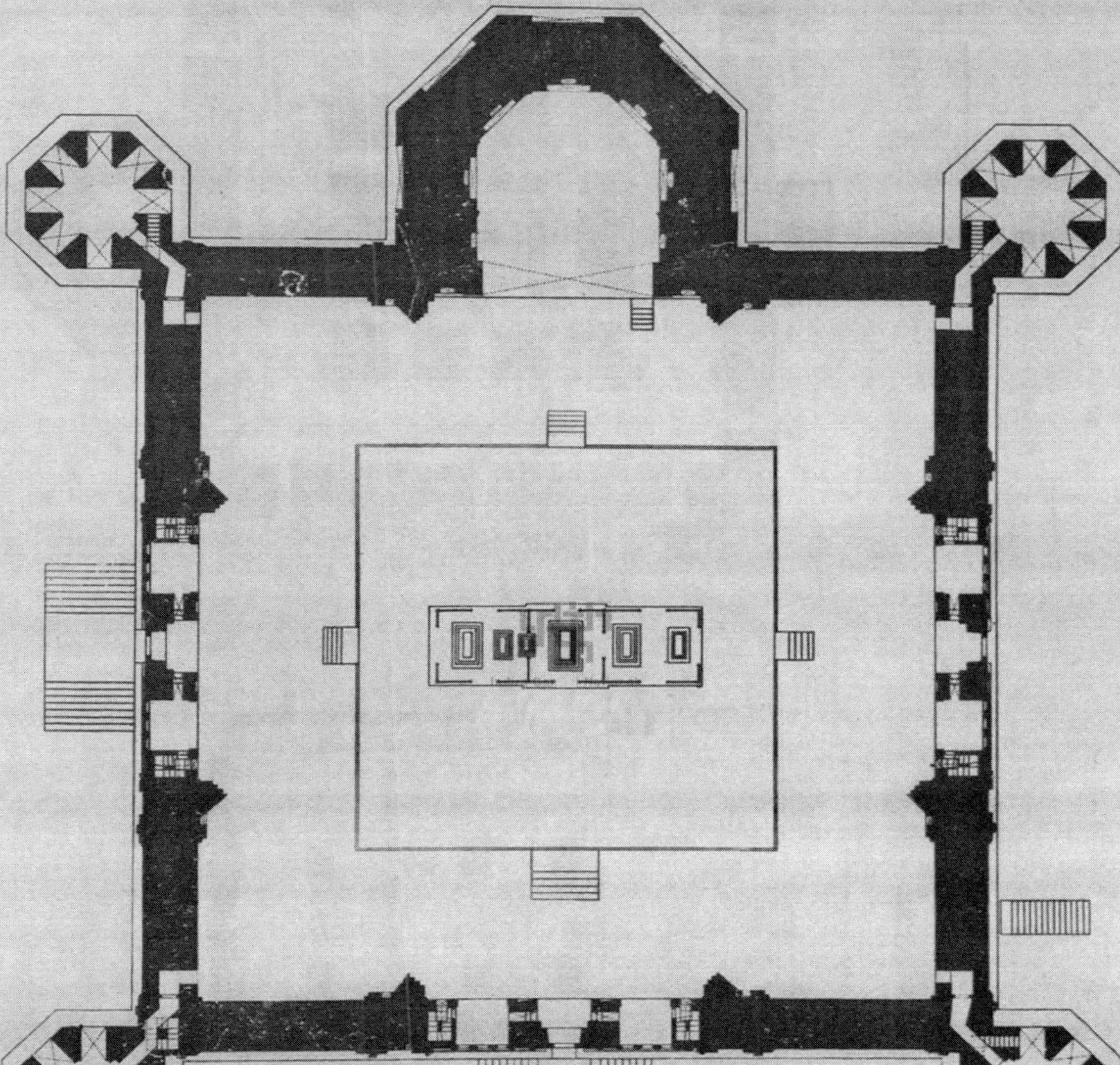

GROUND PLAN OF THE GOL GUMBAZ.

PLATE LXXXIX

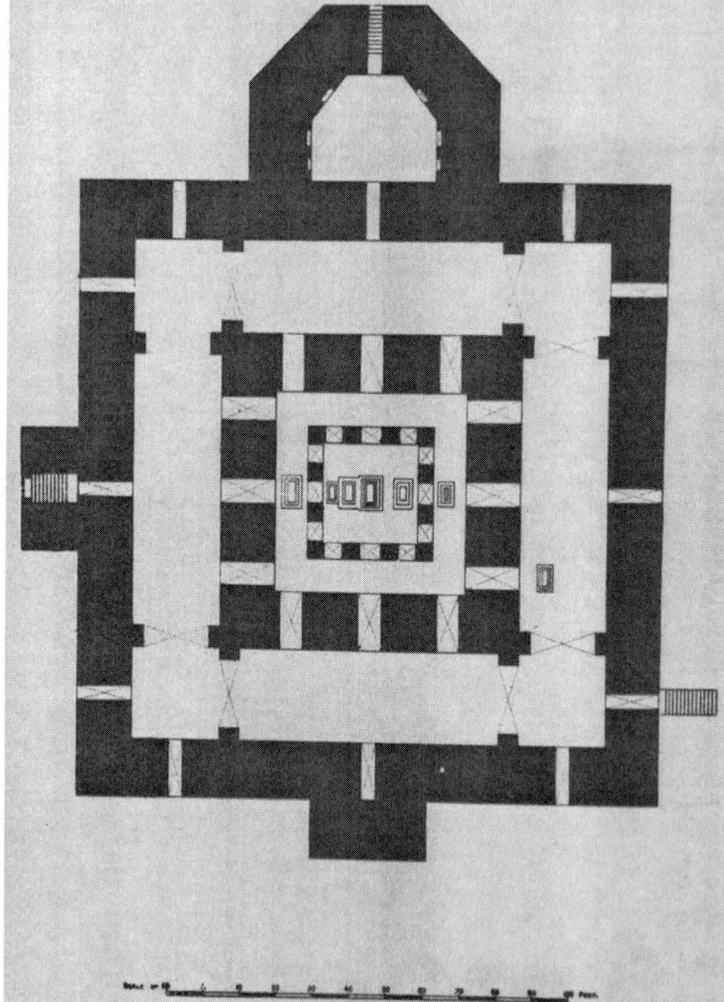

PLAN OF THE VAULTS OF THE GOL GUMBAZ.

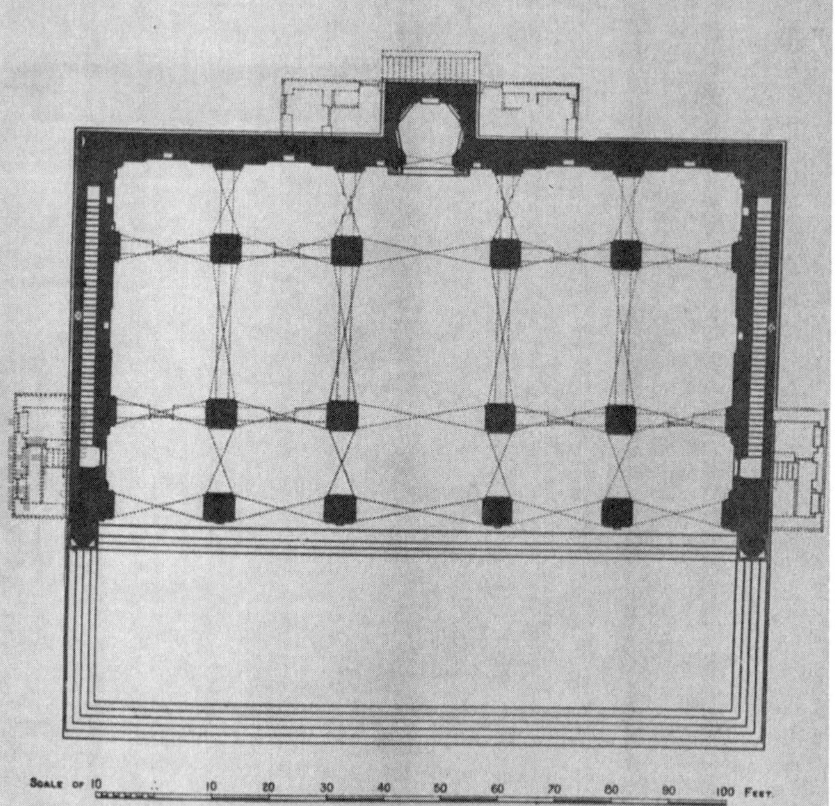

PLAN OF THE MOSQUE OF THE GOL GUMBAZ.

SECTION OF THE GOL GUMBAZ.

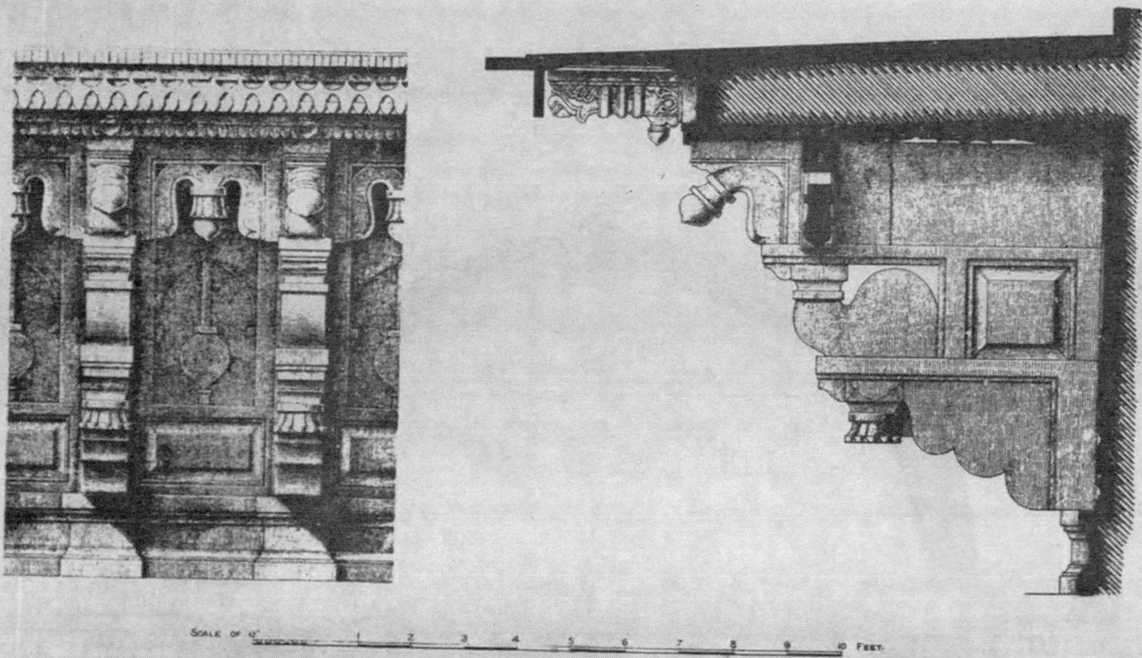

FRONT ELEVATION AND SECTION OF THE GREAT CORNICE OF THE GOL GUMBAZ.

PLAN, LOOKING UPWARDS, OF THE GREAT CORNICE OF THE GOL GUMBAZ.

SCALE OF 12" 1 2 3 4 5 6 7 8 9 10 FEET.

CORNICE OF THE MOSQUE OF THE GOL GUMBAZ.

PLAN OF CORNICE OF MINAR LOOKING UPWARDS

ELEVATION OF MINAR

ORNAMENT ON MINAR ABOVE CORNICE.

SCALE OF 5 5 10 FEET.

SCALE OF 12" 1 2 3 FEET

DETAILS FROM THE GOL GUMBAZ.

DETAILS OF STUCCO ORNAMENT ABOUT THE ARCHES OF THE GOL GUMBAZ.

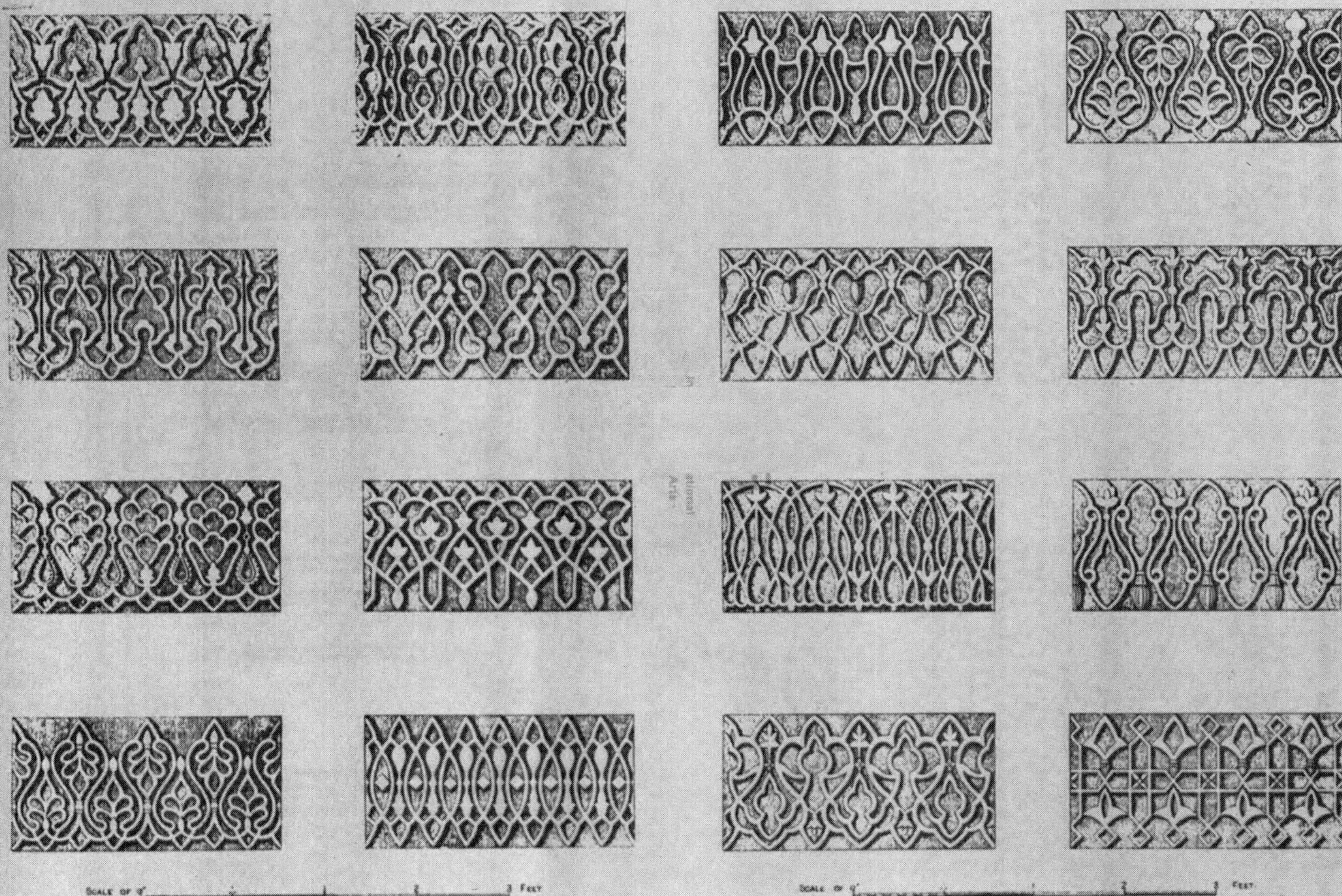

ORNAMENTAL STUCCO BANDS ROUND THE MINARS OF THE GOL GUMBAZ.

PLATE XCV

ORNAMENTAL STUCCO BANDS ROUND THE MINARS OF THE GOL GUMBAZ.

WOODEN CANOPY OVER THE TOMBS IN THE GOL GUMBAZ.

INTERIOR OF JAHAN BEGAM'S TOMB OF AINAPUR.

THE JOD GUMBAZ FROM THE SOUTH-EAST.

PLATE XCVII

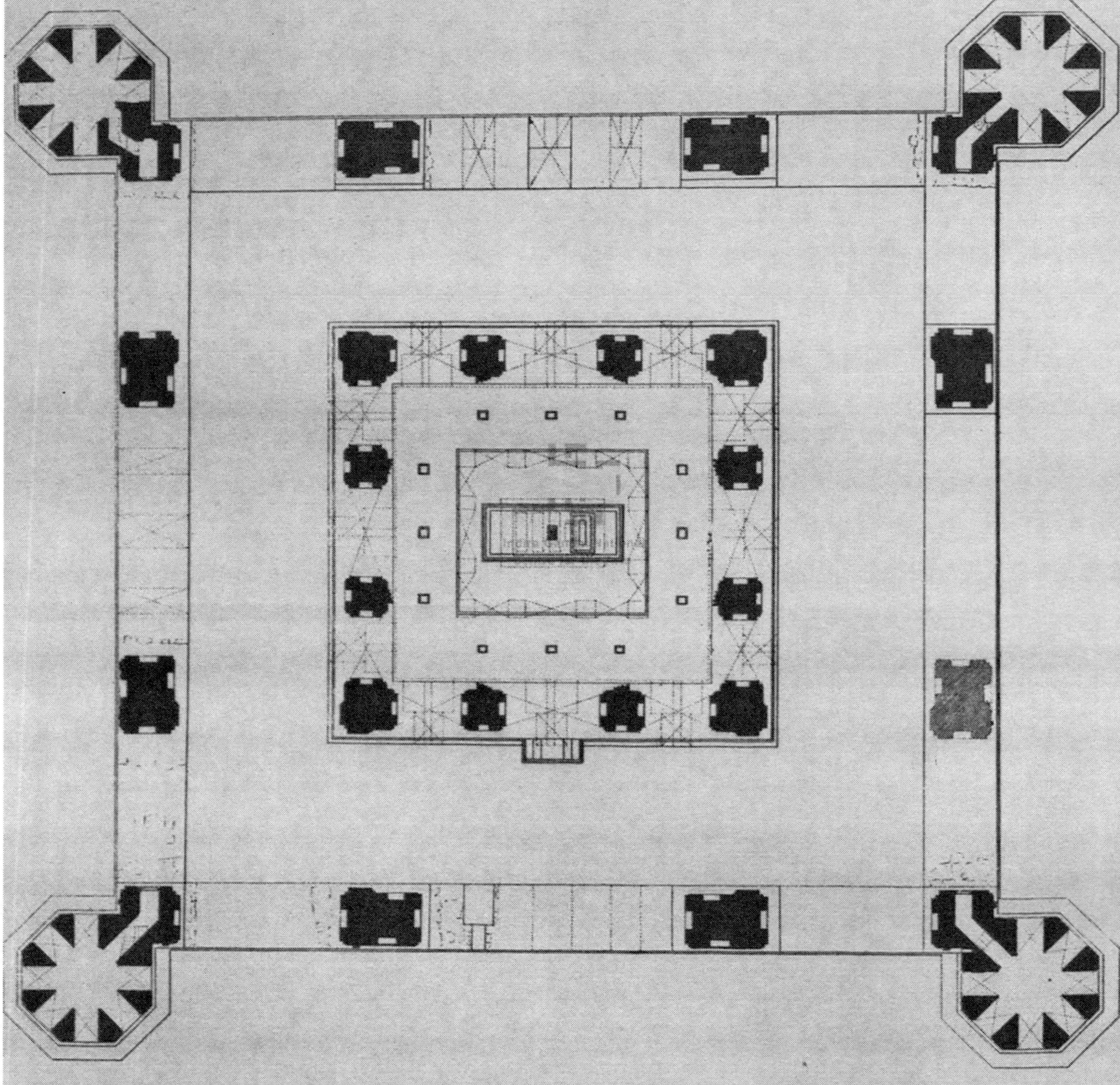

PLAN OF JAHAN BEGAM'S TOMB AT AINAPUR.

GREEN-STONE TOMB.

UNFINISHED TOMB OF ALI II.

PLATE XCIX

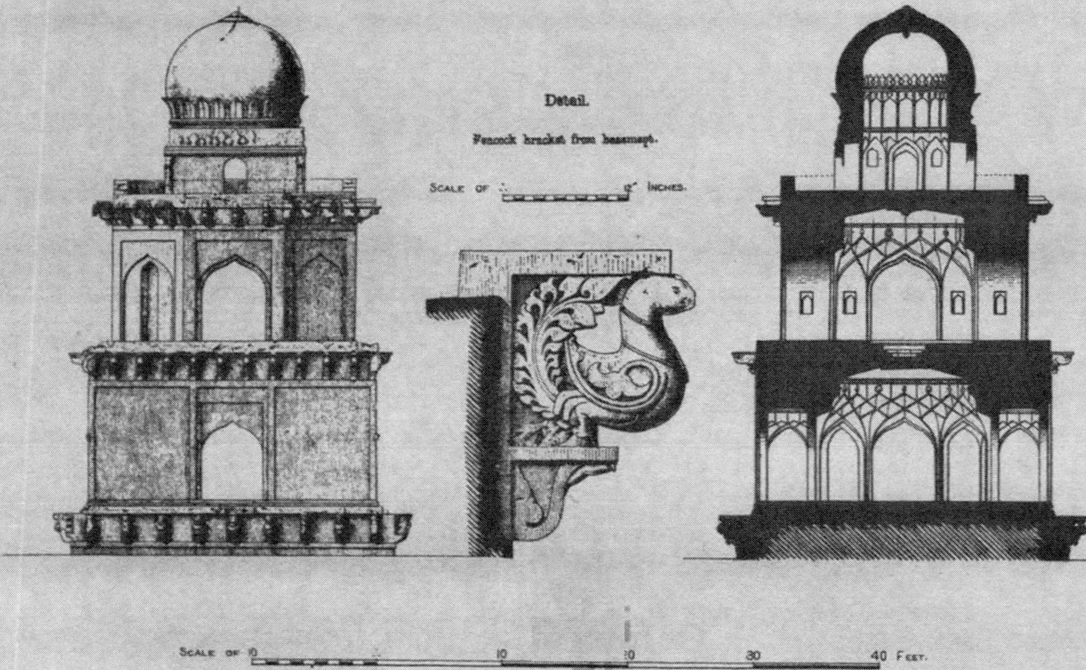

ELEVATION, SECTION AND BRACKET FROM MUBARAK KHAN'S MAHALL.

GREENSTONE TOMB.

PLATE C

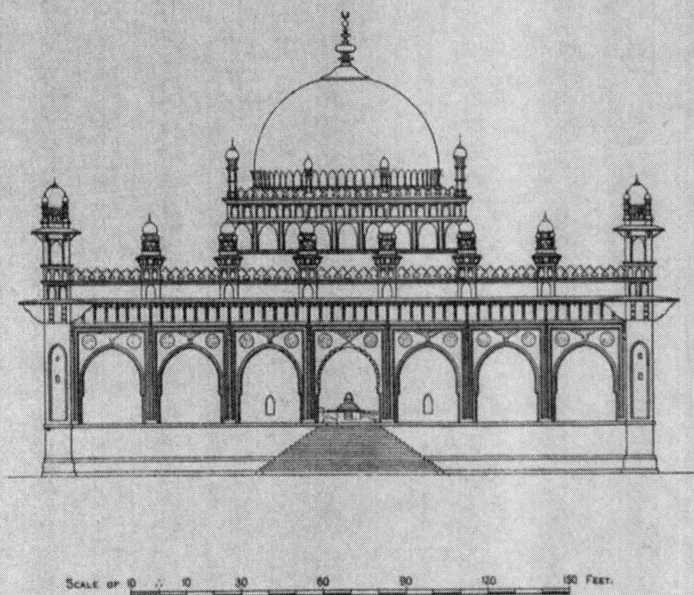

RESTORED ELEVATION OF TOMB OF ALI II.

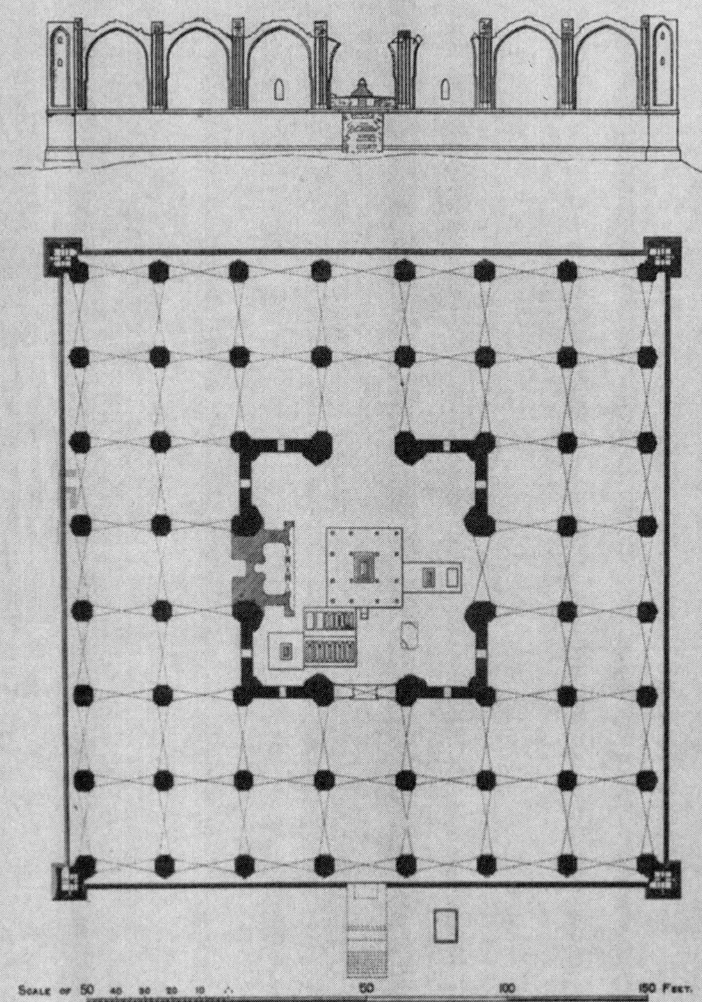

ELEVATION AND PLAN OF TOMB OF ALI II.

THE PANI MAHALL.

THE MAKKA MASJID.

PLATE CII

ELEVATION OF THE MIHRAB OF THE MAKKA MASJID.

ELEVATION OF FRONT WALL OF THE PANI MAHALL.

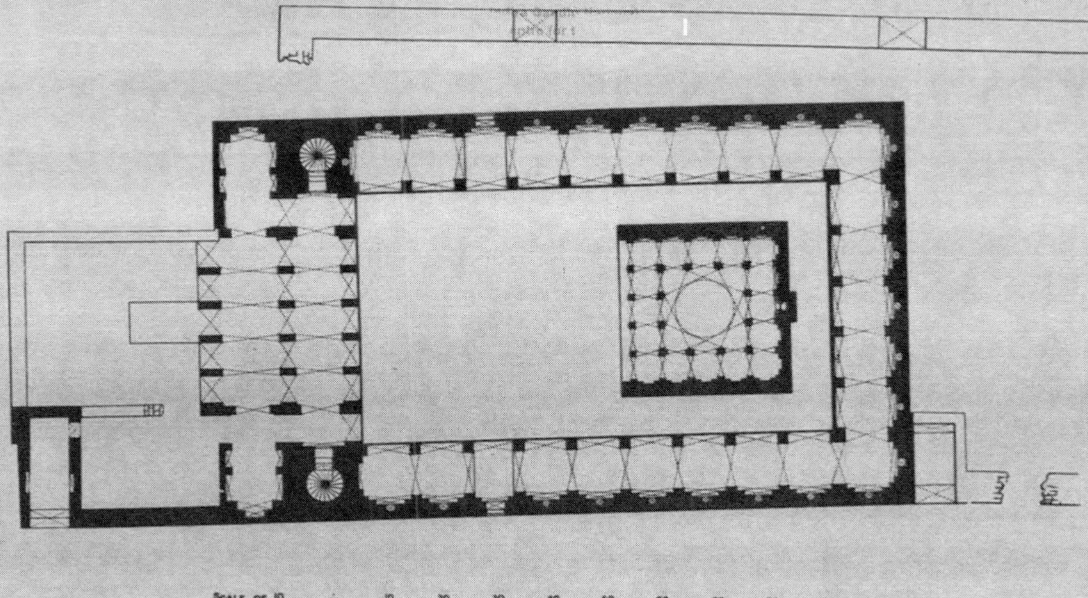

PLAN OF THE MAKKA MASJID.

PLATE CIII

THE TOMB OF SHAH NAVAZ KHAN

MOSQUE AND TOMB OF YAQUT DABULI

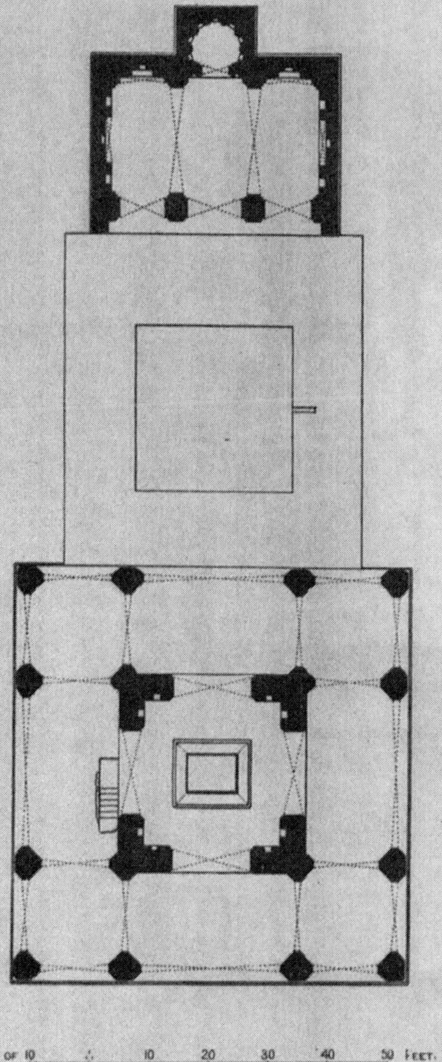

PLAN OF SHAH NAVAZ KHAN'S TOMB AND MOSQUE.

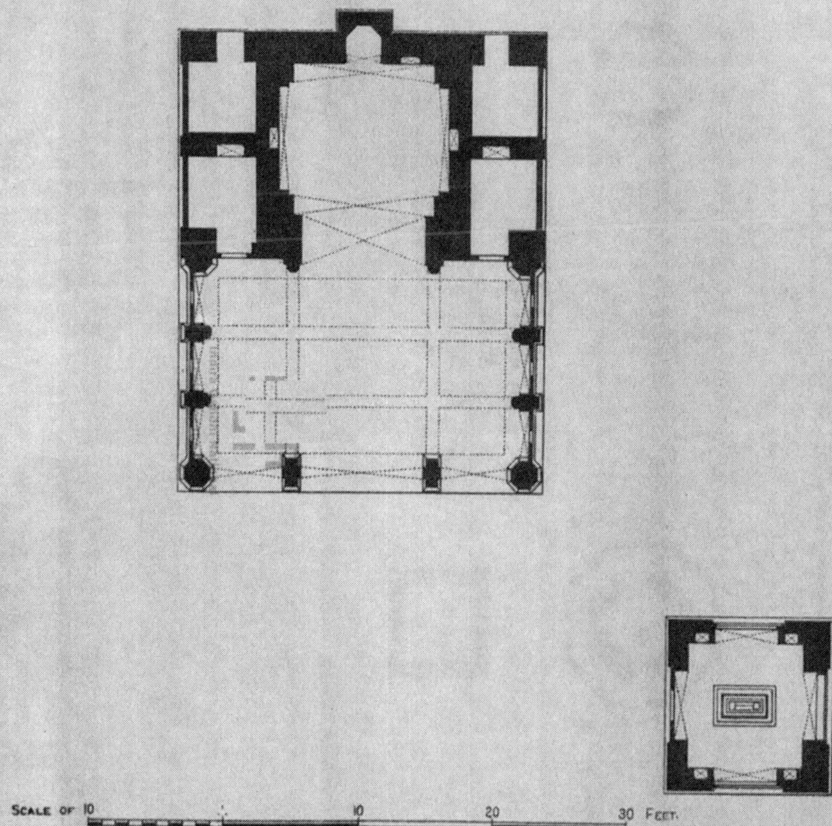

PLAN OF YAQUT DABULIS' MOSQUE AND TOMB.

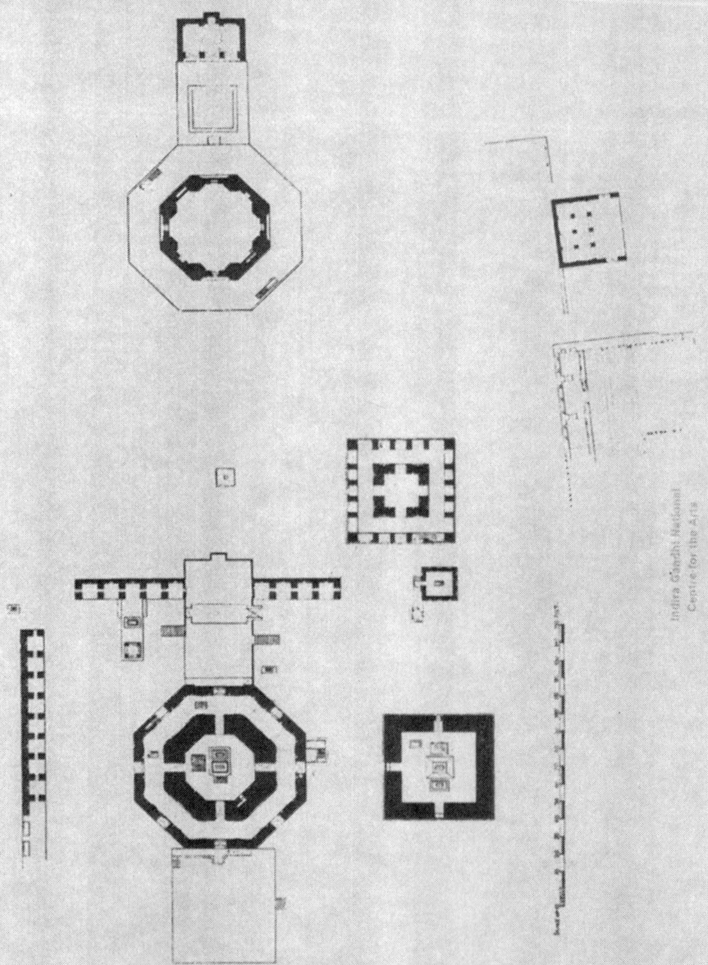

SCALE OF 10 — 10 — 20 FEET

PLAN OF THE JOD GUMBAZ.

SECTION OF ALLAH BABU'S MASJID.

SHAH KARIM'S TOMB.

ALLAH BABU'S MOSQUE AND TOMB.

SECTION OF CEILING IN SAYYID ABDUL RAHMAN'S TOMB.

PLAN OF CEILING IN SAYYID ABDUL RAHMAN'S TOMB.

THE CHINCH DIDDI MASJID.

THE AINAPUR MÀHALL.

PLATE CIX

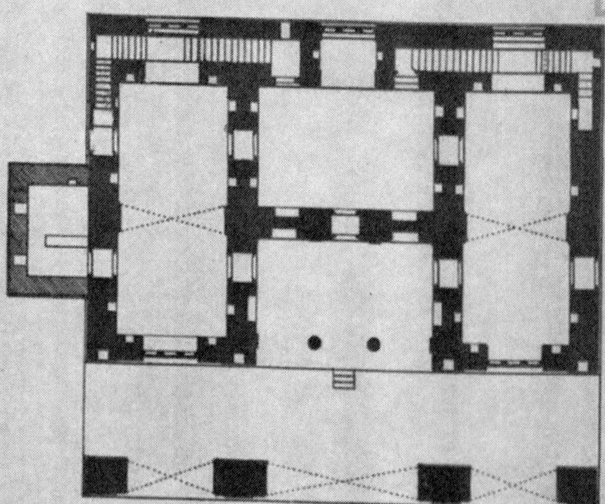

PLAN AND ELEVATION OF PALACE AT AINAPUR.

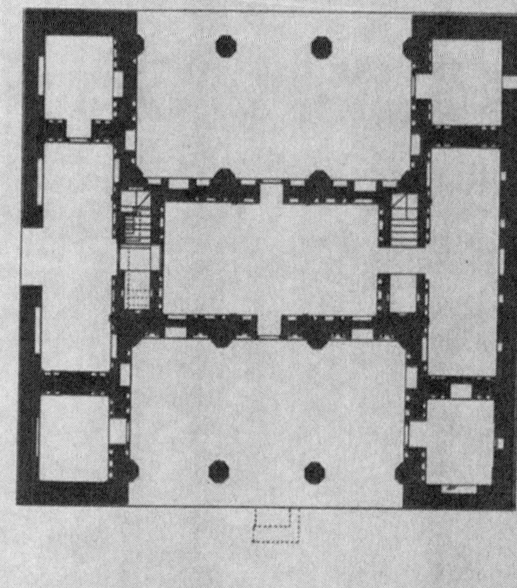

PLAN OF THE DAULAT KOTHI.

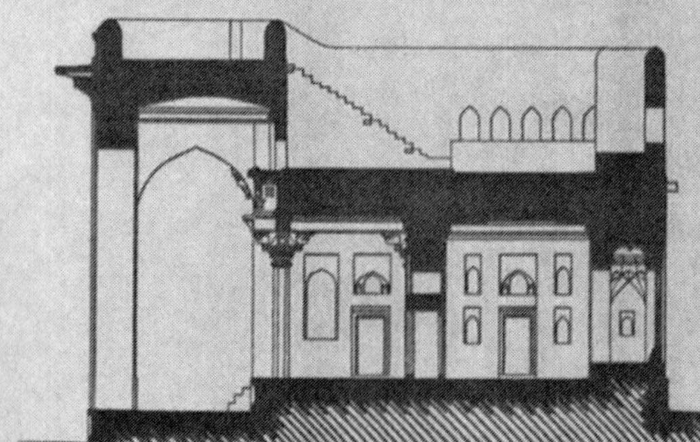

SECTION OF PALACE AT AINAPUR.

THE TAJ-BAURI.

WATER PAVILIONS AT KUMATGI.

INTERIOR OF A WATER PAVILION AT KUMATGI.

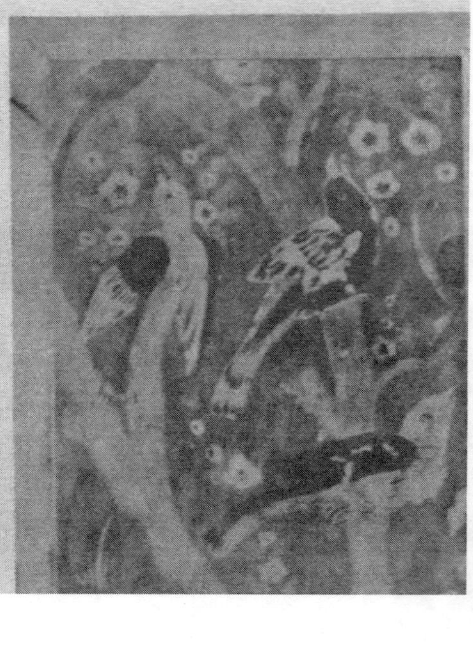

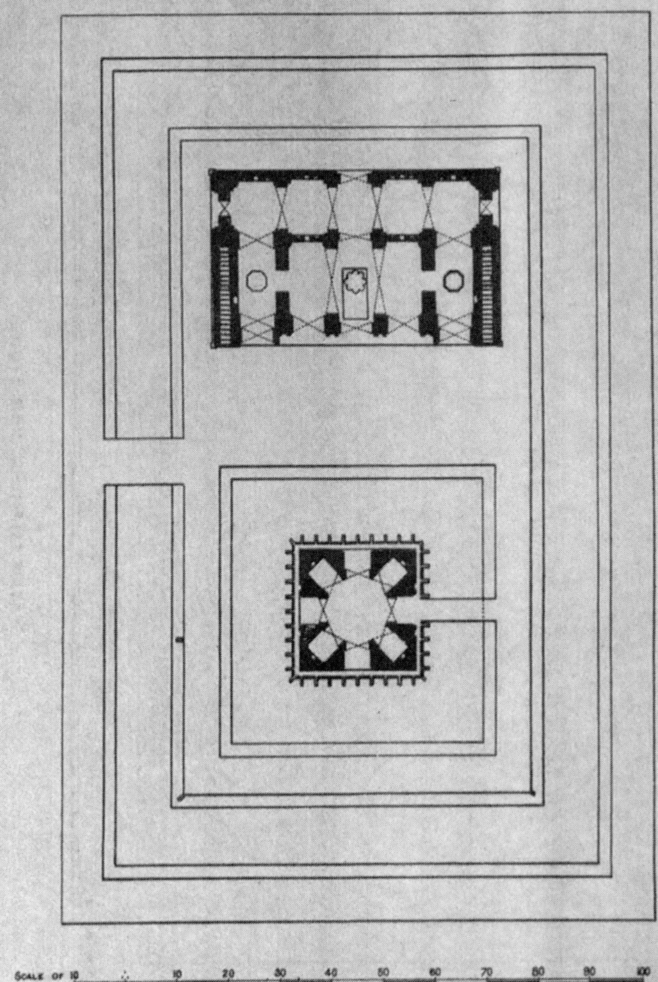

PLAN OF A WATER PAVILION AT KUMATGI.

PLAN AND SECTION OF CEILING IN A WATER PAVILION AT KUMATGI

OUTLINE DRAWING OF PAINTING OF POLO AND OTHER FIGURES IN A WATER PAVILION AT KUMATGI.

WATER CHANNEL BED STONE.

PLATE CXIV

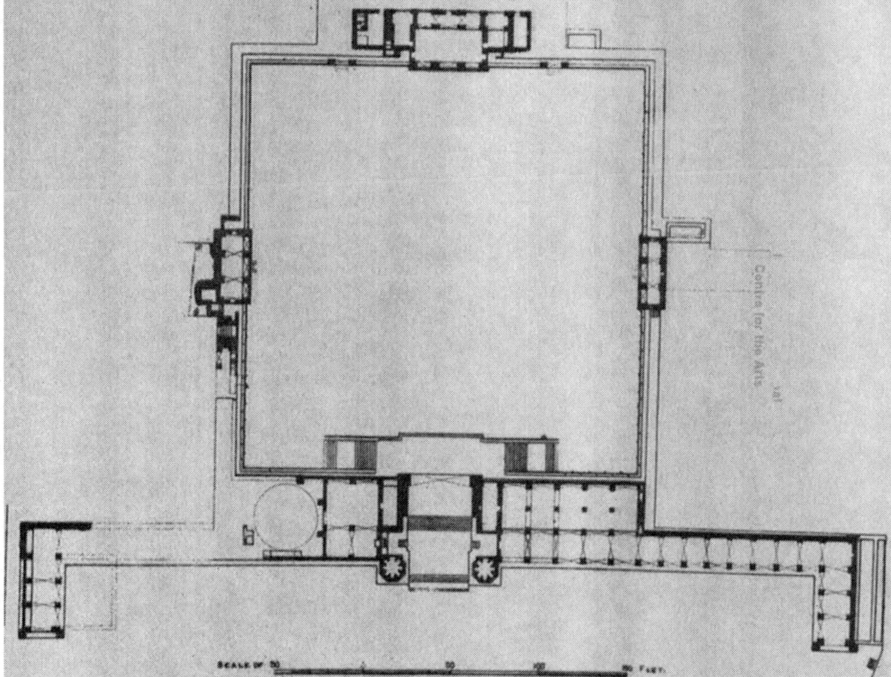

PLAN OF TAJ BAURI.

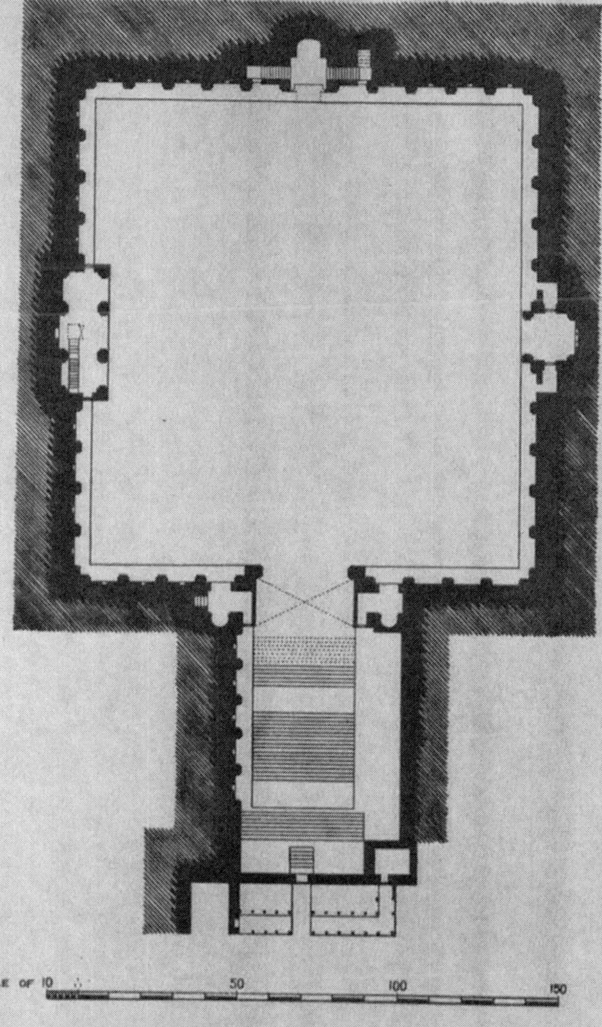

PLAN OF CHAND BAURI.

PLATE CXV

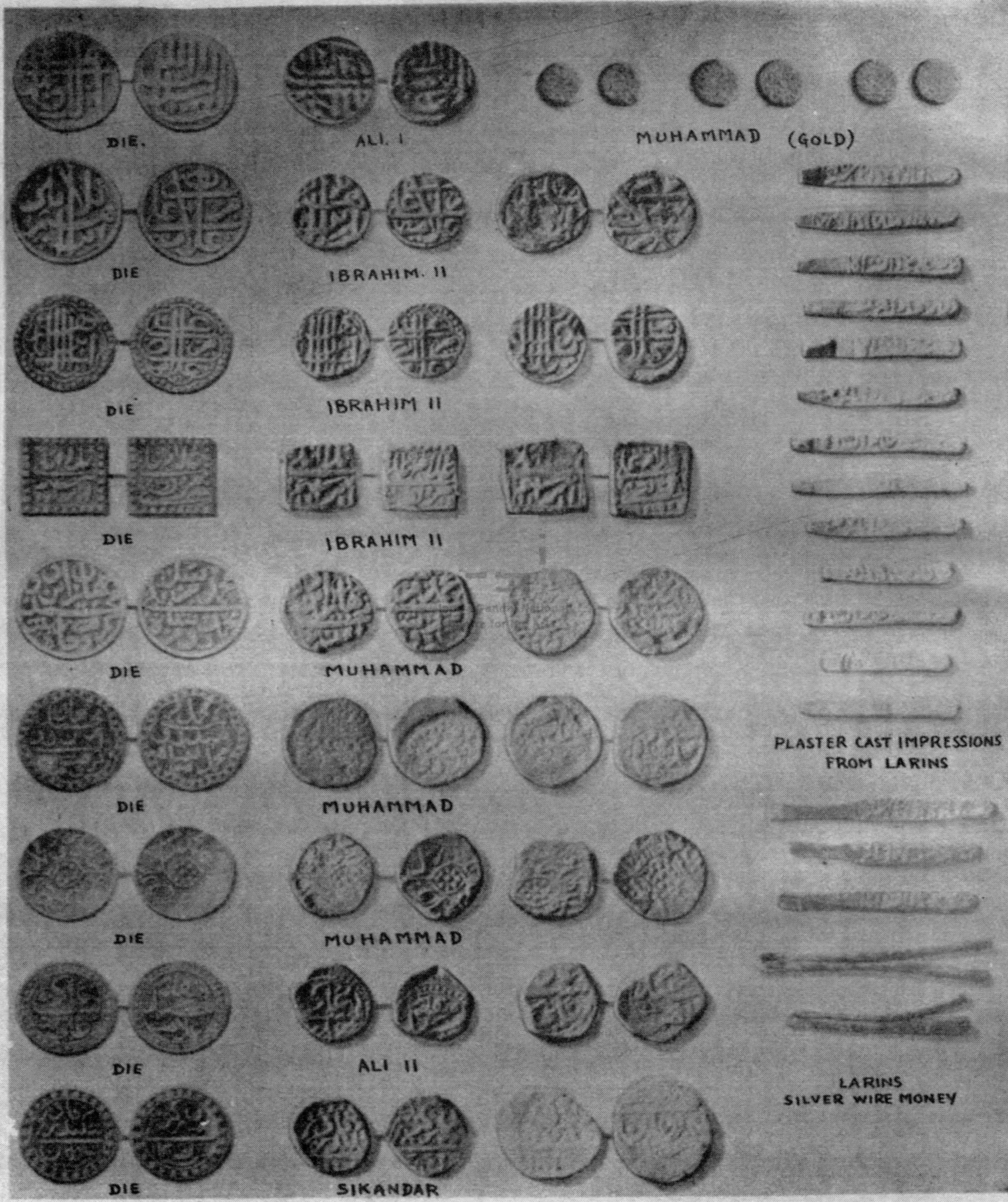

SOME COINS OF BIJAPUR.

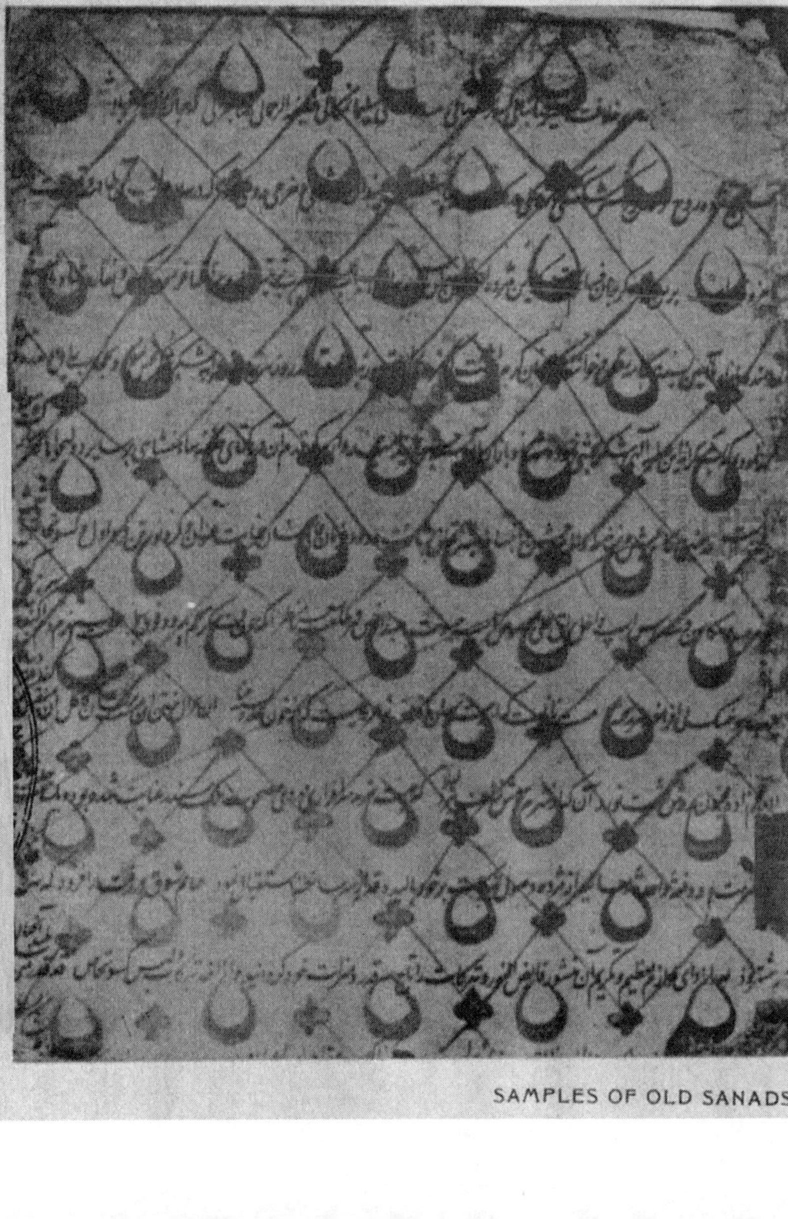

SAMPLES OF OLD SANADS OR DEEDS.